Immigration and Social Equality

Immigration and Social Equality

The Ethics of Skill-Selective Immigration Policy

Désirée Lim

OXFORD
UNIVERSITY PRESS

Oxford University Press is a department of the University of Oxford. It furthers the University's objective of excellence in research, scholarship, and education by publishing worldwide. Oxford is a registered trade mark of Oxford University Press in the UK and certain other countries.

Published in the United States of America by Oxford University Press
198 Madison Avenue, New York, NY 10016, United States of America.

Library of Congress Control Number: 2023938487

ISBN 978–0–19–765809–3

DOI: 10.1093/oso/9780197658093.001.0001

Printed by Integrated Books International, United States of America

This book is dedicated in loving memory of my mother, Wendy Toh, who was at one point a low-skilled migrant worker in Canada (as well as an international student).

20 June 1954–12 June 2020

Contents

Acknowledgments

This book is, above all, a product of the thriving and nourishing academic environments that I've been lucky to be a part of, and the people who I've been even luckier to meet. My research on the ethics of immigration began in Fall 2011, when I first started graduate school at King's College London (KCL) under Andrea Sangiovanni's guidance. I remember pacing around in my kitchen, quite literally muttering to myself about how much I disagreed with certain philosophical arguments about immigration, and realizing how thrilling and absorbing it was to have *something* I really wanted to write about. I am grateful to Andrea for getting the fire started, so to speak, and for teaching me that philosophy is, above all, a joyful and creative activity where we always have much to learn from each other.

I am similarly indebted to Sarah Fine, who was the primary supervisor of my PhD thesis at KCL. As a graduate student trying to find my footing in our (admittedly) strange discipline, I could not have asked for a more dedicated mentor and friend. Sarah continues to advise and cheer me on today, and in my capacity as a professor, I am always trying to model her kindness, good humor, and unfailing precision. It is no exaggeration to say that, without her, this book would never have existed. Sarah also urged me to apply for KCL's Norman Malcolm Fellowship, which allowed me to spend a semester at Cornell University under Richard Miller's encouraging supervision, where Chapter Three was first conceived.

My thesis began its gradual transition into a book project when I started my postdoctoral fellowship at the McCoy Center for Ethics in Society. The two years I spent at Stanford are treasured years that I will remember forever. When making my revisions, I was first guided by the insightful comments made by my viva examiners, Laura Valentini and Zofia Stemplowska. From there, I continued to develop my book's central argument, and our weekly postdoctoral workshops at the McCoy Center were instrumental to this purpose. Rob Reich, Debra Satz, Anne Newman, and Eamonn Callan provided excellent feedback, and so did my fellow postdocs: Bernardo Zacka,

Fay Niker, Hannah Carnegy-Arbuthnott, Johannes Himmelreich, Lindsey Chambers, Oded Na'aman, Prithviraj Datta, and Ted Lechterman.

In 2018, my brilliant and lively colleagues at Penn State's philosophy department and the Rock Ethics Institute showed me that there were topics that were sorely missing from my book. True to its reputation, my department has sparked my interest in decolonial theory and the critical philosophy of race. In particular, Eduardo Mendieta drew my attention to migratorial disobedience and underscored the role that decolonial considerations must play in our theorizing about justice. I have benefited immeasurably from the good counsel of Amy Allen, John Christman, Nancy Tuana, Robert Bernasconi, and Uygar Abaci, whose expertise has helped me to navigate the delicate process of publishing one's first monograph. In this vein, it has been a pleasure to work with my editor at Oxford University Press, Peter Ohlin, whose professionalism and responsiveness has made the process a very smooth one. I also want to thank Ben Jones, for his tireless capacity for offering constructive comments (right down to coming up with the title of this book!), and above all, his steadfast friendship and support. And I must thank Brady Bowman for many animated and invigorating conversations that have profoundly shaped my thinking and continue to influence me today.

I am my own worst co-author, and the truth is that my messy manuscript desperately needed interventions by Joseph Carens, Michael Blake, and José Mendoza in order to remotely resemble an actual book. I've admired these theorists' work for a long time, going back to the days when I first started writing about immigration. It was surreal to me when, owing to support from Penn State's philosophy department, I was able to meet them personally at my book manuscript workshop. Joe, Michael, and José have been committed to asking me challenging questions and pushing me on the arguments that needed the most work, but equally committed to giving me invaluable suggestions on how to move forward, and continuously reminding me of the value of my research. Michael's critiques have been especially important to finessing the final draft of my book, and Joe has generously given me his counsel on other important occasions. Not least of all, I want to thank Michael Ball-Blakely for copyediting and indexing my manuscript, while providing suggestions along the way; I could not imagine entrusting these tasks to anyone else.

Apart from the persons mentioned above, some chapters of my manuscript have been fundamentally shaped by rounds of feedback that I obtained from anonymous reviewers. I am grateful to reviewers at *Social Theory and Practice*, where a version of Chapter Three was published, and reviewers at *the Critical Review of International Social and Political Philosophy*, where a version of Chapter Four was published. Various components of my book were also presented at the University of Washington, the University of Wisconsin-Madison, the 2019 Association for Political Theory Conference (hosted at UC Irvine), the "Philosophy of Borders" conference (hosted by the Central European University and the Hungarian Academy of Sciences), the Stanford Political Theory Workshop, the 2016 Association for Political Thought Conference (hosted at St Catherine's College, Oxford), and KCL's philosophy graduate workshop.

The last two years of my life have been especially challenging, perhaps even excruciating at times. I continue to weather the storm because of the devotion and patience of my oldest and dearest friends, Tiffany and YK.

Introduction

1. Skilled and unskilled migration

After leaving Singapore in 2007, much of my adult life has been spent in transit. A great deal of effort and resources have gone into my goals of migrating to the United Kingdom and, later on, the United States. I first applied to enter the United Kingdom on a university student visa (Tier 4); later, I arrived at the United States as an exchange researcher (J1) and specialty worker (H1-B). In 2020, I became the recipient of a green card, which I am eligible for as a so-called alien of extraordinary ability. Prior to this remarkable stroke of luck, I've been in some sticky situations: these include having to print stacks of bank records that proved I had enough money to support myself in the United Kingdom, dealing with interminable visa delays when I urgently needed to return to London for work, forgetting to pay a mysterious fee to the US embassy and being unceremoniously ejected from it as a result . . . you get the picture. Generally speaking, however, being a "highly skilled migrant" meant that my regular passage through border security was mostly uneventful. An officer would ask me a series of routine questions about where I worked or what I taught, and after taking my fingerprints and a fresh photograph of my scowling, jet-lagged face, send me on my way. While waiting for my turn, I couldn't help but take notice of the ubiquitous signs that encouraged me to sign up for the US Customs and Border Protection's "Trusted Traveler Programs." Like membership in an elite club, being part of the "TSA Pre✓" program and "Global Entry: Trusted Traveler Network" will grant you the privilege of skipping the queue and using a self-serve kiosk instead. Of course, you must be able to afford the membership fees, which go up to $100. Furthermore, not everyone can qualify—only citizens of *certain* countries like India, Germany, Panama, and South Korea, are eligible for Global Entry.

I'm not quite at the end of my journey, but up to this point, I've learned that migration through "legal" pathways is all about having your ducks in a

Immigration and Social Equality. Désirée Lim, Oxford University Press. © Oxford University Press 2023.
DOI: 10.1093/oso/9780197658093.003.0001

row. You need cash on hand to pay for unexpected administrative fees—lots of it. You must plan far ahead and show up to your immigration appointments in the right order, and most of all, you *must not* lose that lone, dog-eared piece of paper from four years ago, because your lawyer will need to take a close look at it. Fall short at any point, and you're in for some trouble. Often, however, trouble comes your way even if you've done your best to ward it off, like in the case of the citizens and long-term residents who have found themselves wrongfully deported from the United States,[1] or a previous student visa-holder who found herself placed in detention after returning to the United Kingdom for a job interview.[2] I think of immigration as a game whose rules are not only always changing, but can also be so baffling and convoluted that the only reasonable human response to them is profound despair. (You always wonder, of course, if immigration rules are purposely designed that way.)

Much has changed since the time I first became an immigrant. In the United Kingdom, I remember noticing the growing suspicion toward international students like myself, who had increasingly become scapegoats for supposedly high rates of immigration fraud. Eventually, all international students were required to register their presence with the local police and attend regular interviews to prove that we were properly enrolled in our courses, lest we inadvertently steal a job or two from an unsuspecting citizen while committing crimes on the side. Much later on, when I was no longer a student, I was unsure if I would qualify to enter the United States on a work visa. As a matter of my occupation, income, and the fact I was not educated in the United States, I would have immediately failed to achieve the requisite number of "points" under the new points-based system initially proposed by Donald Trump. As Muzaffar Chishti and Jessica Bolter describe, Trump's proposal sought to "move the United States away from a system that is predominantly family based and towards one that favors applicants with desirable labor-market attributes, to be selected using a points system" (2019). It is best captured as a set of *skill-selective immigration policies*; that is, a bundle of immigration laws that are designed to prioritize the entry and settlement of highly skilled immigrants who "possess extraordinary talent, professionals and those in specialized vocations, and those with exceptional academic achievement" (2019). Quite naturally—and perhaps not too unfairly—a philosopher like myself would have been deemed too low-skilled to live in the United States.

As my newly minted status as permanent resident of the United States might suggest, Trump's proposal never came to fruition, and I could breathe an enormous sigh of relief after my first employment visa was approved in 2018. Countless other persons, however, were not as lucky. While Trump's points-based system would have been punishing in its exclusion of those deemed to be low-skilled migrants, its basic structure was nothing particularly unique or shocking. Canada, Australia, and the United Kingdom all make use of skill-selective, points-based immigration systems that favor the highly skilled and disfavor the low-skilled, and they've all done so for some time. This is not to say that the United States is any more friendly toward low-skilled immigrants than the other countries I have mentioned. Low-skilled migrants, as I will show, occupy an objectionably precarious and vulnerable status within wealthy Western countries. Extreme as it may have appeared to those unfamiliar with points-based systems, Trump's proposal could only have been drafted in a broader immigration context that endorses skill as a key criterion for admission and exclusion, and has sought to measure and evaluate skill through narrowly construed proxies like occupation, income, and educational level.

This book is all about the precarity of low-skilled migrants, in the world as it presently stands. One illuminating lens for interpreting such precarity is the lens of social egalitarianism, which emphasizes the value of equal respect for all persons. In this vein, my book advances the view that noncitizens are entitled to the right to social equality, and uses social equality as a yardstick for assessing the justice of skill-selective immigration policies. There are many ways where immigration law can violate noncitizens' social equality, such as by racial discrimination, and the reader should not lose sight of such demeaning policies. However, the contemporary philosophical literature has not directly engaged with how *skill-selective immigration policies* can set back social equality, and that's why my book will be focusing on the issue of skill: more specifically, low-skilled migrants and their social subordination at the hands of the states that may receive them. Certainly, the stakes of the "immigration game" (as I've characterized it) are pretty high for me; my occupation as a philosophy professor rests on my playing by its rules, assuming that the United States doesn't choose to block me from participation altogether. But many other migrants—agricultural workers, domestic workers, cleaners, taxi drivers—have much higher stakes yet, and they don't have access to the pathways that are available to migrants who, like me, have also been judged to be "aliens of extraordinary ability." There are persons whose life and limb depend on their ability to migrate, persons who will be torn away from their families if their visa application fails, or people who will lose access to their essential medical treatments or medications if they are told to leave. In the present day, those who fail (or are otherwise unable) to play by the rules of the game are punished with extraordinary cruelty. I say "cruelty" because the practices go beyond the mere use of force itself; it seems that the primary goal is to impose tremendous suffering, rather than effectively enforce a rule. You will likely be familiar with the children who are separated from their parents at the border and held in cages, or the unsanitary conditions and abusive treatment in detention centers, where immigration detainees have died, or the sweeping, unprecedented ICE raids on factories in Morton, Mississippi. In 2021, the freshly constituted Democratic administration suggested some cause for optimism, with President Joe Biden promising to "reverse the Trump Administration's cruel and senseless policies that separate parents from their children at [the] border" and secure a path to citizenship for certain undocumented persons,[3] there is no doubt that the United States has a long way to go in reforming its immigration practices. We may all be "migrants" in theory, but the experience of those affected by these moral atrocities could not be more different from mine.

Before I continue, a number of important points need to be made. Most crucially of all, my book does not seek to make an argument in favor of open borders, although it does not explicitly reject the idea altogether. Its primary focus is not the fact of immigration exclusion in itself, which I believe can be permissible or even necessary depending on the circumstances. Rather, I will be concerned with the *modes* through which immigration exclusion is currently managed and justified. As I'll show, exclusion is carried out in a way that is deeply—and unjustly—hostile to low-skilled migrants. The book draws attention to the social subordination of low-skilled migrants, and it is critical of particular border policies and their underlying logic insofar as they contribute to such subordination.

Secondly, my book does not challenge the legal and philosophical distinction between high- and low-skilled immigrants. There is a separate literature on how occupations themselves are already unjustly sorted, perceived, and assigned.[4] More radically, we might think that the division of occupations into "high" and "low" skill is itself unjust—it is no coincidence at all that jobs regarded as "low-skilled" are often gendered and racialized. We might think that women and racial minorities are trapped in a toxic pattern where (a) they disproportionately take low-skilled jobs because of the persistent inequality of opportunity; (b) "low-skilled jobs" continue to be devalued and denigrated because they are associated with the labor of subordinated groups, and thus tend to be precarious and low-paying; and (c) women and racial minorities in low-skilled occupations lack social mobility precisely because they are so ungenerously and precariously employed, and so the occupations continue to be associated with them *and* also remain devalued/degraded (and so forth). It is not out of lack of sympathy that I do not engage more extensively with the above argument. Clearly, skill categories are socially constructed—often unfairly so—yet they persistently constrain or make possible our material life-prospects. We have good reason to resist the pejorative language of "low skill," which suggests inferiority and deficiency on the part of persons who perform essential labor. That said, it is exactly *because* of the "social realness" of skill, and the hardening of skill-based categories, that my book seeks to understand immigration injustice as it is experienced by those judged as "low-skilled," and how it can be ameliorated even if we fall short of eliminating skill categories altogether. My suspicion is that, for as long as we inhabit a capitalist economy that makes hierarchical distinctions between different modes of labor, and ascribes greater value, remuneration, and autonomy to jobs at the upper rungs, skill categories are not going to disappear anytime soon. It is all the more pressing, then, that we theorize about how to protect the social equality of low-skilled migrants under *nonideal conditions*, rather than focusing too fiercely on a distant utopian ideal of occupational egalitarianism.

Finally, I must note that the low-skilled migrants I have referred to above, in the US context, are predominantly Latino/a/x in origin. There is little doubt that the cruel treatment they are subject to is also partly a result of perceived racial otherness, and majority-race citizens' hostility toward those who are judged to be inferior and undesirable on the basis of their race. We may thus make a distinction between persons who face differential treatment *purely* on the basis of their perceived as low-skilled, and persons who are subject to it because of a combination of their perceived race *and* identity.[5] An example of a "pure" case of skill-based discrimination might have been the experiences of many white Irish migrants to the United States in the 1800s and beyond. While Irish migrants constituted nearly half of all immigrants to the United States in the 1840s, they often "entered the workforce at the bottom of the occupational ladder and took on the menial and dangerous jobs that were often avoided by other workers," and were the targets of attack by organizations like the American Protective Association and the Ku Klux Klan (Library of Congress). It seems fair to say, then, that Irish immigrants were discriminated against on the basis of their perceived low-skill *despite* being recognized as white. The serious marginalization of low-skilled Latino/a/x migrants in the United States, in contrast, seems premised on a combination of perceived racial otherness and low skill. As my book is an exercise in *nonideal theory*—a point that will be elaborated in Chapter One—I will be primarily concerned with cases where race and skill intersect. This is because I wish to focus on the cases of immigrant marginalization that I take to be the most salient today in affluent countries like the United States and United Kingdom, and such marginalization tends to be intersectional rather than "pure."

To highlight the special relevance of skill, I should note the differences between highly skilled immigrants like myself and those who suffer the bulk of immigration enforcement tactics. It cannot simply be the fact that the majority-Latino/a/x migrants held in US detention centers are viewed as racially Other. In the United States and United Kingdom, my racial identity certainly has an effect on the beliefs that citizens of those countries have about my membership in their polity—more specifically, the assumption that I am *not* a member. I am frequently coded as "foreign" because I look Asian, in the sense that I get asked where I'm "really" from or complimented on my proficiency in English, which happens to be my native language. To be sure, *citizens* of color also report similar experiences, where they face differential treatment on the basis of their "foreignness" regardless of their actual citizenship status; this we have in common.[6] But we need more than a summary glance of the *material consequences* that perceived foreignness has on how we are treated. A US citizen, for example, may be ordered to show proof of her legal presence because she is assumed to be a low-skilled migrant, and subjected to the use of force if she cannot produce the required papers. One only needs to look to the numerous instances where citizens of color were accidentally detained and deported. For example, Chandran Kukathas discusses the tragic fate of Johann "Ace" Francis, a young American citizen who was arrested in Oregon after being caught up in a street fight, and deported to Jamaica after he said he was born in Jamaica and could not prove his American citizenship (2021, 66). Ace Francis lived on the beach and streets until he was able to locate his biological father, and it took ten years for the then-high-schooler to go home, due to difficulties in finding the necessary documentation (66).

Here, I want to suggest that, while other persons of color may share my experience of being treated as "foreign" in a general sense, the particular intersection of race *and* skill that is perceived by others can make a significant difference to the character and extent of our oppression. It is, of course, not pleasant to have to fend off assumptions about my linguistic capacities, but I have never had my workplace raided, had ICE called on me, or been stopped by the police to have my papers checked because of purported "Mexican appearance."[7] The point to take home is that presumed "foreignness" and xenophobia have many faces, some of them considerably uglier than others. Usefully, on Ronald Sundstrom and David Kim's account, we should think of xenophobia as a type of "civic ostracism" (2014, 22). For Sundstrom and Kim, being included in the civic mainstream is a "precondition for certain social goods," such as "reasonable and fair access to goods, jobs, relationships, and statuses comparable to those of one's peers," as well as the sense that one's claim to the full array of basic rights within the polity is legitimate (2014, 22). In short, one's ability to access, or have a claim to such social goods can be indexed to the degree that they are perceived as properly "belonging" to the state in question. Here, the very opposite of civic inclusion is the "attribution of the cultural alienness of the subject or the felt sense that the subject does not rightly belong to the nation" (Sundstrom and Kim 2014, 25).

It is abundantly clear to me that, vis-à-vis a sense that they "rightly belong," *highly skilled migrants* like myself (doctors, lawyers, professors, scientists, software engineers) are treated very differently than *low-skilled migrants* (servers, cleaners, agricultural workers, construction workers, and domestic workers). This is not to say, of course, that everyone likes and accepts highly skilled migrants. Some people may sincerely prefer that there be no migration at all. Despite his professed desire to admit immigrants from "good countries" like Norway, US President Donald J. Trump rolled out the "Buy American and Hire American" executive order, intended to overhaul highly skilled immigration programs (like the H1-B) to "create higher wages and employment rates for workers in the United States." Yet, on the whole, highly skilled migrants are regarded as very desirable indeed; various countries have repeatedly expressed the desire for the "best and brightest" to bring over their labor, skills, and capital. There is a *place* in the polity appropriately reserved for "model" migrants of this sort. In contrast, there is no room whatsoever for the "bad," low-skilled migrants who pose serious security threats, finagle their way into leeching off social welfare, and worsen working conditions for citizens by lowering salaries or taking their jobs. The entry of "good migrants" is to be incentivized, while "bad migrants" must be forcefully deterred. Particularly in the wake of a rash of hate crimes against Asian persons in 2021, I want to be careful not to trivialize the violence against Asians, including highly skilled Asian migrants, that civic ostracism can incite. That said, to the best of my understanding, persons like myself who are read as "Asian" are *comparatively* less vulnerable to *state-sanctioned violence* that is perpetrated by law enforcement agents. This is because they are commonly assumed to be "model migrants": docile, law-abiding, and productive in virtue of their perceived high skill. Chapter Three considers the social standing of Asian immigrants and the idea of the "model migrant" in more detail.

We are told over and over, it seems, that skill-selective immigration systems are commonsensical. In theory, they do not discriminate on the basis of race, gender, or religion—you only need a skill set that is economically beneficial to the receiving state. Furthermore, it's a win-win situation: migrants get to pursue their dream careers, while states have much to gain from admitting highly skilled migrants who are ready and willing to work. However, even as a "highly skilled" migrant who benefits from such beliefs, a striking fact of skill-selective immigration policies—which forms the very basis of this book—is that they treat low-skilled migrants as a *socially subordinated* category of persons. The temptation is to think of immigrant selection as a kind of idealized job interview where each candidate is rigorously and fairly evaluated, and the most qualified individual of all gets hired. This picture, however, fails to track how skill-selective immigration policy *actually* operates in the real world. The guiding motivation of my book is to illuminate and make sense of how the process of skill-selection does not occur in an ideal interview room, but a profoundly *nonideal* world, rife with historical injustice that has constructed demeaning stereotypes about low-skilled migrants. In turn, these stereotypes are used to justify their unjust treatment across a range of contexts. Insofar as the subordination of low-skilled migrants (and people coded as such) is deeply unjust, and such injustice is upheld by skill-selective regimes, we have strong ethical reasons to rethink skill-selective immigration policies.

2. Justice and social subordination

Before I continue, I'll provide some theoretical background to the issue of justice and social subordination, especially with regard to noncitizens. As a starting point, Aristotle had a thing or two to say about foreigners and their place in the world. For one, he was a notorious proponent of "natural slavery"—the idea that the majority of human beings could be justly enslaved because they are slaves by nature (Heath 2008, 1). Specifically, he thought that natural slaves lacked the capacity to make reasoned judgments about what they ought to do consistently with their conception of the good life, even if they could be extremely intelligent in other ways (Heath 2008, 8). On Aristotle's view, *foreigners* in particular—that is, non-Greeks—were deemed to be natural slaves, consequent on the dispositions that were produced by different climate conditions. Thus, his test for determining whether or not someone was a natural slave went like this: "if he is a native of an area to the north or east of Greece, he probably is; if he is a native Greek, he almost certainly is not" (Kraut 2002, 291).

The bluntness of Aristotle's argument may sound jarring, but it is not too far removed from the demeaning terms in which people think about low-skilled migrants today. While they may not use the language of "natural slavery," there is an outright assumption in many societies (in the global north and south alike) that the purpose of low-skilled migrants is to "do the dirty work"—the unpleasant, laborious, and unsanitary tasks that are essential to the sustenance of the receiving state. Such tasks include caring for children and the elderly or infirm, which many citizens need help with. Theoretically speaking, however, Aristotle's hypotheses are assumed to have lost all appeal. Philosophers largely subscribe to the principle of moral equality—the fundamental belief that all persons are of equal moral status, which Deborah Hellman describes as a "bedrock moral principle" (2011, 6). Equal moral worth is composed of two secondary principles. Firstly, the worth or value of persons necessitates that they be treated with respect. Secondly, moral worth doesn't vary in accordance with their other features (6). For example, we are not endowed with *more* or *less* worth as a result of our height, age, or intelligence. This widely shared commitment has played into normative claims about what a just society would look like. While the idea of moral equality is too abstract to function as a premise from which we logically *deduce* a theory of justice, it is the yardstick that we use to judge the merits of competing conceptions of justice (Kymlicka 2001, 44–45).

One influential example of an equality-driven theory is John Rawls's theory of justice. For Rawls, moral equality primarily means that no persons should be subjected to arbitrary unequal treatment. While the demands of moral equality imply "justice as regularity" in the administration of institutions as public systems of rules, where similar cases must be treated similarly, it also applies to the *substantive* structure of institutions (1999, 441–442). This means that, under the first principle of justice, institutions assign equal basic rights to all persons that are compatible with a similar scheme of rights for all, while the second principle dictates that social and economic inequalities must be "attached to offices and positions open to all under conditions of fair equality of opportunity" and arranged to the greatest benefit of the least advantaged (Rawls 1999a, 266). Thus, for Rawls, the abstract commitment to moral equality gives rise to two concrete claims: firstly, that no arbitrary distinctions should be made between persons during the assignment of basic rights and duties, and secondly, that distributive shares should not be influenced by factors (like one's race, class, or gender) that are "arbitrary from a moral point of view" (1999a, 63).

Rawls's views have not generally been contested because of skepticism about moral equality per se, but rather, diverging beliefs about how best to capture it. For example, several philosophers have argued that moral equality may demand a form of equality that goes beyond eschewing arbitrary differences in rights or material distributions. Elizabeth Anderson has argued for a conception of social, or relational equality. While Anderson, like Rawls, begins from the equal moral worth of persons (1999a, 312), she contends that the proper aim of egalitarian justice is "to create a community in which people stand in relations of equality to others (Anderson 1999a, 288–289). On this interpretation of the demands of moral equality, it is wrong for the state to treat citizens as if they are "inferior to others in the worth of their lives, talents, and personal qualities," or to "express contemptuous pity" for those stamped as inferior, as well as for it to "stigmatize" and make "demeaning and intrusive judgments" about them (Anderson 1999a, 289).

Here, we can see that moral equality leads to the claim of *social* equality: that citizens ought to relate to each other as *social* equals, not as superiors and inferiors. Although some, including Anderson, have characterized the social approach as in competition with the distributive one, we need not accept this to appreciate its value. Aristotle's beliefs are not just troubling because of their material consequences for slaves, with regard to the rights or distributions they were accorded, but because they *also* presuppose a social order where "from the hour of their birth, some are marked out for subjection, others for rule" (*Politics* I, 5 1254a). On his vision, foreigners are essentially *social inferiors* who can be rightfully subjugated. So, the normative force of moral equality can be said to transcend the demand for political or distributive equality; it also forbids the demeaning or humiliating treatment of persons at the hands of the state. In other words, it entitles them to *social equality*.

3. What is social equality?

It is important to establish what exactly I mean by "social equality." Inegalitarian relationships, as I will understand them, are those where one person or group is *treated as an inferior* in relation to another, to the extent that they are dominated, exploited, marginalized, demeaned, and the targets of violence (E. Anderson 1999a, 313). In contrast, social egalitarians demand that persons stand in relationships to each other that are, at least in certain vital respects, not structured by differences of rank, power, or status (Scheffler 2015, 225). To be sure, my core argument will not be premised on the stronger assumption that social egalitarianism is the only currency of egalitarianism we should strive toward. Rather, I make the weaker assumption that egalitarians in general have strong reasons to object to unequal relationships. At the same time, by its very definition, social equality may be interpreted as presupposing the notion of a society. According to this reading, social equality would be realized within a "society of equals." We see this in Anderson's talk of a "community of equals," as well as in her notion of "democratic equality," which makes explicit reference to law-abiding citizens within a democratic state (1999a, 289). Likewise, Philip Pettit's vision of social equality, which is rooted in the ideal of nondomination, treats nondominating relationships as a "universal ideal for the members of a contemporary society" (1997, 6). From my perspective, however, the word "social" can refer more broadly to social interactions between different agents, whether they are individuals, collectives, or institutions. Many of us regularly engage in such social interactions outside of the context of a bounded community. I do not share a "society" with a Canadian border officer who I may speak with while arriving at the airport, nor am I part of the same "society" as a Filipino call center agent whom I may be relying on to resolve my online banking issues. Attempting to claim that we all inhabit the same society would stretch the definition of "society" beyond recognition. All the same, my interactions with the border officer and call center agent are undoubtedly *social*, and I can be treated by them—or find myself treating them—in ways that are objectionably inferiorizing, fleeting or geographically distant as our interactions can be. As Chapter Two of this book will explain in depth, we can think of social equality as a norm that regulates and constrains how we treat others in our varied social interactions with them, even outside of a bounded social community.

To sharpen the definition of social equality, consider some paradigmatic examples of hierarchical relationships in nonimmigration contexts. Suppose that a man insists that his wife defer to his judgment in major decisions and obey his commands, down to how she dresses, without question. Here, she stands in a relationship of inferiority to him, insofar as she is expected to behave in a submissive and obedient manner when interacting with him. Compare the pair to another hypothetical couple who make major decisions by having respectful and reasonable discussions, rather than attempting to issue unilateral commands to each other. In stark contrast to the previous case, both parties stand in equal relations with each other. Neither of them engages in behavior that designates the other as their inferior.

We need not restrict our theorizing about unequal relationships to small-scale interpersonal cases. Social inequality can also take the form of widespread social practices. Think of the Jim Crow era in the United States, where all persons classified as Black by the "one-drop" rule in place were forced to abide by particular strict rules of etiquette. For example, Black men were not supposed to shake hands with white men because it implied that they were of equal rank. Similarly, Black people had to use courtesy titles when addressing whites, instead of calling them by their first names, while white people did not use courtesy titles when referring to them. These rules of etiquette went hand-in-hand with official Jim Crow laws, which excluded Black people from public transport and facilities; they were not allowed to use the same train carriages, bathrooms, or drinking fountains as white people.

I now wish to highlight at least four distinctions that can be made between various instances of social equality:

a. Interpersonal vs. intergroup social inequality

Looking back at the examples I have chosen above, one happens at the *interpersonal* level, denoting a relationship between two *individuals*, while the other occurs at the greater *societal* level, and denotes a relationship between two *social groups*. The two levels are often closely related; indeed, many interpersonal instances of social inequality are traceable to broader, persistent patterns of behavior between groups. An inegalitarian relationship between a particular man and woman may be significantly influenced by patterns of unequal relationships between men and women as groups. For example, it is difficult to imagine how, within the context of a society where women do not have the right to vote or own property, interpersonal relationships between men and women could be said to be truly "equal." A man who loves his wife very much may do his best to respect her as an individual, but it seems unlikely that his behavior would not be affected by the legal architecture that surrounds their relationship, which would have the effect of encouraging or legitimizing dominating behavior toward women. At the same time, social inequality at the societal level is often reinforced by the individual behavior of people at the interpersonal level; every white person who insisted that Black people behave deferentially toward them, or permitted them to do so, contributed to keeping Jim Crow etiquette alive and well.

b. Formal vs. informal social inequality

The above examples also show that while status hierarchies can be built into a society's formal legal and political framework, they are often also part of informal social structures where particular norms and interactions are routinely reproduced. In this way, we can distinguish between *formal* and *informal* social inequalities. Examples of formal status hierarchies are relatively easy to come by. Think of the system of racial classification in apartheid South

Africa, or the caste system in India. Informal status hierarchies, on the other hand, include banal social practices that many may take for granted, such as the expectation that women be primarily responsible for domestic labor, or even the everyday decisions made by individuals, such as an employer choosing to ignore a job application because the person who submitted it has a name with racially coded associations, or lending discrimination by banks. Indeed, many people who participate in such practices may not even conceive of themselves as reinforcing a social norm or standard (McTernan 2018, 279), simply because the practice is so normalized as to be practically invisible to the agents who maintain it.

c. Direct vs. indirect social inequalities

Thirdly, Carina Fourie usefully distinguishes between *direct* and *indirect* social inequalities. The former is an inequality of status that explicitly and unambiguously confers a higher status to some in comparison to others. An example of a direct social inequality would be the expectation that certain individuals are expected to look down when they are spoken to, or speak only when they are spoken to (Fourie 2012, 114). In comparison, indirect social inequalities are differences or inequalities of nonsocial kinds that indicate or contribute to social inequalities. Racially segregated schools, for example, did not "clearly and unambiguously" confer a higher status to white children any more than gender-segregated schools "clearly and unambiguously" confer a higher status to boys. Nevertheless, educational segregation was rooted in the notion that Black children were inferior to white children and ought not to associate with them. Similarly, while the relative scarcity of women in STEM occupations in Western countries does not "clearly and unambiguously" confer a higher status to men, it is frequently attributed to the demeaning treatment of women in those fields, as well as girls being conditioned to believe that, unlike boys, they lack the scientific rigor necessary for such occupations—a belief that harks back to the stereotype that women are less capable of reason than men. Attention to indirect social inequalities may be regarded as especially important in the current political context. While philosophers previously defined social equality by contrast with ranked societies where each person could be placed in a particular station, and where deference and condescension were considered primary virtues, people's experience of social inequality has changed over time (Miller 1997, 234). Focusing too much on the absence of direct social inequalities may serve to mask the continued presence of indirect inequalities.

d. Intentional vs. unintentional social inequalities

Lastly, we should take care to distinguish between *intentional* and *unintentional* social inequalities. The social inequalities that were reinforced by racially segregated schools seemed to be dependent, at least in part, on the internal motivations of those who crafted and supported educational segregation. Arguably, racial segregation would not have counted as an example of social inequality if it were thoroughly driven by a different motivation: for example, if Black and white children had radically different physiological responses to the same highly contagious flu virus, such that white children would die from it but Black children escaped with a mere cold, and school administrators acted to prevent more deaths (E. Anderson 1999b). Significantly, however, social inequalities can be created *even* if the intentions and motivations of an agent are innocent or driven by seemingly legitimate considerations. Also consider the difficulties that are often faced by parents who travel internationally with their child and do not share their child's last name. Such parents are often subject to additional scrutiny at the border, to the extent that they have been advised to take along supporting documents, such as the child's birth certificate, to avoid being stopped at the border. The higher burden of proof on parents who do not share their child's last name seems to serve a benign purpose: to prevent child abduction and trafficking. However, the policy of requiring further proof of relationship is also known to have a serious disparate impact on divorcées who no longer share their child's last name, married women who decline to take their husband's name (in a world where children often take their father's last name by default), and LGBT households. Furthermore, it has also resulted in the frequent stopping of women of color who are traveling with their multiracial children without the presence of their white partners. The suspicion cast on parents with different last names from their children has sexist, racist, and homophobic consequences, well-intended as it may seem, and that these undesirable consequences give states good reason to pursue alternative policies (like allowing parents to name children in their passport, or creating electronic links between the passports of parents and children).

It is important to make three additional clarifications about the concept of social equality. Firstly, the fact that one person is treated as a superior, and the other as their inferior, does not necessarily mean that the former is treated very well, or that the inferior person is necessarily severely disadvantaged. As Carina Fourie notes, "The point, when we refer to hierarchies of social status, is the nature of the relationship between social positions, not the absolute level of treatment" (2012, 111). In other words, the main problem with social inequality is not that one party is treated badly, or that the other is privileged, but that they are not treated as equals (2012, 112). That said, a person's absolute level of treatment matters for how others relate to them. It might be difficult for the financially destitute, for example, to afford the essential provisions they need (like clean clothing and basic toiletries) to not be treated contemptuously by others in society. Guarding against social denigration, then, might require that everyone is guaranteed a minimum supply of goods or income alongside the demands of distributive justice, but I shall not speculate on what it ought to look like.

Secondly, the observation that one person (or a group) is treating another as their inferior is not wholly dependent on the former harboring a superior attitude toward the latter. I don't have to actually *believe* that you are my inferior in order to *treat* you as such, even though inferiorizing beliefs and actions tend to accompany one another. This is because, quite apart from an agent's actual attitude, we can be justified in regarding an action of theirs—or a series of actions—as *expressing* an inferiorizing attitude of its own. A man may control his wife's expenses for purely benevolent reasons: perhaps because he genuinely worries about her fiscally irresponsible ways and wants her to have enough savings for her retirement. All the same, even if he does not strictly *see her as inferior*, we may say that his decision expresses an infantilizing attitude toward her: a view of her as someone who is too irrational and childish to manage her own finances. As Elizabeth Anderson and Richard Pildes have suggested, "Not everything that expresses a state of mind is caused by that state of mind" (2000, 1508). For example, musicians can play music that expresses sadness without themselves experiencing sadness; "the sadness is in the music itself" (1508). Likewise, lawmakers could pass a law that *expresses* contempt for Black people even though none of the lawmakers personally feel racist contempt and are merely pandering to the hostile demands of their white constituents (1508).

But on what grounds, exactly, would we judge that an action expresses a particular attitude? On one well-known account, expressive meanings result from "the ways in which actions fit with (or fail to fit with) other meaningful norms and practices in the community" (Anderson and Pildes 2000, 1525). Put differently, we do not simply express attitudes of superiority or condescension by intending to express them or believing that our actions express those attitudes. In Rainer Werner Fassbinder's *The Bitter Tears of Petra von Kant*, the emotionally unstable and narcissistic title character subjects another woman, Marlene, to her incessant commands, which include asking Marlene to dance with her intimately. Throughout the film, Petra not only assumes total control over Marlene (who doesn't have a single line of dialogue), but also harshly berates her and takes out her unhappiness on her. Petra is seemingly unaware of her own dominating behavior toward Marlene; she casually dismisses Marlene's unsettling subservience as Marlene's "love" for her. As this rather extreme example illustrates, the standard for what counts as inferiorizing treatment is not subjective, especially when we can be terribly wrong about our own mistreatment of others. Rather, it is set by public and objective criteria for determining what our actions mean (Anderson and Pildes 2000, 1512).

Yet Anderson and Pildes's argument may not seem entirely satisfying. Firstly, it can be said to rely too much on the notion of the bounded social "community" and pay insufficient attention to the possibility that social meanings can trickle in from external sources, leading to a sea change in how particular actions are interpreted by some members of the community. Often, this can lead to confusion, if not outright incredulity, from other community members who have not taken up those meanings in the same way (because they lack exposure, or less charitably, because of willful ignorance). For illustration, consider the controversy over a Singaporean advertisement in 2019, where a majority-race, Singaporean Chinese actor had his skin painted a darker hue in a bid to portray an Indian, minority-race character.[8] Minority-race citizens sharply criticized the advertisement, naming it an instance of "brownface" that expressed the derogatory attitude of Singaporean Chinese toward them. It seemed that they had taken up the social meaning of *blackface* in Western societies, which fundamentally shaped their interpretation of the actor's regrettable "costume." In response, many Singaporean

Chinese denied that the social meaning of Black/brownface held any relevance for Singaporean society, simply because it was a product of *Western* histories, rather than something that could be universally applied to all social contexts. They believed, instead, that the actor's costume ought to be regarded as a benign celebration of multiculturalism. This example shows how, in the age of global communication and exchange, particular communities can find themselves disagreeing over the content of public meanings.

Such disagreement, however, is not neutral. There is a serious worry that the search for "objective meaning" might be obstructed by the well-known tendency to think of the status quo alone as possessing such legitimacy; an uncritical lauding of "objectivity" can risk crowding out the voices of minority groups who have lacked the equal chance to shape the community's social meanings, and therefore have "well-fitting" interpretive standards that may seem unfamiliar or absurd to the majority. Indeed, many Singaporean Chinese behaved as if the offense expressed by minorities was strange and obscure when *their* perception of "brownface" seemed much further off the mark, given the well-documented broader context of racism against non-Chinese. It is not always clear how to interpret a particular action if we cannot, from the get-go, agree about what the relevantly "meaningful norms and practices" actually are. Such instances, however, don't necessarily indicate that "objective" public criteria for social meanings are a lost cause. They just mean that our search for social meanings requires greater recognition of, and reconciliation with, the standpoints of groups who have been previously silenced. What matters, perhaps, is not public *consensus* over what things mean, but the willingness to understand and acknowledge what they mean to other persons—especially those with comparatively less social power—and in turn, the willingness to *allow* others to shape what they *come to mean*. In this sense, public meanings have an important procedural dimension. They don't necessarily track *how we currently perceive things*, but rather, what things *ought to mean* for the community after a fair process of deliberation over the available social meanings that is properly inclusive of *all* its members. As I endeavor to show, an openness to what things *do mean*, if we carefully reflect upon them, will be particularly important in the case of skill-selective immigration policies.

Thirdly, although I have sought to illustrate how social egalitarians oppose many relationships that exhibit a hierarchical character, they do not object to *all* cases of hierarchy. As Samuel Scheffler writes,

> differences of rank, power, and status are endemic to human social life. Almost all human organizations and institutions recognize hierarchies of authority, for example, and most social roles confer distinctions of status which in turn structure human relationships, such as the relationships of doctors to patients, teachers to students, parents to children, attorneys to clients, employers to employees, and so on. (2012, 225)

As a result, for a relationship to qualify as egalitarian, it is not necessary for it to be "altogether unmarked by distinctions of rank or status" (Scheffler 2012, 226). But if social egalitarians condemn hierarchical relationships between men and women, or Black and white people, why *don't* they necessarily condemn the social roles that Scheffler references, such as hierarchical relationships between doctors and patients, or teachers and students?

The relevant difference, I believe, is that the former track distinctions in "recognition" respect, while the latter do not. Gender and racial hierarchies, for example, are based on the assumption that women are *inferior persons* to men, or that nonwhites are *inferior persons* to whites. The latter, however, track what Stephen Darwall calls "appraisal respect," which "consists in an attitude of positive appraisal of [a] person either as a person or as engaged in some particular pursuit . . . the appropriate ground for such respect is that the person has manifested characteristics which make him deserving of such positive appraisal" (1977, 38). We can see that the higher status of the doctor to her patient, within the clinical context, is rooted in a positive appraisal of the doctor's knowledge and expertise relative to the patient, as opposed to an appraisal of the doctor as an overall *superior person* to the patient. In other words, distinctions in rank or status are prima facie compatible with social equality when they simply track particular attributes that an individual has (like experience or skill) that are superior to that of others, rather than an assessment of *superior personhood*, which is clearly in violation of social equality.

However, the lines between appraisal respect and recognition respect can be blurry, as there may be practices of positive and negative appraisal that suggest that persons with a certain attribute are inferior to others—all while hiding behind the language of mere appraisal. This can happen in two ways. The first is when people are given appraisal respect for personal attributes that are *meaningfully loaded* in the current social context. By meaningfully loaded, I mean that the esteem of certain attributes cannot be easily disentangled from inferiorizing attitudes toward others, according to our shared history and social conventions. For example, the academic hierarchy between professors and students is generally unproblematic in this regard, because the deference the students show their professors is typically rooted in appraisal-respect for their expert knowledge on a particular subject. Such esteem carries no corresponding demeaning message about the persons who lack doctorate-level expertise in, say, physics or sociology in the classroom, as no such stigma exists. In contrast, think of colorism, where people with darker skin have historically been treated as inferior to lighter-skinned people, through derogatory representations in society's cultural symbols, and their subjection to discriminatory practices. In this context, social equality is violated when someone is esteemed for having very light skin, because such esteem translates into social privileges that they enjoy at the expense of disrespect for darker-skinned people. Likewise, while distinctions in military rank generally bear no connection to social inequality present-day societies, the widespread glorification of people who serve in the military may also be inextricable from inferiorizing attitudes toward groups who have been deemed too weak and or damaged to serve, like women, transgender persons, or the non-able-bodied. Thus, social inequality refers only to differences in rank, power, or status that are grounded in disrespect and stigma for those at the losing end.

To summarize my main claims so far, instances of social inequality can differ in these four ways: (a) they can be interpersonal or societal; (b) they can be formally or informally enforced; (c) they can be direct or indirect; and (d) they can be intentional or unintentional.

4. Social equality and the claims of economic migrants

Keeping these remarks on social equality in mind, let's return to Aristotle's objectionable views on the so-called natural inferiority of foreigners. I am assuming that the reader will agree that it is deeply wrong to think of noncitizens as inherently inferior. But it is not nearly enough that we *believe* noncitizens are our equals; we must also *act* in ways that duly reflect this fact. If we recognize that social equality has serious implications for how citizens ought to be treated, it is no less necessary that the concern for, and protection of, noncitizens' social equality ought to regulate states' practices and policies toward noncitizens.

Significantly, while social equality is a familiar concept in discussions about the claims of fellow citizens, it has rarely been applied to the claims of immigrants. At best, it seems to warrant a superficial nod. For example, Christopher Heath Wellman dismisses the claim that the right to exclude wrongfully prevents noncitizens from equalizing their opportunities by aligning himself with social egalitarians, who do not necessarily argue for distributive equality between persons. As he writes, "equality demands that we address those inequalities that render people vulnerable to oppressive relationships. If this is correct, then the particular theory of equality required to motivate the egalitarian case for open borders is suspect and should be rejected in favor of a theory of relational equality" (Wellman 2008, 120). Here, Wellman acknowledges that achieving social equality may be important enough to outweigh other values like self-determination (2008, 122), and that "one consequence of the emerging global basic structure is that virtually all of the world's people now share some type of relationship" (2008, 123), so it seems that social egalitarians may have reason to care about unequal relationships between persons in different countries. However, Wellman does not expand on the consequences of social equality for the right to exclude, other than to use it for the purposes of fending off objections to the right to exclude. In contrast, my book develops the idea that a social account of equality is especially well-placed to provide illuminating insights about how states' right to exclude noncitizens ought to be limited.

In this book, I will be primarily concerned with the policies and actions that wealthy Western states have toward noncitizens; in particular, low-skilled economic migrants and the ubiquitous practices of exclusion I have mentioned at the beginning. By "economic migrants," I refer to migrants who fall within the purview of what Sarah Fine and Andrea Sangiovanni term the "pure case" (2014, 193). These persons are not refugees, and need not suffer from severe economic deprivation; neither are they seeking to migrate in order to reunite with their families. Nevertheless, they have a strong interest in residing in the host state because they are seeking "significantly better job opportunities, greater scope for religious or social association, or more wide-reaching political affinities with residents and citizens than they would in their country of origin" (Fine and Sangiovanni 2014, 194).

But why restrict the scope of my discussion in this way? As matters stand, many philosophers already acknowledge that the claims of refugees, or those who suffer from severe deprivation, or those who wish to reunite with their families, can place limitations on the right to exclude. For example, David Miller asserts that states have an obligation to admit refugees when "temporary solutions," like temporary residence and the establishment of safety zones prove insufficient for the protection of their basic rights (2007, 225). However, proponents of a robust right to exclude also tend to assume that states' exclusion of economic migrants is not subject to such constraints. Unlike the other groups mentioned above, those migrating to improve their prospects simply *do not have* moral claims to be included. On the other hand, some theorists have opposed this view by claiming that wealthy Western states *do* have a duty to admit economic migrants from poorer countries. As their arguments tend to go, the moral equality of citizens and foreigners means the entitlement to equal opportunities regardless of one's nationality, and that a global or cosmopolitan view of equal opportunity may demand extremely permissive immigration policies ("open borders," so to speak), although immigration restrictions can also be defended on similar grounds (Higgins 2009, 149).[9] So, economic migrants' right to admission may rest on a more general principle of global justice.

My book focuses on resisting the assumption that receiving states have free rein to exclude economic migrants, and defending the view that the commitment to social equality can place serious constraints on states' exclusion of immigrants in the "pure" case. Yet I also show that the commitment to social equality and its attendant implications for states' treatment of economic migrants is independent of a broader principle of global justice. One does not have to be a cosmopolitan to agree that states should not demean or subordinate immigrants. My overarching goal, rather, is to show that we have strong reasons to rethink skill-selective immigration policies that advantage highly skilled migrants and disadvantage low-skilled migrants *even if* states have an underlying right to control their borders. Furthermore, my objections to states' existing exclusionary mechanisms and how they are used against low-skilled migrants do not necessarily imply a system of open borders. Rather, I believe that the ethical commitment to social equality requires states to *regulate* their exclusionary practices so that they do not demean and subordinate low-skilled migrants.

The core insights of the book are intended to inform philosophical theories of just admissions; in particular, the question of what justice requires with regard to the admission of low-skilled migrants. However, it is worth underscoring that my aims are more diagnostic than prescriptive. Rather than proposing concrete solutions for how immigration policies should be designed, I am far more interested in providing a critique of how and where existing skill-selective immigration policies go wrong, and equipping the reader with a conceptual toolkit for understanding why we should object to immigration policies that may seem so pragmatic and commonsensical at first blush. As I endeavor to show, at present, there is a noticeable gulf between what existing theories of immigration justice have to say about low-skilled migrants and the intricacies of low-skilled migrants' lived experience on the ground. It behooves us to step away from the realm of abstract principles, whether they speak for or against the admission of economic migrants, and supplement it with a more fine-grained social analysis of how skill-based selection may be demeaning in a way that closely intersects with gender, race, and class oppression.

My strategy follows the one Joseph Carens effectively uses in *The Ethics of Immigration*, where the assumption that his audience is motivated by the basic commitment to the equal moral worth of individuals allows him to establish a "shared understanding" between those with a permissive attitude toward immigration, and those with a considerably more restrictive view, rather than treating them as irreconcilable from the ground up (2015, 5). Similarly, my claims in this book are designed to appeal to an audience who is committed to equal respect for all persons, including those who are firmly convinced that states have the right to exclude. When confronted with the demeaning treatment that low-skilled migrants are regularly subjected to by receiving states, our shared belief in the imperative of equal respect ought to unite us in condemning such treatment, more than it divides us over other problems. Below, I outline the overall strategy and structure of the book.

5. My strategy and structure

The book is divided into three parts. Part I focuses on the conceptual grounding of the universal entitlement to social equality. In Chapter One,

I situate the idea of states' right to exclude squarely within the realm of *non-ideal theory.* Rather than focusing on how the right to exclude may be justified within an ideal theoretical realm, we must pay attention to how the right to exclude is exercised today, in a world riddled with social inequality and injustice (much of which has deep historical roots). At present, the most well-known argument against states' right to exclude, made by theorists like Joseph Carens and Philip Cole, is grounded in the foundational principle of equal respect for all persons. This argument, which I call the Argument from Social Contingency, claims that immigration exclusion disrespects noncitizens because it treats them unequally from citizens for a morally arbitrary reason. Exclusion treats noncitizens unequally by denying them access to the wealth of opportunities available in the receiving state and thus blocking them from equalizing their life-prospects. At the same time, it does so *arbitrarily* because they are denied entry on the basis of their citizenship status, which is believed to be a socially contingent feature. The problem with the Argument from Social Contingency, however, is that it does not clearly engage with the particular sites and methods of exclusion that are likely to reinforce objectionable forms of social inequality. A quick survey of other examples of wrongful exclusion reveals a different angle: that immigration exclusion may be disrespectful because it *demeans* at least some noncitizens. Put differently, it wrongfully treats them as the social inferiors of citizens. Consequently, the problem at hand is not that noncitizens are excluded for *arbitrary* reasons, but that they have long been (and continue to be) excluded for *nasty*,[10] morally repugnant ones. I conclude that "equal-respect" arguments for robust constraints on states' right to exclude will have to take a different route; one that has far more to say about the quality of the *social relationships* between citizens and noncitizens.

Continuing with this strand of thought, Chapter Two develops a strong ethical justification for the right to social equality. I note that, much like distributive equality, the entitlement to social equality is typically construed as turning on a special relationship that is held between fellow citizens; for example, the fact that they are coparticipants in a joint cooperative scheme, or that they are unavoidably and involuntarily subject to background rules that shape the terms of their interaction. This "conventional view," I believe, is seriously lacking because it leaves us with no resources to explain the wrong in subordinating *noncitizens.* In contrast, I argue that the claim to social equality is universal; equal status is owed to *all persons* in virtue of the threat that subordinating treatment poses to their *personhood*. Here, social equality can be understood as a necessary precondition for a flourishing sense of self. To make this argument, I draw on a diverse range of philosophical approaches to the self. After this, I examine the implications of a universal entitlement to social equality for the state. As noncitizens have a basic right to social equality, states owe them two correlative duties of justice: Negatively, states must refrain from enacting institutional norms or policies that foreseeably or observably generate social inequalities. Positively, states must create and maintain the existence of institutions that equip persons with provisions or accommodations that enable them to participate in public life as equals or engage in projects that actively counter and resist established patterns of social hierarchy. The duty to preserve social equality is compatible with states owing stronger obligations to particular groups and less demanding duties to others, rather than having onerous *global* duties to minimize social inequality around the world. However, at the very least, it places some limitations on how states may treat noncitizens who are territorially present, as well as those who are attempting to enter it, but are not yet located on its territory.

From here, noncitizens' right to social equality equips us with a novel conceptual toolkit that we can use to evaluate the permissibility of current immigration policies. In Part II of my book, I take for granted the prevailing philosophical view that states have the right to exclude noncitizens. Nevertheless, I emphasize the *limitations* on how they may exercise such a right, given the duty to refrain from enacting laws or policies that generate social inequality. Interestingly, immigration policies that are generally regarded as neutral or even desirable may turn out to be unjust. In Chapter Three, I focus on the widespread phenomenon of direct discrimination against low-skilled migrants. Unlike gender or race-based selection, it is not generally regarded as unjust, for the same reason that it does not express disrespect in the same way that sexist or racist selection criteria does. I argue that this assumption is mistaken, as in the current social context, skill-based discrimination has the expressive effect of reproducing and legitimizing demeaning social beliefs about low-skilled noncitizens.

Chapter Four deepens my analysis of the wrongfulness of skill-selective immigration policies. Having considered the direct effects of skill-based discrimination, I turn to its *indirect* consequences. Although those policies only exclude low-skilled workers on paper, empirical evidence has shown that they may also have a disproportionate impact on the admission of noncitizens who are women. In other words, it indirectly discriminates against them. On my view, such indirect discrimination is wrongful because it ultimately worsens the subordinate position of woman workers in patriarchal societies. Specifically, I contend that immigration policymakers have negligently failed to consider the social meaning of women's difficulty in being admitted under the "skilled" category, which worsens demeaning stereotypes about working women in patriarchal societies. As a result, it gives us a further reason to object to states' employment of skill-selective immigration policies.

In Part III, I consider another significant line of critique for skill-selective immigration policies, while still stopping short of an argument for open borders per se. Turning away from demeaning social beliefs, I move toward the issue of *existing injustice* and its implications for economic migrants. Chapter Five argues that, aside from being wrongfully discriminatory, skill-selective immigration policies may be wrongful because they perpetuate a distinctively colonial harm: the harm of *racial exploitation*. I begin by discussing two familiar arguments for limiting states' right to exclude vis-à-vis immigrants who originate from past colonial territories, explaining how the wrongs of colonialism may cast a shadow over ex-colonial powers' present-day right to exclude. Firstly, the arguments that are typically used to justify the exclusion of noncitizens may simply not apply to members of past colonies. Secondly, inclusion in ex-colonial polities may constitute an important form of reparations to citizens of ex-colonies. A third requirement of a decolonial ethics of immigration, as I will show, is that states must significantly relax their immigration controls with regard to low-skilled migration. Focusing on the case of the United States, I explain how, through their interaction with unjust social structures, existing skill-selective immigration regimes effectively uphold the racial exploitation of migrants. Low-skilled Latino/a/x migrants are systematically rendered vulnerable and have their vulnerability instrumentalized by the state for its own material benefit. If it is true that racial exploitation lies at the heart of colonialism, we must treat skill-based exclusion as a distinctively colonial injustice, albeit one taking place in the here and now.

Up to this stage, my suggestions have focused exclusively on what *states* ought to do in order for their immigration policies to be just. I conclude the book by considering what my prescriptions may mean for *noncitizens* and how they should act under persistent conditions of injustice. If it is true (as I have argued) that immigration laws are generally unjust, are migrants obliged to obey them? To anchor the discussion, Chapter Six reconstructs two well-established views on this issue: the "permissive" and "restrictive" approaches to immigration disobedience. According to the former, migrants permissibly disobey unjust immigration laws in order to protect themselves against threats to their basic rights. For the latter, however, disobedience is permissible only if the laws in question are *egregiously* unjust. I respond to these two arguments by developing a justification for immigration that stands in-between them. I argue that migratorial disobedience is not only morally permissible in the present-day context, but also *morally desirable.* On my view, the desirability of migratorial disobedience is grounded in the vital role that migrants have to play in transforming socially subordinating systems of immigration law; it may be necessary for receiving states to overcome persistent democratic deficits in immigration policymaking.

PART I

SOCIAL EQUALITY AND THE ETHICS OF IMMIGRATION

1
Equal Respect and the Right to Exclude

1. Introduction

It is widely accepted that all persons are entitled to equal respect, by virtue of their humanity. Are states' rights to exclude noncitizens from their territory consistent with noncitizens' claims to equal respect? A cursory look at the ongoing hostile climate toward immigrants, and the subordinating practices they are routinely subjected to, will tell us *no.* As my book will explain, moving forward from justifying a basis for the state's right to exclude, there is a pressing need to focus on how states *exercise* this purported right in the here and now. Immigration controls, as they presently stand, not only routinely license the social subordination of low-skilled migrants, but also harden preexisting forms of subordination, particularly those that result from colonial legacies. From a social egalitarian perspective—the primary framework I will use for my ethical analysis of immigration policies—we have strong reasons to object to several facets of current immigration policies.

This book should be read as an exercise in nonideal theory. In particular, it pays close attention to the immigration-related ethical issues faced by affluent liberal states that continue to grapple with issues of gender-based, racial, and ethnic marginalization.[1] My overarching task is to explain the moral principles that should guide immigration policy against a real-world background of profound social inequalities, where states are not compliant with the basic demands of justice that apply to them, and migration does not occur within a set of natural and historical conditions that are favorable toward justice for migrants.[2] That said, the moral principles themselves

Immigration and Social Equality. Désirée Lim, Oxford University Press. © Oxford University Press 2023.
DOI: 10.1093/oso/9780197658093.003.0002

derive from a certain commonly held "ideal": the ideal of equal respect and, by extension, equal social relationships between persons. So, my theory of immigration justice is, as Joseph Carens puts it, "an ethical account that incorporates both realistic and idealistic concerns" (1996, 156).

Importantly, other philosophers have already argued for the fundamental incompatibility of exclusion with equal respect for noncitizens. In this chapter, as a starting point, I consider one well-known articulation of the incompatibility thesis, which I will call the Argument from Social Contingency. This view focuses on the morally arbitrary, or normatively extraneous properties of citizenship status.[3] Broken down, the argument goes like this: the exclusion of noncitizens is disrespectful because it subjects them to coercion on the basis of a socially contingent, and thus unjustifiable feature; in this case, their citizenship status. Here, citizenship is seen to fall into the same category as other morally arbitrary attributes like gender, race, and class.

However, this interpretation of the requirements of equal respect is incomplete. In particular, close attention to the nonideal realm will reveal that states do not simply exclude noncitizens for poorly justified reasons, but morally repugnant ones—reasons that are closely bound up with socially subordinating beliefs and practices. Put differently, the problem with immigration exclusion is not (only) that it is morally arbitrary, but that it is *demeaning* to noncitizens. Separate from the failure to provide reasonable justification to noncitizens for their exclusion, which the Argument from Social Contingency focuses on, exclusion harmfully subordinates noncitizens. To equally respect noncitizens, we will have to take a different route from the Argument from Social Contingency; one that has far more to say about the structure and character of *social relationships* between citizens and noncitizens.

I proceed in this order. Section 2 begins by distinguishing between the realms of ideal and nonideal theory, and clarifying the location of my normative analysis of immigration in relation to the two. There, I note that immigration theorists have generally adopted a more abstract approach toward immigration justice, asking *how* the right to exclude noncitizens can be justified in a way that is compatible with liberalism. In contrast, I prefer a concrete, grounded approach that begins with the recognition of entrenched injustice: given a world rife with troubling and persistent social inequalities, many of which are suffered by immigrants (and sometimes, persons of immigrant descent), *which* particular sites and methods of immigration exclusion are likely to reinforce such forms of social subordination? In Section 3, following the "ideal" at the center of my analysis, I explain the demands of equal respect and how it places limits on the actions of states. I also offer an account of moral arbitrariness that explains why states are prohibited from treating persons unequally for morally arbitrary reasons. Next, drawing from instructive arguments by Joseph Carens and Phillip Cole, Section 4 sketches out the Argument from Social Contingency. Section 5 highlights the limitations of the Argument from Social Contingency by explaining how, like in other well-known cases of exclusion, immigration exclusion may disrespect noncitizens because it *demeans* them. I conclude by briefly examining the implications of my arguments for the rest of the book.

2. Nonideal theory and immigration justice

I have suggested that my book should be understood as a contribution to nonideal theory. Importantly, my approach marks a departure from the dominant paradigm of the philosophy of immigration, which has tended to focus on the ideal realm and therefore formed conclusions and made policy recommendations on that basis. To be sure, this is not to say that the majority of immigration theorists have completely neglected nonideal issues and circumstances, or that my normative analysis of immigration policy will reject ideals of justice altogether. Quite the opposite; I argue that the ideal of *equal respect*, properly fleshed out as equal social relationships between persons (citizens and noncitizens alike) has a good deal to say about what's wrong with immigration policy and how we ought, if possible, to change it. At the same time, I want to be attentive to the possible real-world costs of adopting more permissive immigration policies in the name of equal respect, especially when immigration may have a substantial impact on the receiving's state economy and society, including (but not limited to) outcomes in the domestic labor market and levels of expenditure on social services (Yong 2018, 467). In this sense, my book occupies a specific—and I believe, desirable—location in relation to ideal and nonideal theory. In this section, I sketch out the distinction between ideal and nonideal approaches to the ethics of migration, which can lead us to very different normative conclusions. Without altogether dismissing the value of ideal theory, I argue that we ought to prefer the nonideal approach to immigration justice.

a. Immigration and ideal theory

Imagine a world entirely devoid of immigration injustice. The flow of movement around the world, where persons from other countries arrive at, take up residency in, or decide to become citizens of, other countries is governed by principles that are fully just. What would those principles for just migration look like? And what, exactly, would they require of states, citizens, and would-be migrants? Under the lens of *ideal theory*—in particular, the lens famously developed by John Rawls in *A Theory of Justice*—we might focus on working out the principles characteristic of a just migration regime with the assumption of "strict compliance" from all relevant agents to whom the demands of justice apply, as well as "reasonably favorable circumstances" under which the state's historical, social, and economic conditions make the realization of justice possible (1999a, 216; 1999b, 5). On this view, principles of just migration are formulated for an international system of states that is generally compliant with their duties of justice toward migrants, and circumstantially equipped to discharge those duties.

Indeed, as I will explain, several theorists of immigration justice have adopted exactly this standpoint. Broadly speaking, many theorists have begun with the abstract question of whether an "ideal" liberal state—just like the one Rawls has in mind—may justly exclude noncitizens. Put differently, they have aimed to demonstrate that immigration restrictions are compatible with the idea of equal respect, and that states may in theory exercise their right to exclude noncitizens without falling afoul of "perfect justice." Typically, the right to exclude is justified by states' interest in self-determination and its ancillary requirements. This foundational principle is then applied one level "upward" and used to answer more concrete questions about the contours of just immigration policy. To show how the principle operates, I briefly elaborate on three interpretations of self-determination below.[4]

One notable argument from self-determination appeals to the strong interest that states have in maintaining a particular public culture or national identity. David Miller assumes that states "require a common public culture that in part constitutes the political identity of their members, and that serves valuable functions in supporting democracy and other social goals" (2005, 199). He defines a common public culture as a "set of ideas about the character of the community which also helps to fix responsibilities," which is to some degree the result of political debate between citizens, and disseminated by mass media (1995, 68). For example, the public culture of some states may attach more value to individual self-sufficiency, while others will emphasize the value of collective goods (1995, 69). Immigration may have a significant impact on the common public culture, as immigrants who are admitted may do so with different cultural values, including political values that differ from the public culture of the community that they are admitted to (Miller 2005, 199). In a similar vein, Michael Walzer observes that "the distinctiveness of cultures and groups depends upon closure, and without it, cannot be conceived as a stable feature of human life." Acknowledging cultural distinctiveness as a value means permitting closure on *some* level, and it seems appropriate for a sovereign state to "take shape and claim the authority to make its own admissions policy, to control and sometimes restrain the flow of immigrants" (1983, 39). Arguably, without the right to exclude, there could not be "communities of character," which are historically stable, ongoing associations between persons who have a special commitment to one another and their shared life (Walzer 1983, 42).

In contrast, Christopher Heath Wellman interprets the "right to exclude" rather differently. He chooses to focus on an entirely different component of self-determination: the oft-touted value of freedom of association. Wellman begins by identifying the shared conviction that we enjoy a "morally privileged position of dominion over our self-regarding affairs, a position which entitles us to freedom of association in the marital and religious realms" (2008, 110). For example, we assume that everyone has the right to choose their marital partner, or the people they practice their religion with (110). At the same time, the freedom of association includes the right to *reject* potential associations, as well as the right to disassociate (110). I may decide on who I wish to associate with, but also on who I wish to avoid. Wellman suggests that the state has an analogous right to the freedom of association:

> just as an individual has a right to determine whom (if anyone) he or she would like to marry, a group of fellow-citizens has a right to determine whom (if anyone) it would like to invite into its political community. And just as an individual's freedom of association entitles one to remain single, a state's freedom of association entitles it to exclude all foreigners from its political community. (2008, 110–111)

Importantly, none of the above theorists do stop at providing a liberal justification for immigration restrictions. Indeed, their justifications for immigration exclusion have direct bearing on how they believe we should respond to real-world problems. For instance, Miller and Walzer evince a particular view on immigration that tracks their primary concern with the state's right to preserve its culture. For example, Walzer acknowledges that refugees are a group of "needy outsiders whose claims cannot be met by yielding territory or exporting wealth; they can be met only by taking people in," and that "the victims of political and religious persecution, then, make the most forceful claim for admission" (1984, 48–49). Yet, while the claims of refugees may be strong, this does not entirely remove the receiving state's right to exercise discretion over refugee admission by preferring those with a "ideological as well as ethnic affinity," such that states may choose those with a "more direct connection with [their] own way of life.[5] Miller's view on refugees is somewhat different. He concludes that it is "generally indefensible" for states to prioritize refugees on the basis of common culture *unless* there is a background against which cultural selection can be successfully used to divide responsibilities to admit refugees between states (2016, 92). That said, for Miller, refugees constitute a special case; he joins Walzer in concluding that economic refugees may be permissibly selected on the basis of cultural commonality. Both theorists flag the potential costs that cultural differences may impose on the receiving state, such as decreased support for the welfare state as the result of disidentification with newcomers (Miller 2016, 108; Walzer 1984, 38).

Wellman's emphasis on the freedom of association rather than cultural preservation, however, leads him to depart from Miller and Walzer on the issue of refugees. He states that "every legitimate state has the right to close its doors to all potential immigrants, even refugees desperately seeking asylum from incompetent or corrupt political regimes that are either unable or unwilling to protect their citizens' basic moral rights" (2008, 109). This is not to say that Wellman thinks that states lack duties to refugees altogether. Rather, if states choose not to admit refugees, they are morally required to discharge their duties through alternative means. That is, they may "export justice" and assist refugees from afar through the use of military force to create safe havens and no-fly zones (2008, 129). As I have suggested above, this rather stark conclusion seems to be an immediate consequence of his insistence that the receiving state's freedom of association constitutes a legitimate reason for exclusion in itself. Much like in Miller and Walzer's case, we can see how Wellman's grounding principle for permissible exclusion directly informs his concrete prescriptions for present-day immigration policy.

b. Immigration and nonideal theory

So far, I have pointed out two things. Firstly, a number of philosophers have attempted to develop principles for immigration justice by proposing a basic justification for legitimate exclusion. As I have indicated, these justifications are supposed to apply to a liberal state, presumably under conditions of full compliance and reasonably favorable circumstances. Furthermore, these philosophers have tried to answer questions about present-day immigration policy through the lens of their preferred justification for exclusion (whether it is cultural preservation or the freedom of association). The problem with the "ideal" approach, however, is the sizable chasm between the realm of the ideal and the world that migrants actually inhabit. By starting from the "bottom" and focusing on what an ideal liberal state might be permitted to do, it leaves aside the specific character of immigration in the here and now. Take the issue of compliance, for a start. Significantly, Rawls remarks that "[w]e are confident that religious intolerance and racial discrimination are unjust." In comparison with other trickier matters, such as the question of fair distribution, "[t]hese convictions are provisional fixed points which we presume any conception of justice must fit" (1999a, 17–18). We might assume that, within Rawls's view of the ideal realm, agents "strictly comply" with the basic duty of justice to not discriminate on the basis of race or religion (Rawls 1999a, 216), and that his theory of justice is designed to apply to such circumstances. We must be wary of extending these assumptions to our theorizing about immigration justice when it is well known, on the contrary, that states' immigration policies have been (and continue to be) famously racist and intolerant. It bears remembering Australia's self-explanatory "White Australia" immigration policy, or the United States' Chinese Exclusion Acts, or the United Kingdom's "Commonwealth Immigration Act" whose exclusionary impacts, according to the Home Secretary at the time, was "intended to, and would in fact, operate on coloured people almost exclusively." As José Jorge Mendoza has observed, "denying admission or citizenship to certain groups of people is closely correlated to a denial of *whiteness*" (2016, 202). More recently, think of the "Muslim ban" introduced by the Trump administration in 2017, which targeted the citizens of several Muslim-majority countries. These examples merely scratch the surface of a long, tarnished record of injustice toward migrants. As Sarah Fine observes,

> race, racism, and racial and ethnic discrimination are embedded in the history of migration, in public responses to immigrants, in the apparatus of immigration controls, and in migration flows. And this is not just a regrettable historical fact; it remains true, even pervasive. (Fine 2016, 131)

Given these considerations, it is not clear why we should try to "idealize" the realm of immigration, when injustice *itself* is often the cause of mass migration. To see the problem, imagine pondering the right to bear arms for purposes of self-defense under the assumption of strict compliance. In this (admittedly more extreme) case, it strikes me as wrongheaded to adopt the assumption of strict compliance because it logically precludes the existence of the very injustice that it is supposed to help us address. To be sure, I do not deny that persons may, in an ideal world, have injustice-free reasons for deciding to migrate, nor am I saying that persons *only* migrate today as a response to injustice. The point, rather, is that today's immigration trends—the very trends that make immigration a serious political issue in the first place—are generally driven by injustice. For example, the UNHCR recorded that at least 79.5 million persons were forcibly displaced as a result of "persecution, conflict, violence, human rights violations, or events seriously disturbing public order." If the goal is to develop guiding principles for immigration justice, it is not clear how instructive it would be to abstract away from the fact of immigration-related noncompliance by state actors, both in the past and the present.

One reply might go like this: ideal theory is a "necessary precursor" to nonideal theory (Stemplowska and Swift 2016, 374). As a starting point, ideal theory "identifies the objective at which nonideal theory ought to aim and thereby gives nonideal theory its ultimate target." Put differently, it plays a "target role" by telling us what to do in the here and now, given the ideal endpoint that we wish to arrive at (376). Furthermore, as Stemplowska and Swift suggest, ideal theory can also play an "urgency role": by observing the extent to which they deviate from our notion of "perfect justice," (2012, 376) we can make assessments about the relative urgency of particular injustices and which we ought to prioritize. I don't disagree that, in some cases, ideal theory can be used as a yardstick for evaluating the seriousness of particular injustices and giving us a sense of the direction that we ought to be moving in. My goal in this chapter is not to deny or undermine the value of ideal theory as a philosophical enterprise. The issue, rather, lies in the specific *site* of injustice that I am trying to address. At least within the sphere of immigration, I worry that overuse of the ideal standpoint would lead to our "abstracting away from realities crucial to our comprehension of the actual workings of injustice in human interactions and social institutions," therefore moving us further away from what we would consider to be ideal rather than closer to it (Mills 2005, 170). As Charles Mills points out, ideal theory may be *antithetical* to justice in scenarios when its neglect of social realities leads us to endorse abstract normative concepts that turn out to be illegitimate or harmful in practice (2005, 176).

In my view, the grounding principles endorsed by Miller, Walzer, and Wellman already suffer from this limitation. As abstract justifications for exclusion, the ideas of cultural preservation and freedom of association may sound very attractive at first glance. Matters look different when we rethink these normative concepts in conjunction with the legacies of racism that have fueled immigration policy—specifically, the well-known historical tendency to exclude immigrants of color on the basis that they were culturally inferior and unassimilable, or that they were racially undesirable and therefore not fit for association with citizens of the state. In sum, without taking full account of immigration-related noncompliance, we may place a good deal of weight on normative concepts that risk propping up immigration injustice in practice, rather than decisively tending away from it. To be clear, I am not saying that Miller, Walzer, and Wellman themselves *endorse* racist immigration policies, or that exclusion on the basis of culture dissimilarity or the state's freedom of association is necessarily racist. One way around the problem might be to argue for an additional regulative principle that forbids exclusion on the basis of race, or to define "cultural preservation" or "freedom of association" in a way that precludes racially exclusionary interpretations of the concepts. Yet, even if we can pull this off, the normative concepts themselves seem wanting. On their own, they leave us without an understanding or diagnosis of past immigration injustice and how related forms of immigration injustice might continue to be perpetuated in the present day, albeit sometimes in more indirect and insidious forms. Quoting Mills, "it may be that the non-ideal perspective of the socially subordinated is necessary to generate certain critical evaluative concepts in the first place" (2005, 177). In order for us to inch closer to immigration justice, we will need a set of "critical evaluative concepts" that we can use to interrogate past and present-day immigration policy, not normative concepts that are prone to appropriation and abuse by noncompliant agents.

As I see it, the goal of my nonideal approach to the ethics of immigration is precisely to offer a "critical evaluative concept" of this sort. Firstly, the concept in question must be grounded in our knowledge of existing injustices that migrants experience under conditions of noncompliance—and the circumstances that produce them. Secondly, it should help us to understand the relationship between myriad forms of immigration injustice—for example, why they are similar in character or how they may systematically uphold each other over time. It is worth noting, here, that the nonideal approach does not require aversion to *ideals* in themselves. The target of my criticism has the tendency to neglect wealthy Western states' legacy of crafting racist and discriminatory immigration policies, which has led them to proffer foundational principles for migration that do not respond to, or worse still, threaten to reinforce those injustices. Nevertheless, the most valuable critical evaluative concepts are often accompanied by a corresponding ideal that we believe society ought to strive toward. One example of a critical evaluative concept might be that of the *patriarchy*, which seeks to describe the subordination of women across multiple domains of social life. While the concept of "patriarchy" has developed out of nonideal theory that seeks to illuminate the reality of women's subordination, it carries the treasured "ideal" of gender equality: the vision of a society where women and men can stand in relation to each other as equals, rather than as inferiors and superiors. Notice, however, that we can only arrive at this ideal by observing and analyzing the specific forms of gendered discrimination and violence that have taken place under conditions of noncompliance. In this case, a nonideal approach may be able to better realize the ideal of equality by "realistically recognizing the obstacles to [its] acceptance and implementation" (Mills 2005, 181).

I believe that we should take a similar approach to immigration justice. The "ideal" can only be properly understood and realized if we pay sufficiently close attention to the "nonideal." Keeping this in mind, as I have suggested in the Introduction, one powerful ideal that unites many philosophers and foregrounds their theories of justice is the principle of *equal respect for all persons*. To reiterate, by virtue of our equal moral worth, all persons should be treated with equal respect. It is from this timeless and appealing ideal, I think, that we can successfully derive much-needed guidance for (more) just immigration policies. I will assume that, at its core, immigration policy cannot be just if it is *disrespectful* to noncitizens; we can agree on this much. However, as I will show, the concept of equal respect will only have teeth if it has more to say about the distinctive ways in which noncitizens are routinely subordinated and relegated to an inferior status, and how these demeaning relationships between citizens and noncitizens are effectively reproduced by present-day immigration policies that may seem "neutral" or "desirable" on paper.

Up to this point, I have mainly attended to well-known philosophical arguments—namely those by Miller, Walzer, and Wellman—that support a robust right to exclude noncitizens. In what remains of this chapter, I want to focus on a well-known objection to the right to exclude, which I call the Argument from Social Contingency. Importantly, this objection, which has been most famously articulated by Joseph Carens and Phillip Cole, strongly appeals to the idea of equal respect. By pointing to the *moral arbitrariness* of citizenship, it makes the case that exclusion is *disrespectful* to noncitizens. Put differently, the disrespectful treatment in question lies in a failure to properly justify exclusion (and the coercive treatment it entails) to noncitizens on the receiving end. However, while the Argument from Social Contingency rightly identifies equal respect as a moral consideration that can limit states' right to exclude, it is insufficiently attentive to nonideal conditions and the nature of the reasons for which many noncitizens have been excluded. As I will show, the violation of equal respect doesn't lie in states having *insufficient reasons* for exclusion, but rather, *nasty* ones that are deeply harmful to noncitizens.

3. Equal respect and the right to exclude

States' right to exclude noncitizens may ultimately be blocked by a competing ethical consideration: the equal moral status of noncitizens. In this vein, Michael Blake has suggested that one of the most basic ethical questions for immigration theorists is whether restrictions on prospective migrants can be consistent with our commitment to the equal moral worth of persons

(2008, 965). But how, exactly, should immigration policy be responsive to the demands of equal respect? What does it mean to treat someone as an equal in the immigration context? In this section, I look to one widely shared interpretation of the demands of equal respect: each person's right to be treated in accordance with reasons are *reasonably justifiable* to them.

a. Justification as a requirement of equal respect

Following Stephen Darwall's influential view, we are required to show each and every person *recognition respect*. As Darwall writes, having recognition respect for someone *qua* their humanity is to "give appropriate weight to the fact that he or she is a person by being willing to constrain one's behaviour in ways required by that fact" (Darwall 1977, 45). But which features of persons are appropriate objects of respect, and how do we act in ways that are consistent with those features? For Rawls, the answer lies in our individual possession of what he calls the two moral powers: the capacity for a sense of justice, and for a conception of the good. Firstly, we can rely on each other to understand and act in accordance with principles of justice (Rawls 1999a, 125). Secondly, we are able "to form, to revise, and to pursue a conception of the good, and to deliberate in accordance with it" (Rawls 1993, 72). Individuals are therefore understood as self-authenticating sources of value who are able to give value to plans and allegiances through freely exercising their moral abilities (Blake 2001, 271). Furthermore, while persons have legitimate aims and interests, they also have a "highest-order interest" in developing and exercising their moral powers, and securing the conditions under which they can further their determinate conceptions of the good, whatever they may be (Rawls 1993, 105–106). In sum, as equal persons, we have valuable interests that stem from our individual conceptions of the good, coupled with a *highest*-order interest in cultivating and exercising our moral capacities, and we treat others respectfully when we constrain our behavior in light of their individual interests. As Rawls writes, "[m]utual respect is shown in several ways: in our willingness to see the situation of others from their point of view, from the perspective of their conception of their good; and in our being prepared to give reasons for our actions whenever the interests of others are materially affected" (Rawls 1999a, 297).

For Rawls, then, equal respect is fundamentally a matter of *equally recognizing* each person's *moral capacities* by justifying actions in a way that recognizes and speaks to their conception of the good. For states to fulfill the requirement of equal respect, their exercise of political power must be justified to each citizen by appealing to reasons that citizens can reasonably be asked to endorse (1993, 217). Rawls's point is echoed by Carens, who suggests that "[i]t is never enough to justify a set of social arrangements governing human beings to say that these arrangements are good for us, without regard for [other persons].... We have to appeal to principles and arguments that take everyone's interests into account or that explain why the social arrangements are reasonable and fair to everyone who is subject to them" (2015, 227).

b. Moral arbitrariness as disrespect

Conversely, power-holders disrespect power-subjects when they exercise power over them in the absence of reasons that the latter can reasonably endorse; that is, when they fail to *justify* their actions. In the style of Rawls, we might characterize the failure of justification as *moral arbitrariness*. For example, as Rawls writes, "conceptions of right have a certain content and exclude *arbitrary and pointless principles* [my emphasis]" (1999a, 130). What, then, are some examples of morally arbitrary actions? As a starting point, a power-holder may act arbitrarily when she fails to give reasons at all. Imagine a scenario where a tyrannical head of state imposes a strict curfew on her citizens, under the penalty of shooting-on-sight. When terrified citizens demand to know why the curfew has been imposed, the tyrant may simply respond that she "felt like it." Here, the tyrant *disrespects* their moral capacities by refusing to give reasons for her decision. On the other hand, the tyrant acts just as arbitrarily if she gives the citizens *bad reasons*. For example, she may say that the curfew was imposed in order to satisfy her own aesthetic preference for quietness and empty streets while idly touring the village in her Lamborghini. While the tyrant certainly furnishes the citizens with *a* reason, the reason is disrespectful. The citizens cannot reasonably be asked to endorse a reason that factors in the aesthetic interests of the tyrant while thoroughly ignoring their own interests in not being subject to the curfew, or worse still, losing their lives over it.

Yet disrespect-as-moral-arbitrariness can manifest in less overtly tyrannical forms. More specifically, in Rawls's theory of justice, it is morally arbitrary for distributive outcomes to be influenced by "social circumstances and such chance contingencies as accident and good fortune," such as one's social class (Rawls 1999a, 62–63). I will have more to say about the idea of social contingency in the section that follows, but for now, it is easy to see why Rawls is suspicious of luck and the role it often plays in shaping our outcomes. As Zofia Stemplowska writes, "[L]uck's victims are not chosen because they ought to be affected; luck strikes with no purpose" (2013, 390). In contrast, we normally also believe that equal respect does not require the elimination of chosen or avoidable disadvantages that are of people's own making (390). Suppose that Angela and Brian start out with equal degrees of advantage. In his prime, Brian is suddenly struck down by a debilitating genetic illness and becomes penniless due to the escalating medical fees. But there is no sense in which Brian *deserves* to have less than Angela; his unequal share of goods cannot be *justified* to him. Consequently, while Rawls does not go as far as to claim that we should be wholly insulated from the effects of luck on our life-prospects, he famously argues that inequalities between persons must be *regulated* by the Difference Principle in order to be justified: they must be arranged by the greatest benefit of the least well-off. On the other hand, suppose that Brian becomes penniless because he knowingly makes a series of high-risk financial investments. In this case, Brian can be reasonably asked to endorse the differences in holdings between him and Angela because the inequality arose as a result of his own aims and interests, and the conscious decisions that rose out of them.

To conclude this section, I have sketched out the requirements of equal respect. It requires states and other power-holders to *justify* their actions to their power-subjects. In particular, the use of force can only be justified if it takes account of, and subsequently appeals to, each person's conception of the good. As a corollary, persons suffer disrespect when they are treated *morally arbitrarily*; that is, when power is exercised over them in the absence of reasons they can reasonably be asked to endorse. I now turn to how immigration exclusion can *disrespect* noncitizens by failing to justify states' exercise of power over them.

4. The argument from social contingency

In the previous section, I have explained how equal respect for persons prohibits power-holders from treating them in an arbitrary manner. I now reconstruct the claim that the right to exclude is wrongful precisely because it enforces states' power against noncitizens in a morally arbitrary way. I assume, here, that noncitizens who wish to enter the state's territory are subjected to the state's coercive powers; "borders have guards and the guards have guns" (Carens 1987, 251). But it is not just the use of force in itself that calls out for justification. It is the current *social arrangements* that forceful immigration exclusion serves to uphold—a global structure where citizens in the global north command the lion's share of wealth, resources, and opportunities. Under present circumstances, receiving states' decision to include or exclude an individual can have enormous consequences on their life-prospects, mainly because the "general well-being, quality of services, safety, and scope of freedoms and opportunities" available to those in affluent polities are far greater when compared to those born in poor countries (Shachar 2009, 26). For these reasons, opening borders to these noncitizens would help to equalize these staggering inequalities in life-prospects by enabling large numbers of people to travel from the poor world to the rich, to make use of the opportunities there (Seglow 2005, 327). On the other hand, the forceful exclusion of noncitizens would mean that they are forced to accept significantly fewer opportunities in their homelands. For this reason, Cole asserts that the global migration regime plays an essential role in maintaining "present global patterns of inequality of power and resources"—inequalities that were profoundly shaped by colonial histories (2011, 221). Given the nature of the stakes involved in exclusion, states must not only justify their use of force on noncitizens, but the inegalitarian social arrangements that are upheld and preserved by it.

This is where Carens and Cole's central claim comes in: the charge of social contingency. In line with the Rawlsian view discussed in the previous section, inequalities of life-prospects that arise from mere social contingencies cannot, on their own, be justified to noncitizens. Like gender, class, and race, they argue that citizenship should be viewed as "such a contingency" (Cole 2012, 123). If this is true, exclusion disrespects noncitizens by coercively subjecting them to inegalitarian social arrangements on the basis of a morally arbitrary feature.

It bears clarifying what "social contingency" means in the context of citizenship. To begin with, there are at least two different ways of understanding "contingency." We may say that something is contingent because it is *unchosen* and subject to mere chance—for example, we may say that my natural hair color is contingent. For Cole, citizenship may be viewed similarly. It is essentially unchosen, as we exert no control over where we are born or who our parents are (Cole 2000, 151). Similarly, Carens relies on an analogy between feudalism and citizenship. Under feudalism, opportunities were shaped by sheer *luck*; they largely depended on which class you happened to be born into. As he asserts, citizenship has a good deal in common with feudal status, as both statuses are assigned at birth, cannot typically be changed by the individual's willpower and hard work, and also have major consequences for the person's life-chances (1987, 26). If we agree that it is wrong for class to shape an individual's opportunities because it is *unchosen*, how can someone's seriously unequal life-opportunities be justified on the basis of their citizenship, which is arguably just as random and unchosen?

On the other hand, there is a closely related, but conceptually distinct sense of contingency. We may say that something is contingent when it is *conditional* on other factors. My job prospects, for example, are contingent on whether or not I have research publications. This might be a merely descriptive claim; it is just something philosophy professors are supposed to do. However, in other instances, the claim of contingency is normative—it is used to undermine the desirability of a given state of affairs. For example, we may negatively judge an agent's decision and its outcome to be "contingent" because it is conditional on external factors and circumstances, rather than decided by principled ethical reasoning or commitments that are internal to the agent's deliberations. Suppose that Carol is no longer in love with her husband, Don. While Don remains blissfully ignorant of Carol's true feelings, she plans to leave him as soon as she possibly can. Unfortunately, to Carol's shock, she finds out that she is pregnant and that it is too late for her to undergo an abortion. Unwilling to parent the child on her own or give them up for adoption, Carol decides to remain in the loveless relationship with Don. Given these facts, we might say that Carol's decision to stay with Don is merely contingent because it is wholly dependent on the circumstances of her accidental pregnancy. *If* Carol had not gotten pregnant, she would certainly have left Don, who she has no underlying commitment to. But consider an alternative scenario. Despite Carol's waning romantic feelings for Don, she cares enough for Don that she would never want to upend their life together and break his heart. Ultimately, Carol decides to honor her lifelong commitment to Don out of concern for his well-being. It is safe to say that we would not describe Carol's decision as "contingent" in *this* case. Rather, her choice to continue her relationship with Don is grounded in a deep and unshakable commitment to him.

Likewise, the claim that citizenship is contingent may refer to the fact that citizenship, as a construct, depends on facts that were decided by the vicissitudes of history rather than anchored in the long-standing ethical commitments of its architects. As an example of such an argument, consider Cole's comments on the placement of national boundaries. The location of borders is important for the present discussion because our relationship with the territorial space contained within the borders plays some role in determining membership (Cole 2014, 507). It is not just which side of the border I am born that matters, but *where* the border itself is located. Cole claims that even if borders fall where they are through intention and planning, they *could* be different from the way they are, and there is no "natural" reason why they must be this way (507). They are a matter of historical contingency, rather than fixed by a practice that is "ethical or rational" (Cole 2014, 507). As an example of this, Cole cites how nation-state borders were fixed in Africa by colonial powers: Lord Salisbury, the British Prime Minister, commented on how "we have been engaged in drawing lines upon maps where no white man's foot ever trod; we have been giving away mountains and rivers and lakes to each other, only hindered by the small impediment that we never knew exactly where the mountains and rivers and lakes were" (2014, 518). The fact that borders could theoretically have been drawn up in totally different locations, because they were simply *not* guided by any kind of principled considerations, seems to undermine their normative significance in the present-day. In turn, noncitizens may reasonably ask why they should be expected to accept more disadvantageous life-prospects as a result of boundaries that were created without any regard for their interests and well-being. The historical contingency of those borders, it may be argued, means that their exclusion and its consequences cannot be justified.

To sum up, critics of the right to exclude have argued that citizenship is a morally arbitrary feature that fails to justify states' use of force to exclude noncitizens and the unequal life-prospects that are upheld by it. This is because citizenship is socially contingent in two ways. Firstly, in a world dominated by birthright citizenship, one's state of citizenship is often a matter of luck that one has no real "choice" in. Secondly, our citizenship is determined by borders that were not created on the basis of principled reasoning, but are the products of historical accident (and in some cases, historical injustice). As a result, immigration exclusion *disrespects* noncitizens.

5. Nonideal theory and the incompleteness of social contingency

Above, I have considered one influential explanation of why states' right to exclude may violate the requirements of equal respect with regard to noncitizens. According to the Argument from Social Contingency, noncitizens are excluded on the basis of a socially contingent feature: their citizenship status. In light of the purported social contingency of citizenship, states fail to justify their use of force on noncitizens through "guards and guns," as well as the social arrangements that are maintained by exclusion. In the absence of a justification that considers and appeals to their conception of the good, the moral powers of noncitizens are disrespected by states—or so the argument goes.

Yet how successful is the Argument from Social Contingency in responding to proponents of the right to exclude? Bringing back the discussion to Section 2, where I argue that we need to adopt a nonideal approach to the ethics of immigration, I suggest that the Argument from Social Contingency focuses on the wrong target. We cannot just look at arbitrariness in itself, but the ways in which *some* arbitrary differences have been used in our societies to ground hierarchical social structures. Similar to the arguments proffered by Miller, Walzer, and Wellman, it focuses too narrowly on the subject of *reasonable justification* while neglecting noncitizens' real-world experiences of social subordination. Furthermore, we should not primarily understand social subordination as a failure to recognize noncitizens' capacity for the conception of the good, but rather, a phenomenon that threatens to damage it.

a. Nonideal theory and the argument from social contingency

Returning to the distinction between ideal and nonideal theory, in which theoretical space should we situate the Argument from Social Contingency?

It is evident that Carens and Cole are attentive to important aspects of nonideal theory. Central to the Argument from Social Contingency, for example, is the causal connection between immigration exclusion and global inequality, which has stemmed from an extensive history of colonial domination and exploitation.[6] The comparison to feudalism speaks volumes. At the same time, by pointing out the contingency of territorial borders, Cole in particular highlights the role of colonial injustice in determining their placement. These nonideal conditions do not, in themselves, invalidate Miller, Walzer, or Wellman's normative justifications for immigration exclusion. After all, a state's right to exclude might remain justified by cultural preservation or the freedom of association in the *absence* of historical injustice and its long-term consequences on global social arrangements. Nonetheless, the Argument from Social Contingency says that a world devoid of such injustices is *not* the world we live in, and *until* historical injustices have been redressed, we need guidance from an ethics of immigration that can properly account for, and respond to them.

All the same, as I have framed it, the Argument from Social Contingency relies on a particular interpretation of *disrespect*: namely, disrespect as a *failure of justification to persons who are subject to coercion.* The main problem with exclusion, on Carens and Cole's reading, is that states have not "given appropriate weight" to noncitizens' moral powers—in particular, their equal capacity for a conception of the good—by neglecting to give justification for their exclusion that they can reasonably be asked to endorse. There is no doubt that it is disrespectful to treat someone unreasonably. However, it is possible to develop a richer account of disrespect, and this is the task that I take on in my book. Disrespect, as I will understand it, does not just involve unreasonable behavior, but demeaning and subordinating attitudes toward members of particular social groups. In fact, a closer look at the phenomenon of discrimination will help to illuminate this. I elaborate on the second sense of disrespect below.

b. Disrespect and social subordination

A cursory look at quintessential cases of discrimination will reveal that persons rarely seem to protest their exclusion on the basis of social contingency. Social contingency, I suspect, doesn't fully explain why token cases of exclusion are so morally troubling. Consider, for example, the exclusion of gay persons from the Boy Scouts. It is unlikely that the gay people who wish to join the Boy Scouts would challenge their exclusion on the basis that sexual orientation is a socially contingent feature. They would be more likely to say that the exclusion policy expresses a demeaning attitude toward gay people and reinforces homophobic stereotypes about them. It does not matter, for example, whether or not sexual orientation is chosen; even if a prospective Boy Scout has *chosen* to be gay, it doesn't make his exclusion from the group any more permissible. Similarly, consider the historic exclusion of women from political decision-making, or the Trump administration's recent decision to ban transgender persons from serving and enlisting in the military. Would women and transgender persons mainly contest their exclusion on the grounds that their gender is unchosen, and not because these exclusionary policies reflect demeaning attitudes toward them—the view that women are too irrational and emotional to vote, or that transgender people are inherently damaged and deficient and hence unable to serve in the military as functionally as cisgender members? The claim that a mode of exclusion is demeaning in this way, I believe, can be formulated into an appealing alternative to the Argument from Social Contingency. The wrongfulness of demeaning treatment can have strong explanatory power, and as I show in the remaining chapters of my book, it can help us understand a good deal of immigration injustice today that would not be fully accounted for by the Argument from Social Contingency and the charge of moral arbitrariness.

To see the difference between the two interpretations of disrespect, consider a person who is excluded from a job on the basis of race. To go with the initial interpretation of disrespect-as-arbitrary treatment, we could say that racist exclusion is disrespectful due to its denial of equal citizenship on morally arbitrary grounds (Shelby 2003, 1709). Here, we may use Kwame Anthony Appiah's framework, which defines racism as the belief that race is a morally relevant distinction and hence a "legitimate basis for treating people differently" (Shelby 2012, 338). We may distinguish between "extrinsic" and "intrinsic" racism. *Extrinsic* racists, on one hand, make moral distinctions between races because they believe that racial essences entail, imply, or causally determine morally relevant properties that lead to differences between members of particular races. In turn, those affect one's moral duties to members of other races to license differential or negative treatment

(Ikuenobe 2010, 164). Such properties may include, for example, character traits and tendencies like honesty, laziness, or intelligence (Shelby 2012, 339). On the other hand, *intrinsic* racists morally differentiate between members of different races simply because of the belief that "each race is intrinsically morally significant or that each race has a quality or a status that is morally significant to the race," but this intrinsic moral quality is independent of any moral characteristics that may be implied or entailed by the racial essence of the specific race (Appiah 1990, 5).

Regardless of this difference, it seems that what racists essentially have in common, on Appiah's view, is that they believe that race is a *morally relevant* feature that should factor into their actions and decisions. Suppose that we reply to the racist by pointing out that race is, in fact, socially contingent: it is *unchosen*, and the very construct of race is dependent on legacies of colonial injustice.[7] So, we should not exclude or treat people differently on the basis of race. This seems to suggest that the opposite of racism would be the commitment to treating people equally *regardless of race*; perhaps something like the endorsement of *color-blindness*, which holds that "race should never be a consideration in determining how government institutions treat persons regardless of the purpose or rationale behind such race-conscious measures" (Shelby 2012, 342). Yet it is not *always* disrespectful for race to factor into our deliberations. For example, as Appiah himself acknowledges, differential treatment based on race might sometimes be justified if the goal is to increase racial diversity or integration in public schools, against advocates of color-blindness (Shelby 2012, 344). Race might also be highly relevant to some policies insofar as it is an accurate proxy of particular forms of historical disadvantage, given legacies of slavery and colonialism. The use of race seems to be morally desirable in these cases even if it is no less socially contingent.[8] If this is true, it cannot be the case that racist exclusion is disrespectful simply because race is socially contingent.

An alternative explanation for the wrongfulness of racial discrimination is that it is *demeaning* and *stigmatizing* to people of the affected racial background. I now examine the idea of stigmatization in greater detail. According to Erving Goffman, "society establishes the means of categorizing persons and the complement of attributes felt to be ordinary and natural for members of each of these categories" (1963, 11). When we encounter strangers, we assign a *virtual social identity* to them by anticipating the categories they belong to and the attributes they have. Put differently, virtual social identity involves making certain assumptions about "what the individual before us ought to be." However, virtual identity and *actual* identity can diverge systematically in a given individual's social experience (Loury 2003, 60). While virtual identity is constructed "from the outside," through social imputations based on a person's physical presentation, actual identity is constructed "from the inside," through the accumulation of facts that are specific to a person's life-history that are more or less independent of conventional ascriptions (Loury 2003, 60). As Goffman continues,

> When a stranger is present before us, evidence can arise of his possessing an attribute that makes him different from others in the category of persons available for him to be, and of a less desirable kind—in the extreme, a person who is quite thoroughly bad, or dangerous, or weak. He is thus reduced in our minds from a whole and usual person to a tainted, discounted one. Such an attribute is a stigma, especially when its discrediting effect is very extensive; sometimes it is also called a failing, a shortcoming, a handicap. It constitutes a special discrepancy between virtual and actual social identity. (1963, 12)

In short, to stigmatize someone is to impute to them a virtual social identity that is disreputable or "spoiled," and we can understand the stigmatized as people who "[carry] bodily marks (stigmata) that incline others to judge them negatively, but also people with less visible markings who live at constant risk of being 'exposed'" (Loury 2003, 60). Drawing from Goffman's insights, Glenn Loury proposes that we can understand racism as a form of stigma. In his words, "When the meanings connoted by race-symbols undermine an observing agent's ability to see their bearer as a person possessing a common humanity with the observer—as 'someone not unlike the rest of us'—then I will say that this person is 'racially stigmatized,' and that the group to which he belongs suffers a 'spoiled collective identity'" (2003, 67). If we accept Loury's characterization, the prospective employer racially *stigmatizes* the Black job applicant by expressing the belief that Black persons are inferior to white persons—for example, that they are less intelligent, more idle, and thus less likely to perform the job as well as a white applicant. Thus, it seems that the Black applicant is disrespected because she is *demeaned* by the employer's act of exclusion, and not merely because race is a socially contingent feature.

But aren't demeaning practices just another form of morally arbitrary behavior? Perhaps social subordination is just another way of treating someone unreasonably. That you believe someone is "naturally inferior" is simply not a good reason for excluding them—it is not a reason that any person can be asked to reasonably accept. Against this, I believe that we have good reason to separate *unreasonable behavior* from *demeaning* behavior. As I have suggested, they constitute two distinct forms of disrespect. The disrespect shown to the Black applicant who is not given a job on the basis of her race is not merely a failure of justification. In fact, she cannot make sense of the reasoning in defense of her rejection unless she accepts her own social inferiority. As Patrick Shin has observed, the problem is not that the act of racial discrimination is insufficiently justified, but that it relies on an objectionable judgment about "how the differently treated individuals are related to each other" (Shin 2009, 7). The employer's disrespect does not lie primarily in their *unreasonableness*, but rather, the morally objectionable judgment they have made about the inferior social standing of Black persons in relation to white persons (7). Like Shin, I think that the complaints of the gay persons excluded from Boy Scouts, or the transgender persons excluded from the military, amount to more than just the assertion that exclusion is unreasonable. Rather, they are objecting to a social practice that treats them as the social inferiors of heterosexual or cisgender people. As a result, it is not clear that we need to frame demeaning treatment in terms of arbitrariness at all; demeaning or stigmatizing behavior is in itself a specific—and commonplace—form of disrespect.

To conclude this section, I have suggested that violations of equal respect do not necessarily take the shape of social contingency and moral arbitrariness. Put differently, disrespect does not necessarily lie in the failure to justify one's actions to others who are affected, but in subjecting them to demeaning or stigmatizing treatment.

6. Conclusion

In this chapter, I have argued that we ought to adopt a nonideal approach to the ethics of immigration. We cannot come up with a satisfactory account of immigration justice unless we duly respond to the nonideal circumstances that have colored and left their mark on immigration in the present day: specifically, the world's history of racism and colonial injustice. That said, nonideal theory does not preclude our being guided by a certain ideal (or set of ideals). I have looked to the ideal of equal respect as a potent source of "critical evaluative concepts" that can help us to understand the injustice of past immigration policies and how they may be reproduced in the present. While theorists like Carens and Cole have objected to immigration exclusion on the grounds that it is disrespectful, they have focused on one interpretation of disrespect: the failure of reasonable justification to noncitizens who are subject to the state's coercive power. However, I have argued that there is another compelling interpretation of disrespect: disrespect as demeaning or subordinating treatment toward members of particular social groups.

Naturally, my interpretation of disrespect raises more important questions. Firstly, why is it so wrong to demean someone? Secondly, do states really have a duty to show noncitizens equal respect? Thirdly, are states obliged to avoid demeaning noncitizens at any cost? These questions will be addressed in Chapter Two.

2
Noncitizens and the Demands of Social Equality

1. Introduction

In the previous chapter, I considered the possibility that immigration exclusion violates noncitizens' right to equal respect. To this end, I reconstructed an influential argument by Joseph Carens and Philip Cole, which I termed the Argument from Social Contingency. As Carens and Cole argue, exclusion on the basis of noncitizenship is disrespectful because it is morally arbitrary and therefore fails to justify noncitizens' subjection to the state's exclusionary powers. Furthermore, exclusion is arbitrary because of the *contingency* of one's citizenship status, whether it is one's luck in the "birthright lottery," as Ayelet Shachar has termed it, or the historical contingency of borders themselves.

Despite its undeniable force, I've noted that there is a second possible interpretation of moral disrespect. Think, for example, of classic cases of discrimination, where persons have been excluded on the basis of their gender, race, sexual orientation, or gender identity. Those cases are instructive because they involve *demeaning* or *subordinating* treatment of excluded persons. As I have suggested, the wrong of such exclusion is aptly captured by its fundamental violation of *social*, or *relational equality*: the idea that persons ought to relate to each other as social equals, rather than superiors and inferiors. The Boy Scouts' initial decision not to admit gay members expressed stigmatizing beliefs about gay people; for example, that homosexuality is morally impure and perverse, running counter to the Scouts's purported aim to be "morally straight and clean in thought, word and deed."[1]

The question, then, is whether states' exclusion of noncitizens could be wrong for the same reasons. Notably, Grant Silva makes a comparison between borders and racial categorizations that, to some degree, echoes Carens and Cole's remarks on contingency. He criticizes the popular narrative that

Immigration and Social Equality. Désirée Lim, Oxford University Press. © Oxford University Press 2023.
DOI: 10.1093/oso/9780197658093.003.0003

racial differences are "older than history itself, a part of nature" by noting that the main goal of the "color line" is to protect privileges that are "based in relations of domination, where advantages come at the expense of disadvantage" (Silva 2015, 79). As he continues, "borders operate this same way but secure *national privilege*"—specifically, a "national imaginary" oriented toward whiteness (79). The conceptual overlap is clear: Silva's words resonate with Carens's sentiments on the preservation of national privilege, such as between serfs and feudal lords, as well as Cole's observation that borders are often established for unjust purposes. Yet, by highlighting the parallels between *race* and *citizenship*, Silva's comments introduce something new: the fact that our analysis of border exclusion must be thoroughly informed by other types of social subordination *and* its existing relationship to them. In this spirit, the ambition of my book is to demonstrate the structural similarity between the status of noncitizens and other socially subordinated groups, as well as explore the paths through which border exclusion reproduces those unequal relations.

There is a tricky matter, however, that a convincing social egalitarian critique of immigration exclusion (i.e., the kind I'm interested in providing) will need to address. On what I will call the "conventional view," the ideal of social equality is believed to only apply between citizens, within the context of a bounded society. Many have assumed that it is citizens of the same state who ought to relate to each other as social equals, rather than as superiors and inferiors. Alongside the state's redistributive duties to its citizens, this ideal gives rise to a further set of duties of justice that are directed at minimizing social inequalities. In this chapter, I argue that noncitizens share a right to social equality. This includes noncitizens who are territorially present within the confines of the state and, more controversially, noncitizens who remain outside of the state's territory. The entitlement to social equality, on my account, is not derived from one's citizenship status, but the distinctive harms that social subordination pose to our moral personhood. As I will show, inferiorizing treatment may seriously inhibit our ability to develop and pursue our conception of the good. Nevertheless, recognizing a universal entitlement to social inequality is compatible with states owing stronger obligations to particular groups and less demanding duties to others, rather than having onerous *global* duties to minimize social inequality around the world.

My argument proceeds in these steps. In Section 2, I consider the possibility of a *moral right* to social equality. On one hand, states may have a negative duty to refrain from creating or maintaining rules or norms that contribute to social inequalities. On the other hand, states may also have the positive duty to ensure the continued existence of institutions that protect social equality or take active steps to counter patterns of social subordination. This leaves open the question, however, of whether the right to social equality is a *general* or *membership-based* right; we have yet to address the proper scope of social equality. Section 3 shows that broad conceptions of social equality as a membership-based right, which allow some noncitizens to qualify as "members," remain too underinclusive and risk leaving many noncitizens vulnerable to social subordination. In Section 4, I argue that we should recognize a general right to social equality. All persons have a basic interest in being treated as social equals, because social equality is a necessary condition for developing and pursuing our conception of the good. In Section 5, drawing from the analogy of human rights, I show that states have negative and positive duties to minimize social inequalities experienced by citizens *and* noncitizens located within their territory, alongside negative duties to refrain from harming the social equality of noncitizens located *outside* of their territory. This has significant implications for the ethics of immigration, which I explore in the rest of my book. I conclude in Section 6 by considering the relative weight of the right to social equality and the costs that states can reasonably be asked to absorb as a consequence of its provision to noncitizens.

2. Social equality and the state

In this chapter, I contend that states have duties of justice to protect the social equality of all persons subject to their coercive power. This includes noncitizens who have migrated to reside within the state's territory, as well as noncitizens who are *not yet* located on the territory, but are applying to enter the state in question. As it is usually understood, by "coercive power," I refer to states' capacity to use physical force on citizens and noncitizens alike. States may *directly* or *indirectly* apply such force, and we can see this distinction within systems of immigration law. On one hand, there are immigration laws that are directly coercive toward noncitizens; they establish the state's right to use force on migrants (e.g., by means of detention and deportation). On the other hand, there might be immigration laws that are indirectly coercive;

while their content does not directly relate to practices of coercion, they delineate the categories of migrants on whom exclusionary force can be used. For example, following the "Muslim ban," would-be migrants from a number of Muslim-majority countries were coercively subjected to an unjust immigration law, albeit not in the "direct" sense. They were rendered straightforwardly ineligible for admission; as a result, they would have been detained or removed if they tried to enter the United States. In this sense, the "Muslim ban" indirectly licensed the use of force on would-be migrants from the listed countries, even if it did not directly pertain to coercion.[2] I begin by constructing a more demanding conception of the state's duties to minimize social equality that goes beyond the preserve of ensuring equal rights and liberties. In particular, states should recognize that noncitizens have the right to social equality. After this, I establish the grounds of individual claims to social equality. The right to social equality does not derive from one's citizenship status, but rather, the significant threat of damage to the self that persistent and pervasive subordination may cause.

a. Duties of justice to minimize social inequality

The normative valence of social equality has been understood to correspond to certain nondistributive duties of justice that the state is responsible for discharging on top of its redistributive duties of justice. Of course, there is room for disagreement over the exact content of those duties. On one relatively minimal conception, social equality demands that, on top of maintaining some level of distributive equality, states also ensure that everyone has equal basic rights and liberties. In the conventional sense, "basic rights and liberties," as defined by Rawls, refer to the right to political liberty (the right to vote and to hold public office); freedom of speech and assembly; liberty of conscience and freedom of thought; freedom of the person (such as the right to bodily integrity); the right to hold personal property, and last of all, freedom from arbitrary arrest and seizure (1999a, 53). It is important that everyone's right to these things is *equally* protected and upheld, because the unequal provision of basic rights can have serious downstream effects on one's standing in the sphere of politics. Rawls is careful to note that a publicly affirmed distribution of fundamental rights and liberties is necessary for citizens to have a "similar and secure status when they meet to conduct the common affairs of the wider society" (1999a, 477). Inequalities in political rights or inequalities in opportunity, for example, would have the consequence of publicly establishing the inferiority of particular groups and giving them a "subordinate ranking in public life" (477). For this reason, he concludes that "the hardships arising from political and civic inequality, and from cultural and ethnic discrimination, cannot be easily accepted . . . it is the position of equal citizenship that answers to the need for status" (Rawls 1999a, 478).

If Rawls's ultimate goal is to ensure "equal citizenship" as such, it is not clear that equal basic rights and liberties would be *sufficient* for his purposes, although they may indeed be *necessary*. As we have seen in the Introduction, social inequality can take many diverse forms—some of them less visible and more insidious than others. It is simply not enough that states eschew formal and direct social inequalities. *Informal* and *indirect* social inequalities between groups may continue to exist even if all persons formally enjoy equal "basic rights and liberties" in the way that Rawls construes it. That is, states may continue to enact laws and policies that have inferiorizing consequences for particular groups, to the extent that it profoundly affects their standing in public life, *even* if equal basic rights and liberties are guaranteed on paper. It is far too quick to assume that unequal standing could only be a problem for societies that outright tyrannize particular groups by refusing to recognize their rights and liberties, such as apartheid South Africa, the antebellum south of the United States, or in the case of colonial domination. As Iris Marion Young has pointed out, persons can continue to suffer serious social inequality because of the "everyday practices of a well-intentioned liberal society"; that is, its "unquestioned norms, habits, and symbols, in the assumptions underlying institutional rules and the collective consequences of following those rules" (1990, 5).

Consider the disproportionate incarceration of African Americans in the United States, which Michelle Alexander has aptly termed the "new Jim Crow" (2012). Arguably, this phenomenon does not count as a *formal* social inequality; there is no law that formally calls for the imprisonment of African Americans in particular. It is not Jim Crow per se, but a modern incarnation that is the logical consequence of everyday social practices that fatally intersect with racial inequalities that persist in the wake of Jim Crow. Mass incarceration, it has been agued, is brought about by the combination of extremely heavy penalties on drug offenses that are formally race-neutral, yet remain accompanied by the *informal* disproportionate policing of Black communities. Neither does it count as a *direct* social inequality. The disproportionate incarceration of African Americans, in itself, does not "explicitly and unambiguously" signify their inferiority as it could theoretically be compatible with unaffected African Americans having an equal social status to whites. Yet, because those labeled as "criminals" are disenfranchised during the course of their sentence and typically suffer very poor life-opportunities even after they are released, disproportionate imprisonment *indirectly* reinforces the group's inferior status by constraining the rights of many African Americans to political participation and equality of opportunity. It also worsens stereotypes about African Americans that have deemed them *punishable* in the eyes of (majority-white) society; that they are inherently dangerous, criminal, and must be contained to protect the security and well-being of the general public, even if this means severely constraining the life-opportunities of African Americans themselves. Similar undesirable properties have been ascribed to low-skilled migrants, and Chapter Three and Four will expand on these in more detail. Overall, given the nonideal context of pronounced racial inequality, we may regard heavy penalties on drug possession in the United States as an example of institutional norms that seriously affect social equality.

b. The pro tanto right to social equality

I have tried to show that, in order to truly minimize social inequality, states must go beyond ensuring equal basic rights and liberties in the conventional sense. It is clear that social equality plays a foundational role in our sense of what makes a society *just*. Equality of *status* matters enough that it can motivate demands of equality made in other "currencies." For this reason, instead of skipping around the idea, it makes sense to explicitly recognize a pro tanto *right to social equality* held by all persons who are subject to the coercive power of the state. As we have seen, the right to social equality can only be realized under circumstances where other basic rights and liberties are equally recognized and protected. Yet it comprises two additional demands of justice. Firstly, I propose that states have *negative duties of justice* to refrain from enacting institutional norms or policies that foreseeably lead to social inequalities. The types of policies that states have a duty to refrain from imposing may extend far beyond those that directly affect basic rights and liberties. We must also take care to consider the indirect effects of their potential interactions with existing inequalities. Secondly, the state may also have *positive duties of justice* to create and maintain institutions that protect social equality, give people provisions or accommodations that enable them to participate in public life as equals, or even take active steps to counter established patterns of social subordination between its citizens. Roughly, these can be understood as corresponding with Elizabeth Anderson's view that "negatively, egalitarians seek to abolish oppression—that is, forms of social relationship by which some people dominate, exploit, marginalize, demean, and inflict violence upon others," while "[p]ositively, egalitarians seek a social order in which persons stand in relations of equality" (1999, 313).

Before I continue, I want to address a number of initial objections that can be made to the right to social equality. The first concerns the issue of *vagueness*. There cannot be a right to social equality, it may be said, because the concept of social equality is too indeterminate. As matters stand, there is too much room for disagreement over what it means for people to stand in equal relations with each other in the context of public life. Furthermore, the exact requirements for social equality depend too much on the social meanings and circumstances of particular societies. In response, it's worth pointing out that other kinds of basic rights—rights that are not typically contested in the philosophical discourse—are not exempt from the same charge of indeterminacy. One only needs to turn to the current discourse on abortion, for example, to see that the justification for the right to bodily autonomy and its proper limits remain matters of public, as well as philosophical debate. The same can be said about the right to the freedom of speech: does the right to free speech preclude, or provide a case for the right to *hateful* speech? My point, here, is that the indeterminacy of what a particular basic right might demand from society doesn't necessarily stop us from making stipulations about it.

Secondly, it might be said that the right to social equality is too *demanding*. Given the complexity of social inequality, especially the kind that is indirect and unintentional, it may require considerable resources to address—resources that could be channeled into more valuable causes. I fully agree that social equality may be a difficult goal to undertake, and that we must be aware of the opportunity costs. Again, however, there are several other recognized basic rights whose realization might also be very demanding.

Arguably, in order for the right to political liberty to be genuinely held by *all*, or for everyone to have a meaningful right to the freedom of speech and assembly, society might have to provide disadvantaged groups with relevant provisions, or on a deeper level, reorganize the very structure of society. Yet this does not hinder us from assuming that political liberty or the freedom of speech and assembly are basic rights. Every right has its *costs*, and it isn't clear why we should think of social equality as being uniquely costly for society. It is also worth noting that, at this stage of my argument, I am not yet proposing that any particular *legal* rights or duties ought to follow from the right to social equality. Social equality, as I understand it, is a *moral right*—the fact that a moral right is burdensome is compatible with its existence. Demandingness simply shows that we may have reason to limit the scope of the right in light of other valuable moral or political considerations.

But perhaps this answer is too glib. In particular, when applied to the concrete realm of immigration policy, the robust recognition of noncitizens' right to social equality might require the imposition of heavy costs on receiving states and their citizenry. The reader is likely to be familiar with these potential costs. If it is true that the pro tanto right to social equality requires states to limit their exercise of the right to exclude (which is exactly the argument I seek to make in this book), a more permissive immigration policy might threaten to harm the socioeconomic prospects of the most disadvantaged citizens, especially those from marginalized racial and ethnic groups. For example, Stephen Macedo worries that immigration to the United States may undermine social justice and heighten domestic economic disparities by lowering wages, particularly for low-skilled Black workers, and eroding support for social welfare (2011, 302–308). How should we negotiate these trade-offs? What if the social equality of noncitizens is inherently in competition with that of citizens?

Here, I want to emphasize that the right to social equality is a pro tanto right—not a right that must be realized at any cost. Barring empirical facts about the long-term economic consequences of increased migration, if it *does* turn out to be true that more permissive immigration will have serious costs, I follow Kieran Oberman's view that "[r]estrictions might be justified in extreme circumstances in which immigration threatens severe social costs that cannot otherwise be prevented" (2016, 32). Here, the key lies in "cannot otherwise be prevented." It is not clear why we should characterize immigration and domestic social justice as a zero-sum game when states have the capacity to offset the negative effects of immigration on vulnerable citizens with institutional interventions. Take, for example, the possibility that increased immigration might weaken citizens' support of the welfare state. Instead of assuming that this outcome is set in stone, states could work to maintain support for welfare programs by incorporating immigrants in a manner that current citizens see as fair, *and* to actively reconstruct "communities of shared identity needed to maintain distributive justice" (Pevnick 2009, 149). A similar approach could be adopted with regard to the worsening of vulnerable citizens' economic opportunities. It may be necessary for states to pair permissive immigration policies with additional policy reforms that protect the wages of local workers, or otherwise distribute the economic benefits of immigration in a way that advances social equality for other marginalized groups in society.[3] There is a real worry that the "zero-sum" view of immigration and domestic social justice limits our imagination, as well as our willingness to seriously consider such reforms.

3. The proper scope of social equality

Up to this point, I have not said very much about the scope of social equality. Even if we accept that states do have duties to minimize social inequality, it is not obvious if they should only be concerned with social inequalities between citizens, or if they should also be concerned about the unequal social status of noncitizens. Should we treat social equality as a *general* right that all persons have, or is it something that only *citizens* can be entitled to?

a. The "conventional view" on social equality

Noncitizens are curiously absent from the literature on social equality. In the above passages I have quoted from, it is clear that Rawls is mainly concerned with the subordination of some *citizens* to others. Promisingly, Anderson suggests that "[e]galitarians base claims to social and political equality on the fact of universal moral equality" (1999, 313)—presumably a moral status that noncitizens also possess. Nevertheless, her influential account of social egalitarianism focuses only on working out the implications of social equality for the entitlements of citizens. Arguably, noncitizens could be absent from the discussion for a good reason. On what I will call the "conventional view," states are obliged only to minimize the social inequalities that obtain between its citizens. Christopher Heath Wellman, for example, asserts that we have a "special duty to respect our fellow citizens as equal partners in the political cooperative" that is not equally owed to foreigners (2008, 39). The consequence of this view is that, while it may be deeply insulting for Black noncitizens to be denied entry to the state, a racist immigration policy of this nature would only be unjust insofar as it subordinates *existing citizens* who are Black, sending a clear message that they are second-class citizens (Wellman 2008, 139–140). Furthermore, it implies that racist immigration policies would not be unjust if no citizens belong to those excluded groups. In short, the duty to minimize social inequality is a *special* one, not one owed to all persons regardless of their citizenship status.

Here, we can see a clear parallel to the scope of the state's redistributive duties of justice. Some have insisted that it is the state's exercise of coercive force that entitles citizens to some level of distributive equality; without it, the exercise of power cannot be justified to its subjects.[4] Because states do not exercise comparably intense coercive force on *noncitizens*, they are not entitled to distributive equality, although they may qualify for some minimum threshold of material entitlement. Alternatively, following Wellman, you might think that it is citizens' joint participation in a cooperative scheme—and by extension, their entitlement to be treated as equal partners through fair (and hence justified) terms of cooperation—that entitles them to distributive equality. Noncitizens, however, cannot be considered equal participants in the cooperative venture. The same line of reasoning may well apply to the claim to social equality. The grounds of the claim to be treated as a social equal, whether it is rooted in coercion or cooperative participation, could simply fail to apply to noncitizens.

b. Expanding the scope of the "conventional view"

i. General and membership-based rights

To lay out the groundwork for my own argument, I want to take the opposite view—that social equality depends on political membership—very seriously. This is especially important given how pervasive the "conventional view" seems to be. Suppose that it is correct to say that only members of the same political community (which might include long-term resident migrants) are entitled to be treated as social equals. Why does it make sense to hold this view? Or—to frame it differently—why should we see social equality as the kind of good that depends on membership in the state?

To answer these questions, I turn to Carens's instructive comparison between the legal rights of citizens and noncitizens. Carens observes that states are enjoined to uphold the "general human rights" of both groups; we have a bundle of rights that the state must grant to everyone who falls within its jurisdiction" (2015, 93). General human rights include rights that are designed to protect people from others within the state (e.g., the right to personal security), as well as rights that give them claims against the state itself; interestingly, even visiting tourists are entitled to rights like the right to freedom of thought, religion, and speech. Here, Carens seems to be suggesting that *noncitizens* who fall within the state's jurisdiction are entitled to something like Rawls's equal basic rights and liberties. What's more, in order for states to act *justly*, they must acknowledge that noncitizens have "legitimate interests and moral claims that [states] must respect whether the people in question are citizens or not" (2015, 93).

At the same time, however, Carens accepts that states can legitimately give citizens or long-term residents a larger bundle of rights than mere visitors. He proposes a *second* category of rights, which I will term "membership-specific rights." Visitors can initially be denied such rights, although they may eventually acquire an entitlement that strengthens as their roots to the state sink in more deeply. In turn, membership-specific rights can be divided into "membership-specific *human* rights" and "membership-specific discretionary rights" (2015, 97–98). Firstly, membership-specific human rights are basic rights that everyone is entitled to, but only certain states have a duty to deliver on those rights: states that they are members of. For example, even though everyone has the right to seek employment in virtue of their humanity, it is only the states they *reside in* who are obliged to protect this right. Quoting Carens, "[i]t is widely accepted as fundamentally unjust and a violation of human rights if a regime makes it impossible for someone who lives in its society on an ongoing basis to find work or if it arbitrarily restricts her employment opportunities" (Carens 2015, 97). Nevertheless, at the same time, it doesn't seem particularly wrong to deny a passing tourist the opportunity to work, even if the tourist might be greatly upset or inconvenienced by the rule. (A parallel argument might be made for the right to vote.)

Secondly, membership-specific discretionary rights are rights that "states are not obliged to establish in the first place and could abolish without acting unjustly (at least within certain procedural constraints)" (Carens 2015, 97–98); hence the term "discretionary." States may legitimately decide *only* to allocate such rights to members, although they may of course prefer to be more generous. Typical examples of membership-based discretionary rights might be rights to various social provisions, such as educational grants, that states only owe to citizens and residents (Carens 2015, 98). Again, states do no wrong by denying these rights to short-term visitors.

ii. Social equality as a membership-based right

Suppose we agree that social equality is a membership-specific right, much like the right to employment or certain social provisions. Following Carens's terminology, should we think of the right to social equality as a *membership-specific human right* or membership-specific *discretionary right*? We should begin, I suggest, by rejecting the latter view. States cannot legitimately decide to subordinate particular noncitizens, or to tolerate their subordination. The discretionary approach seems to license societies where demeaning messages about particular racial, religious, or ethnocultural groups are permissibly broadcast by the state, simply because no *current* member of the state belongs to any of those groups. Indeed, this is a counterintuitive conclusion of Wellman's view, which essentially allows states to enact immigration policies that discriminate against minority groups who are not yet equal partners in the political collective. To be sure, Wellman claims that, in practice, no state would be able to do this because "no state is completely without minorities who would be disrespected by an immigration policy which invoked racial/ethnic/religious categories" (2008, 140). It is not clear, however, why Wellman thinks this. Suppose that, at some point in history, State X contains only citizens who are Christians and Muslims. Suppose that State X decides to spread denigrating messages about Buddhists, and ban them from entering its borders. This policy, I think, is clearly unjust; it *wrongs* would-be Buddhist immigrants, and it would be wrong even if there are no Buddhist citizens. This intuition seems to be grounded in the belief that all socially salient groups have the right to not be subordinated in public life *even if* they are not yet members of the collective. As matters stand, social inequality is simply not a matter of state discretion.

Perhaps the conception of social equality as a membership-specific *human right* is more successful. On this view, all persons are entitled to social equality *within* a state that they are presently members of, much like their entitlement to voting and employment rights. All the same, they cannot demand recognition of social equality from states that they have no special relationship to. Put differently, states are only enjoined to protect and uphold the social equality of persons who presently stand in some politically relevant relationship with them. Significantly, echoing Carens's comments about the right to employment, this view is compatible with the claim that many noncitizens do already stand in such relationships with the state.[5] I will briefly outline two complementary views that fall into this category, one by Michael Walzer and the other by Rekha Nath. While both are insightful, I conclude that they are ultimately unsatisfying.

Walzer is primarily concerned with the social status of guest workers—temporary migrants who are typically admitted for the purposes of filling labor shortages in low-skilled industries like agriculture, caregiving, and construction. They perform essential jobs that are widely regarded as unappealing to citizens. As I have claimed in the Introduction, low-skilled migrant workers are often treated more disadvantageously than highly skilled migrants. For example, while at least some categories of highly skilled migrants are eligible for a path to citizenship, and are also permitted to bring their family members with them, guest workers are generally denied such rights. For this reason, it is possible for guest workers to have worked in the receiving state for significant periods of time, yet remain in a state of permanent alienage. I will have more to say about the differential treatment of high and low-skilled migrants in Chapters Three and Four, but for now, I focus on Walzer's view. As he sharply observes, guest workers are "locked into an inferior position that is also an anomalous position; they are outcasts in a society that has no caste norms, metics in a society where metics have no comprehensible, protected, and dignified place" (Walzer 1983, 59). Furthermore, Walzer believes that their position of inferiority is directly attributable to their lack of access to political rights. Specifically, guest workers are "exploited or oppressed at least in part because they are disenfranchised, incapable of organizing effectively for self-defence" (59).

Suppose, however, that those who hold a *discretionary* view of the right to social equality are unimpressed. They may argue that we have little reason to regard guest workers' subordination as unjust in the first place. What if receiving states simply have no nondiscretionary duties to protect their equality? Walzer's response is enlightening: we should be troubled precisely because guest workers perform "socially necessary work," and are "deeply enmeshed in the legal system of the country to which they have come" (1983, 60). In this sense, guest workers are, like citizens, subject to the state's coercive laws *and* perform work that is necessary for the state's "cooperative scheme." So, rather than the *grounds* of the entitlement to social equality, citizenship is a *proxy* for subjection to coercion and participation in the state's cooperative scheme. To see why these properties are relevant from the perspective of social equality, we may briefly return to the issue of political justification. Recall that, on a popular interpretation, equal respect for all persons fundamentally requires power-holders to engage in *reasonable justification* for their actions that affect power-subjects. In other words, power-subjects must be offered reasons for action that they can reasonably be expected to endorse. Walzer seems to be suggesting that noncitizens only have adequate reason to comply with state coercion and participate in its cooperative scheme if they are able to co-exist with others in society without being subjected to demeaning treatment. Guest workers may say: "Like everyone else, I am subject to the state's coercive force and participate in the system of cooperation. Just like everyone else, my life-prospects are fundamentally shaped by them. How can I be reasonably expected to support and endorse basic institutions that disadvantage me?" In short, there is no sufficient *reason* through which social inequality can be justified to guest workers in this position.

A further worry, however, is that conceiving of social equality as a membership-specific human right will have the effect of excluding the claims of noncitizens who are not yet territorially present, as would-be migrants are not "participants in economy and law" (Walzer 1983, 60); they are merely *seeking* to become participants. Certainly, they are also subject to the state's coercive force, insofar as they can be forcibly barred from entering. Yet this limited notion of coercion only subjects would-be migrants to "primary immigration laws"—that is, the regime of laws that regulate their entry into and residence in the receiving state's territory (Yong 2018, 460). It seems very different from the type of coercion experienced by noncitizens who already live *within* the state's confines and are therefore subject to the full range of background laws that regulate many other areas of their lives. We do not yet have an argument for why it would be unjust for *would-be immigrants* to be the targets of a racist immigration policy, if no persons from that group presently already reside within the state.

In response to this concern, Nath provides a novel view that expands substantially on the *cooperative* aspect of Walzer's view. On her account, recognizing the relevance of cooperative participation ought to bring at least some noncitizens within the scope of social equality, even if they do not presently reside on the state's territory. Like other theorists I have covered so far, Nath is concerned with the reasonable justification of noncitizens' coercive subjection to the rules of background institutions. Similar to Rawls, Nath observes that "[w]ithin the context of the state, individuals are subject to the rules of background institutions that define the character of their political, social, and economic interaction" (2015, 190). In this vein, citizenship tends to be regarded as the basis of social equality because, under common institutional arrangements, citizens' lives are assumed to be densely interconnected with one another (Nath 2015, 191). As fellow participants of shared structural practices, citizens unavoidably define their social and political standing in relation to each other (191). For persons whose lives are "bound together in this way," their "shared social meanings, attitudes, and perceptions can play an important role in informing what it means for them to enjoy equal standing vis-à-vis one another" (Nath 191–192). In sum, states are vested with the power to define the terms on which "densely interconnected" individuals relate to one another. In order to be justifiable to all participants in the cooperative scheme, shared social practices must not perpetuate social equalities between them. From here, however, Nath derives a surprising conclusion; there are nonresident noncitizens who have the right to social equality precisely because their lives have become interconnected with citizens through the forging of cross-border relationships (2015, 197). Consider a US-owned sweatshop that operates on Mexican territory and subjects the Mexican workers to deeply disadvantageous terms of employment. In this case, the Mexican workers do not reside on US soil. Yet, through close economic ties that are mediated by US trade policy, the Mexican workers and American owners have lives that are no less "densely interconnected" than those of US citizens who participate in cooperative enterprises. At the same time, it seems plausible that the Mexican workers and U.S. owners might come to define themselves in relation to each other. A pattern of labor exploitation in Mexico at the hands of wealthy American businessowners may objectionably position Mexicans as social inferiors in other aspects of social life.

Like Walzer, Nath is right to suggest that the "special relationships" that generate claims to social equality may hold between citizens and noncitizens. Unfortunately, her view continues to suffer from several major limitations. First of all, only a relatively small group of noncitizens have lives that are relevantly interconnected with citizens. Would-be immigrants who are subject to racist exclusion would, again, not meet the minimum requirements for a claim to social equality. Even so, there is a deeper problem. It is worth underscoring that, for Nath, only those who are *unavoidably* subject to the rules of the state's background institutions are entitled to social equality (2015, 192). By building unavoidability into her criteria, Nath risks excluding swathes of noncitizens who *could have* avoided or escaped such subjection by simply choosing *not* to enter the receiving state in the first place, or to return to Nath's own example, participate in cross-border interactions.[6] Most of all, her view of noncitizens' claims to social equality risks begging the question. It succeeds in showing that significant cooperative ties can enmesh noncitizens in inegalitarian relationships with citizens even when they live on a foreign territory. It doesn't explain, however, why we have reason to care about social inequality between citizens and noncitizens. Of course, we may return to the well-established importance of *political justification*: if a cooperative scheme does subject noncitizens to disadvantageous terms, it must give them a good reason to accept it. As I've already suggested in Chapter One, however, the failure of justification does not seem to be the *primary* consideration that animates our objection to commonplace instances of social inequality. The main issue with the disrespectful exclusion of gay persons from Boy Scouts, for example, is not that the persons are treated unreasonably. Rather, the problem is that exclusion is *demeaning* and threatens to *harm their self-conception*.

In the next section, I address these limitations by adopting a different strategy. Namely, I argue that the entitlement to social equality is held by *all persons*, rather than a product of special relationships. For this reason, the justification for entitlement to distributive equality and social equality may come apart. In the next section, I clarify that while the grounding for treatment as a social equal is something that applies to *all persons*, the proximity of those individuals to a particular state and the relationship they have to it helps to determine the content of the state's duties to them. Before I attend to these details, however, I will establish the case for treating social equality as a general right.

4. Social equality as a general right

A general, or universal entitlement to social equality can be justified in virtue of the serious harms that people experience when they are treated as social inferiors. Persons, as we already acknowledge, have certain basic interests that states must protect. I believe that the entitlement to be treated as a social equal is justified by the very same interests. In particular, having the range property of moral personhood generates a claim to be treated as a social equal because social equality is required for us to properly *develop and pursue our conception of the good*, here defined as "a conception of what is valuable in human life." Our sense of the good normally consists of "a more or less determinate scheme of final ends, that is, ends that we want to realize for their own sake, as well as attachments to other persons and loyalties to various groups and associations" (Rawls 1993, 19).[7]

But why is social equality necessary for developing and pursuing our conception of the good? Simply put, our conceptions of "what is valuable in human life" are not cultivated in a social vacuum. Our pursuit of our conception of the good occurs within a social world, where others have the ability to enable or constrain it. Proponents of relational autonomy have already underscored that our self-concepts contain social components, and background social dynamics and power structures play a significant role in the enjoyment and development of autonomy (Christman 2004, 143). In other words, paying due attention to the inherently social nature of our personhood should incline us toward considering how our relationships to others can effectively thwart or support central aspects of it. The point, here, is that our identities are partly shaped by the recognition or *mis*recognition of others, such that "a person or group of people can suffer real damage, real distortion, if the people or society around them mirror back to them a confining or demeaning or contemptible picture of themselves," imprisoning them in a "false, distorted, and reduced mode of being" (Taylor 1994, 25).

We need a thorough explanation, however, of how other person' attitudes or dispositions toward us can threaten to damage and distort our sense of self in this way. To begin with, having a conception of the good seems to presuppose a minimal *sense of self*.[8] In having a particular conception of the good, I also have a particular sense of *who I am as a person*—that is, a sense of myself as a self-governing agent with a scheme of ends that are properly *mine*. In contrast, we often speak of "losing our sense of self" when we become madly infatuated with someone and lose sight of the ends we pursued before they entered our lives, because we now want nothing else but them. As the writer and socialite Vita Sackville-West wrote of her overwhelming love for Virginia Woolf, "I am reduced to a thing that wants Virginia." We make similar complaints when we are so bogged down by helping others pursue *their* ends that we have no room for our own, like the case of the new mother who complains about "losing herself" because she must attend to the needs of her infant round-the-clock.

a. The sense of self

As a starting point, Andrea Sangiovanni provides a rich and insightful account of our sense of self. He defines the self as "one's self-conception, one's conception of the values, commitments, concerns that are central to one's life, the relationships and roles that makes one the kind of person one is, including the qualities and defects of one's personality and character" (2017, 58). According to him, our sense of self emerges from the interplay between two points of view: the point of view of ourselves as creators and enactors (the "self-conceiver") and the point of view of ourselves as what has been created and enacted ("the self-conception") (2017, 59). For example, there is the point of view of myself who has become a scientist, and there is the point of view of myself who regrets this and aspires toward a career change, like becoming an artist. In our lives, we constantly move between one and the other: "by acting, deciding, and pursuing, we shape the kinds of people we are and can become, and by reflecting on who we are and can become, we give rise to our actions, decisions, and pursuits" (59). Here, the self-conceiver chases pursuits and ambitions that give rise to a particular self-conception, which in turn shapes the self-conceiver's future pursuits and ambitions, and so on, and it is these cycles of interaction that lend us a sense of authorship over our own lives.

Importantly, for Sangiovanni, our sense of self only emerges if the interplay between the two selves is minimally *integrated* and has some baseline degree of coherence, continuity, and consistency among the roles over time, with no radical disjuncture between the self-conceiver and self-conception (2017, 5). My current self-conception (of, say, myself as a scientist) may look very different from my future pursuits and ambitions as a self-conceiver (the desire to paint like Jackson Pollock), but the two remain *continuous* insofar as it is the stress of publishing research that has led me to desire the career change.[9] On the other hand, a radical disjuncture that disrupts my sense of self would occur if my country were ravaged by civil war and I was forced to flee to a new state, where my qualifications are not recognized and I must instead work as a taxi driver. In this case, I wouldn't just be leaving my career as a scientist behind: I would be leaving behind a life I have built, guided by *a particular conception of the good* that I must now abandon, simply because it is not available to me in the new country.

It may be objected, at this stage, that Sangiovanni's view of the self is problematic. There are two issues a critic may point to. Notably, Galen Strawson draws a key distinction between what he calls "diachronic" and "episodic" self-experience (2004, 430–431). Diachronic persons experience their selfhood as "something that has relatively long-term diachronic continuity, something that persists over a long stretch of time." In contrast, "episodic" persons have barely any sense, if at all, that their self "was there in the (further) past and will be there in the future, although one is perfectly well aware that one has long-term continuity considered as a whole human being." While Strawson hypothesizes that a predominantly diachronic self is more commonly experienced, he suggests that there is a great deal of individual variation between persons, or even the same individual, depending on their circumstances (2004, 431). Not everyone apprehends their self as something that persists in time, or sees the "remoter past or future" as *their* past or future (2004, 433). The worry at hand for Sangiovanni's view is that "coherence, continuity, and consistency" are attributes of *diachronic*, rather than episodic selves—and it is false to presume that diachronicity rings equally true across the board.

Being somewhat episodically inclined, I am sympathetic to Strawson's claims, but I don't think that the "episodic" sense of selfhood is at all incompatible with endorsing the claim that my selfhood lies in the interplay between myself as self-conceiver and self-conception. My instantiation of *multiple selves* over the course of my biological lifetime does not in itself suggest that those episodic selves each lack a minimum sense of "coherence, continuity, and consistency." Perhaps I (as my current self) am not the same person who I (as a biological individual) was in the past, but as of the *present moment*, my self-conception fits together with the self I am *conceiving of right now*. Désirée 2009 and 2023 may not be parts of the same unified self; I can quite reasonably think of Désirée 2009 as a different person from the individual editing this chapter. At the same time, I may consistently hold that Désirée 2023, for as long as she exists, continues to be (at least in part) the product of her own ongoing actions, decisions, and overall outlook. At a deeper level, the disagreement posed by Strawson may be merely semantic. I take Strawson's claim to be primarily *phenomenological*: he is concerned with accurately describing *how* we experience our sense of self. He simply doesn't *feel* that he has a single self that spans his overall lifetime. But Sangiovanni's notion of the "sense of self" doesn't require that we personally identify with our past and future selves. Rather, what he's identifying is something much more like the experience of autonomy and control, which may remain *constant* over time even when the "selves" it creates are separate and distinct. Our sense of ongoing authorship need not be tied to a specific self.

Secondly, it might be complained that Sangiovanni's account inaccurately presumes that we have a determinate sense of self, when many persons have a sense of self that is constantly shifting and changing depending on their social location, with components that do not always fit together neatly. Here, it's useful to look to Mariana Ortega's notion of "multiplicitous subjectivity": a "self that is pulled in different directions by norms, practices, beliefs, etc., of different 'worlds'" (2008, 71). As I read her, a "world" can be bigger or smaller—it refers to a set of social norms and practices that may be upheld by a dominant group within an actual society, or subgroups within it. Because we may inhabit different worlds at different times, or perhaps even live in-between worlds, the individual may have to negotiate two or more "cultural and/or racial views/understandings/values" at once. Throughout the process of negotiation, a multiplicitous subject may have "a set of norms and practices from different cultures that are not consistent with each other; consequently, she may experience contradictions and feel fragmented" (1984, 73). For example, a French Muslim woman may feel torn between her cultural identities because she is simultaneously expected to keep her religious commitment out of the public sphere, yet also live a life in which religious commitment plays a central role. Perhaps fragmentation of this sort is not always a defect of the self. For at least some people who indeed live and travel between worlds, fragmentation is *constitutive* of their being. Therefore, it seems false to assume that the self-conceiver and self-conception must be coherent, continuous, and consistent.

Note, however, that Ortega is *not* claiming that multiplicitous selves lack coherence, continuity, and consistency altogether. This would be a serious misunderstanding of her argument. Rather, multiplicity should be accompanied by subjects' *negotiation* of their multiple identities (Ortega 2008, 74). As I read her, persons with multiple identities, in particular, must engage in a reflective process of deliberation and redeliberation over who they wish to become. I should not deny or erase my multiplicity, but rather, *negotiate* it by coming to understand the different worlds I inhabit, the expectations or possibilities that they carve out for me, and how I wish to respond to them. Eventually, I may end up prioritizing one world over another, or develop a new consciousness that synthesizes both at once. Furthermore, even if synthesis is ultimately impossible, this need not stop me from constantly and critically negotiating my identities (Ortega 2008, 78). Ortega's emphasis on the *procedural* elements of self-making, then, seems consonant with Sangiovanni's claim that the sense of self arises from the *interplay* between the self-conceiver and self-conceived. On this view, we can certainly recognize and accommodate some degree of ambiguity, contradiction, and fragmentation in the sense of self, but this is perfectly compatible with multiplicitous subjects having a *minimal degree* of coherence, continuity, and consistency that derives from their negotiation of their "history and circumstances" (Ortega 2008, 78). In other words, it is the deliberative process of making sense of one's conflicting identities, and adjusting who we are or who we want to become accordingly, that produces a baseline sense of self-authorship.

b. The social elements of the self

Above, I have defended Sangiovanni's account of the sense of self, showing that it is compatible with multiplicitous or episodic senses of self. I now want to analyze the circumstances under which our senses of self can suffer serious disjunctures. Importantly, I will not be considering the cases where persons simply *lack* a sense of self. It's possible for a person to totally lack a sense of who they are or what they value, but I assume that those people are idiosyncratic. Rather, I am more interested in the situations where persons *do* have a minimal sense of self, but have to battle to overcome constant rupture and distortion that results from their subordinate status in the broader social context. We can think of the sense of self as something like a musical composition that we are constantly playing. To be clear, the claim is not that members of socially subordinate groups have *no composition to play at all*, but that their attempts to play their compositions are consistently drowned or tuned out, so that they must put in additional effort to keep the music going. In the same way that a successful musical performance requires an audience, we don't develop or enact our self-conception in total isolation, but in communication and interaction with other social beings (Sangiovanni 63). There has to be some unity between the self I conceive of and the self-conception that is *received by other persons*. As your friend, for example, I may regularly affirm your sense of self as a dedicated artist by demonstrating my appreciation for your painting skills and dutifully turning up to your exhibitions. It would be challenging to conceive of yourself as an artist unless your pursuits were recognized to some degree by people engaged in similar pursuits, if not your immediate social circle. However, the degree of your success in *communicating* your sense of self to others doesn't just depend on your *performance* of artist-like properties, but on their attitudes and dispositions toward you. You will not be recognized as an artist, no matter how skillful your painting, by persons who are (for some reason) invested in denying you that very identity.

To be sure, I am not arguing that we have an obligation to recognize others in *exactly the light* they wish to be seen. It's true that people can be utterly wrong about who they are, like the quintessential talent-show contestant who claims to be a fantastic singer but can barely hold a tune. Perhaps, in such cases, we are morally obliged to *not* enable the delusion. Nor am I claiming that, under ideal conditions, I must always succeed in bringing across my ideal sense of self to others. Social uptake can fail for various reasons unrelated to injustice, whether it is an innocent misunderstanding, my audience's lack of relevant knowledge, or simple artlessness on my part (e.g., mispronouncing "hors d'oeuvres" when I'm trying to sound sophisticated). But there is a world of difference between a scenario where my attempt at self-presentation *accidentally* falls flat, and one where my self-presentation is likely to fail because it is systematically rejected by others. No injustice occurs when I accidentally fail to recognize you as an artist because I am under the wrongheaded impression, for example, that abstract art is not "real" art, but matters change when I fail to recognize you as an artist because you are a member of a socially subordinated group. The rationale could be that people of your gender or race are highly unlikely to be artists; by dint of their inferior status, they are simply not capable of such valuable projects or achievements. In other words, other people may send us the message that we *cannot* be, or become, who we want to be—that we are aspiring too high for our real station. Particularly illuminating, I believe, is this passage by Elijah Anderson:

> There comes a time in the life of every African American when he or she is powerfully reminded of his or her putative place as a Black person. Among themselves, Black people often refer to this experience after the fact in a light-hearted manner and with an occasional chuckle as the "n***** moment." It is something of an inside joke. At the time it occurs, however, the awareness of this act of acute insult and discrimination is shocking; the victim is taken by surprise, caught off guard [. . .] Emotions flood over the victim as this middle-class, cosmopolitan-oriented Black person is humiliated and shown that he or she is, before anything else, a racially circumscribed Black person after all. No matter what she has achieved, or how decent and law-abiding she is, there is no protection, no sanctuary, no escaping from this fact. She is vulnerable. Whatever the educated and often professionally successful person previously thought her position in society was, now she is challenged, as random white persons casually but powerfully degrade her. (Anderson 2012, 253)

What is so harmful about the racial slur is that it brings about a sudden *reduction* of the self; a sudden diminishment of who the insulted parties take themselves to be, and a flat-out rejection of the face they believed they were successfully presenting to the rest of the world. I want to suggest that similar moments are frequently encountered to varying degrees of severity by women, as well as members of other socially subordinated groups.[10] This includes my own experience at a philosophy conference where a white male professor, immediately after my talk, asked me if I "knew who Kant was" (presumably because I am of Asian descent, and thus could not be expected to know anything about Western philosophy, despite the actual content of my talk strongly indicating otherwise). In that moment, it seemed as though the self-conception I prized so much—that is, of myself as a political philosopher whose work was well-informed by the analytic tradition and legitimate in the eyes of a predominantly Anglo-American audience—had fallen away. This alluring possibility had been foreclosed by my Asian appearance, which meant that I would often be perceived as an "Asian philosopher" who was, by definition, ignorant of the schools of philosophical thought that I wanted to have proficient knowledge of. Though phrased more civilly, the effect was really not too different from routinely having "go back to China!" shouted at me on the streets of London, which again led to an abrupt sense of diminishment: no matter how well I believed I was playing the part of a seasoned Londoner, I was nothing more than an undesirable foreigner in the harasser's eyes.

These cases show that being treated as an inferior tends to foreclose the range of possibilities of *who we can be* to other people. It is highly unlikely that you will be appropriately recognized as the person you have tried (or are trying to) become if you are located in a social world that rejects that possibility on the basis of stereotyping and discrimination. When read as a social inferior, my status is likely to be fixed in other persons' minds as someone who is only narrowly suited for certain purposes, rather than engaging in the meaningful goals or projects that are central to my identity. But why, exactly, is such foreclosure so harmful? Think, again, of the musician who is valiantly trying to perform their composition to an audience who is covering their ears to block out the sounds while simultaneously blasting other musical pieces. Perhaps the musician might still manage to play the song. But it's more likely than not that she will be thrown off by her surroundings; the noise might make her lose her rhythm or play the wrong notes, or she might be so discouraged by the audience's reaction as to walk off the stage entirely. The point, here, is that misrecognition can harmfully interrupt the interplay between the self-conceiving and self-conceived parts of ourselves. As a socially subordinated subject, I may find it deeply difficult to enact the self that I value; worse still, my material successes may be drained of their significance because of others' negative reactions to them. (For another example, we may imagine a prize-winning Black poet being repeatedly told that they only won the award because of racial tokenism, not the merit of their writing.) Such harm to one's sense of self does not only occur when individuals experience overt discrimination or hatred. As mentioned in Section 2, the experience of social inequality has changed over time, and tends to take more indirect forms today.[11] Much like the professor's inference I did not know who Kant was because of my perceived racial background, members of historically subordinated groups often receive subtle signals that members of the dominant groups have failed to recognize their self-conception. It is well documented, for example, that doctors who are read as women or persons of color are often presumed to be nurses. While this error may strike some as trivial or harmless, it originates from the stereotype that members of "inferior" groups do not have high-status occupations; again, their group membership is assumed to foreclose the possibilities of *who they can be*. Worse still, a persistent gap between how we see ourselves and the way others see us may compel us to adjust or adapt in response (Sangiovanni 2017, 63). We may even begin to view ourselves in others' demeaning terms or find ourselves unable to do otherwise from the start. As W. E. B. Du Bois famously put it, "[i]t is a peculiar sensation, this double-consciousness, this sense of always looking at one's self through the eyes of others, of measuring one's soul by the tape of a world that looks on in amused contempt and pity" (2007, 8).

In sum, I have tried to explain why, as moral persons, we have a basic interest in being treated as social equals. Chiefly, there is a set of social conditions that are necessary for developing and pursuing our conception of the good. In order to have a minimally stable sense of self, through which we create and enact our ends, not only must our self-conceptions align with how *others* see us; they must also treat us as self-conceivers, rather than mere tools or playthings. We can justify a robust universal entitlement to social equality by pointing to the demands of moral personhood. Importantly, my claims do not ride on *every* instance of subordinating treatment necessarily posing the threat of damage to an individual's sense of self. Some instances may be too trivial to cause any alarm; some individuals are unusually resilient. The argument is not a priori but a posteriori, ultimately relying on documented observations about the forms that inferiorizing treatment has taken and how it is experienced by members of subordinated groups. On this account, all persons, regardless of their citizenship status, are entitled to social equality in order to protect them from the serious harms of inferiorizing treatment. I attend to the implications of this claim in the remaining sections.

5. What do states owe to noncitizens?

I have argued that social equality ought to be understood as a universal entitlement that is also held by noncitizens. This contrasts starkly with the "conventional view" that only citizens fall within the scope of social equality. However, treating social equality as a universal demand does not mean endorsing the unpalatable view that states have duties to minimize the social inequalities experienced by persons *all over the world*. It would be counterintuitive to proclaim that the United States has duties to minimize gendered social inequalities between men and women in, say, Malaysia, just as much as the Malaysian state itself does.

It is useful to consider an analogous duty of justice: the protection of human rights. Even if human rights are (by definition) universal entitlements, according to the current global order, states are primarily responsible for actively protecting the human rights of citizens *and* noncitizens who are located on *their* territory. In Michael Blake's words, "Although human rights are defined as those rights that are held by human in virtue of being human, this does not entail that all human rights are equally pressed against all human institutions at all times"; in a world divided into distinct jurisdictions, human rights impose distinct obligations on distinct political communities (2013, 110). At the same time, even if states are not strictly responsible for protecting the human rights of those located outside their territory, they also have a more limited obligation to refrain from violating their human rights. Similarly, under the current global order, states may be primarily responsible for minimizing the social inequalities experienced by persons located on their territories, whether they are citizens or noncitizens. To use Carens's language, they are *general* rights, not membership-specific rights. As I outlined in Section 3, states not only have negative duties of justice to refrain from creating institutional norms or policies that lead to social inequalities, but also have positive duties of justice to protect the social equality of these groups (e.g., by granting provisions or accommodations that enable them to participate as equals in public life). Much like in the case of human rights, they acquire new responsibilities to noncitizens who have arrived upon their territory and hence fall within their jurisdiction, including those who are undocumented. Furthermore, in contrast to Walzer and Nath's claims, noncitizens' entitlement to social equality does not arise in virtue of their subjection to the state's coercive laws, performance of "necessary labor," dense interconnections with the lives of citizens, or unavoidable and involuntary subjection to the state's institutions. It is their *moral personhood* alone and, by extension, the threat of damage to their fundamental sense of self, that entitles them to treatment as social equals—an entitlement that generates corresponding duties on the part of receiving states to minimize their social subordination.

Notice that accepting the analogy to human rights leads to a surprising consequence. States are not off the hook with regard to noncitizens who are located outside of their territory. Recall that states are obliged to *defend and protect* the human rights of those within its territorial jurisdiction, yet also refrain from violating the human rights of noncitizens outside of it. Similarly, even if states do not have demanding positive duties to minimize the social subordination of territorially absent noncitizens (who ought to be protected by their own states), states *at the very least* have negative duties to refrain from enacting norms or policies that harm their social equality. It is well documented that noncitizens located on the state's territory are often demeaned and humiliated in the name of immigration enforcement.[12] At the same time, however, immigration policies may effectively subordinate noncitizens who are *not yet* territorially present. In one specific case, would-be immigrants and refugees are sometimes directed to *extraterritorial* detention centers, where they are subjected to degrading and inhumane treatment. The Australian state, for example, was responsible for subordinating the refugees that it sent to encampments on Nauru, even if the refugees were located outside Australian territory. The decision to exile the refugees to Nauru could itself be read as demeaning: it expressed the desire to contain perceived inferiors within a distant space, lest their presence pollute Australian land.

In the remaining chapters of my book, I argue that receiving states can socially subordinate would-be migrants even if those would-be migrants (unlike the refugees who have traveled toward Australian soil) have not left their countries of origin. As I will argue in the next two chapters, this is because would-be migrants can be socially subordinated by *wrongfully discriminatory* immigration policies that exclude them from the outset. States have a duty not to *wrongfully discriminate* against noncitizens, including those who are not yet located on the territory, due to the distorted and contemptible images of themselves that discriminatory policies generally reflect back at them. To be clear, I will not be arguing that *every* form of immigration discrimination will necessarily have this effect on would-be migrants' sense of self. My analysis will be confined to wealthy Western states' discriminatory treatment toward members of *socially salient groups*.[13] Groups are socially salient when one's perceived membership in it is "important to the structure of social interactions across a wide range of social contexts" (Lippert-Rasmussen 2006, 169), and thus holds a correspondingly strong sway over our self-perception. Paradigmatic examples of socially salient groups are those that pertain to their members' gender, race, sexual orientation, and gender identity. Chapter Three makes the case that, similar to those cases, low-skilled migrants constitute a socially salient group whose sense of self may be harmed by states' preference for highly skilled migrants, and Chapter Four investigates the disparate impact that this seemingly "neutral" preference can have on women.

At the same time, states must refrain from enacting policies that produce or maintain colonial relationships between noncitizens and the state. In my view, colonialism is a clear-cut example of a state-implemented policy that has succeeded in harming the social equality of noncitizens outside its territory. For example, in the following passage, Jean-Paul Sartre powerfully describes the destruction of colonial subjects' *sense of self* that often accompanied their violent subordination:

> Violence in the colonies does not only have for its aim the keeping of these enslaved men at arm's length; it seeks to dehumanize them. Everything will be done to wipe out their traditions, to substitute our language for theirs and to destroy their culture without giving them ours. Sheer physical fatigue will stupefy them. Starved and ill, if they have any spirit left, fear will finish the job; guns are levelled at the peasant; civilians come to take over his land and force him by dint of flogging to till the land for them. If he shows fight, the soldiers fire and he's a dead man; if he gives in, he degrades himself and he is no longer a man at all; shame and fear will split up his character and make his inmost self fall to pieces. (in Fanon 1963, 15)

Harm to noncitizens' social equality need not involve active invasion of their land. One of the central wrongs of colonialism was Western powers' *racial exploitation* of the native populations. Through its intentional legal exclusion of low-skilled migrants, present-day immigration policy reproduces "colonial" relationships through interlocking systems of racial exploitation. I discuss this phenomenon in Chapter Five.

Before concluding, I wish to address two potentially worrying objections to the requirements of justice that I have articulated above. First of all, a skeptic might claim that our sense of self need not be fundamentally "social" and other-dependent in the way I have just described. Someone who is persistently treated as a social inferior may simply choose to harden themselves against the demeaning treatment they experience at the hands of states or other agents, and thus fortify their sense of self against the harms of inferiorizing treatment. One could thus opt for the path of *independence* rather than relationality vis-à-vis their sense of self. For this argument to succeed, we don't have to claim that it is *desirable* that people resort to that; we could quite reasonably prefer a society where the state chooses to protect social equality, over one where socially subordinated groups are compelled to seek what Avishai Margalit calls "autarchy"—"the ability to be self-sufficient in satisfying one's needs" (1996, 53). All that matters is that autarchy can be meaningfully *chosen*, and one's sense of self thus detached entirely from the terms in which others may see us. Though it may require the cultivation of considerable mental strength, persons may choose to reorient themselves toward an autarchic mode of existence in a way that they cannot simply choose, for example, to become more materially comfortable. For this reason, states are *not* required to protect persons' social equality as a matter of justice, even if it may be morally preferable that they do so.

In order to address this objection, it is instructive to look to the response to autarchy that Margalit himself considers in his discussion of humiliation. Specifically, he lays out the Nietzschean sentiment that it is truly "impossible for anyone of inferior social status to be truly immune to external humiliation" (1996, 57). The insistence on such immunity, Nietzsche suggests, is a mere defense mechanism adopted by "slaves" at the very bottom of the social rung. It is those who are most lacking in social recognition and affirmation who profess a kind of "false independence that is the essence of slave morality"—that is, an orientation toward the world that centers around self-righteous resentment of the more powerful (57). In sum, Nietzsche's belief is that those of inferior social status are "psychologically incapable" of extricating themselves from the harms of subordination. We need not, I think, adopt a view that is as strong as Nietzsche's. The sweeping empirical claim that no human is psychologically capable of autarchy seems unconvincing and unnecessary. A more plausible response might concede that some psychologically resilient individuals *could* be autarchic in theory. However, the proposal that someone has a right to X doesn't require us to demonstrate that X is important to *each and every individual's* well-being. This would set too high of a bar for what may count as a moral right, and we don't typically enforce this expectation when it comes to commonly assumed moral rights; the entitlements we understand as moral rights have more to do with *general* human interests than psychological possibilities. In the case of the right that promises be kept, for example, there might also be idiosyncratic individuals who have built up robust psychological armor against broken promises and therefore rendered themselves invulnerable to the harm of such offenses. So it goes for other basic moral rights like bodily autonomy, or the right to property-ownership.

A second objection is that, even if the sense of self *is* to some extent other-dependent, state institutions are, by their very nature, not generally capable of affecting our capacity for a sense of self. This could ring true especially in the case of foreign states, which often do not have any direct impact on our lives. The upshot of this argument is that, while demeaning state policies may be wrongful, they are not generally unjust unless they *actually* affect our capacity to develop and pursue our conception of the good. To go back to the concrete case of immigration policy, consider this hypothetical example: suppose that Hungary decides to exclude all philosophers, on the grounds that philosophers are corruptors of the young. It is perhaps wrong for Hungary to do this because they are relying on inaccurate and unfair visions of a profession that is meaningful to many persons and figures nontrivially in their conception of the good. (Such persons include myself and probably most readers of my book). Nonetheless, it's not obvious that Hungary is *actually* affecting our ability to pursue that conception of the good if we don't have a prior wish to move to Hungary, and there exist other countries where we may continue to philosophize in. From this perspective, Hungary's law is more absurd than unjust, wrong as it may be.[14] Even if Hungary acts unjustly on some standard, it's not clear that the injustice in question has anything to do with philosophers' sense of self. What if this were also true of immigration policies that seek to exclude a particular social group—that if they act unjustly at all, it is not for the main reasons that I have attempted to establish?

In my view, Hungary's imaginary exclusion of philosophers differs quite a lot from the real-life examples of immigration exclusion that I will elaborate on in the remainder of the text. There are at least two reasons why they are not comparable. Firstly, unlike *low-skilled migrants* (as well as persons who face discrimination on the basis of their social identity), philosophers do not constitute a *socially salient* group. Recall that a group is only socially salient when one's perceived membership in that group structures how they are treated by other persons across a broad range of social contexts.[15] In a world where being a philosopher does not generally determine how I am treated by other persons, Hungary's singling out of philosophers would be an aberration that is amusing at best and inconvenient at worst, rather than part of a continuing legacy of subordinating and demeaning treatment that cuts across many different spheres of our existence.

Secondly, notice that the example relies heavily on the assumption that philosophers do not generally have a pressing desire to move to Hungary. The point is that Hungary's decision will have little effect on most philosophers' life-prospects, unlike wealthy states' exclusion of low-skilled migrants who wish very much to gain entry, and will go to astonishingly dangerous lengths to do so. For example, the desire of many Central Americans to work in the United States, and possibly build a better life there, has become vital to their self-conception, to the extent that subjection to demeaning exclusion would be profoundly harmful to the development and pursuit of their conception of the good. The same could be said for a citizen of a previously colonized nation, who has (as a result of said colonization) developed an attachment to the metropole, and has therefore also cultivated a conception of the good that involves immigration to the metropole, only to experience what I call a severe disjuncture in their sense of self when they are promptly rejected. Following the Commonwealth Immigrants Act of 1962 and the Immigration Act of 1971, it became very challenging for Indian citizens to enter the British Empire. What is significant, however, is that they were once freely received due to the British Nationality Act of 1948, which had created the new legal status of "citizen of the United Kingdom and Colonies," and eventually led to much opposition to the entry of British colonial subjects.[16]

At this stage, a critic may object that the relative desire of a person to be included has no underlying relationship to how demeaning an act of exclusion is. The fact I actively *want* to go to your party does not make my exclusion on racist grounds any more demeaning than the racial exclusion of a person who is positively uninterested in social gatherings. This is undoubtedly correct. All the same, the desire of the abovementioned migrants to enter wealthy states—unlike philosophers and Hungary—*is* relevant insofar as exclusionary mechanisms targeted at them are usually *responses* to their widely known desire to enter. Racially discriminatory immigration policies like White Australia, the Chinese Exclusion Act, or the "Muslim Ban" were typically introduced when nonwhite persons were, in fact, attempting to enter or had been living in those states for some time, and their presence was commonly interpreted as threatening or otherwise undesirable to citizens. Put differently: for our present purposes, it does not seem fruitful to consider the hypothetical prospect of discriminatory state policies that have exactly no effect on our sense of self, when we are attempting to analyze and understand the injustice of real-life immigration discrimination designed to keep out groups who have much to lose in the way of strongly valued life-prospects.

6. Conclusion

As this chapter has underscored, states have *negative* and *positive* duties to minimize the social inequalities suffered by territorially present noncitizens, as well as *negative duties* not to harm the social equality of territorially absent noncitizens. These pressing duties are justified by noncitizens' moral personhood. Social equality is one of the preconditions for our ability to successfully develop and pursue a conception of the good, rather than an entitlement that we only acquire in virtue of standing in particular political relationships. The philosophical literature on states' treatment of noncitizens must take into account their entitlement to social equality. In particular, we have strong reason to reject immigration policies that have subordinating effects on noncitizens, even if they have not yet been admitted. A recent example that proves this point is the United States' "Muslim ban." Many citizens of the eight Muslim-majority countries who find themselves unable to enter the United States on the basis of this policy may never come close to stepping foot on US soil. It is not just Muslim Americans, but the affected *noncitizens themselves* who are also wronged. It is not at all obvious why the distant location of the would-be immigrant should make a moral difference. Islamophobic immigration discrimination sends the same message that may disrupt our sense of self: that regardless of the positive attributes they present to the authority in question to prove that they are worthy of admission, the applicant will never be anything more than an undesirable or unassimilable inferior in the eyes of the receiving state. The harms of subordination to our sense of self can be carried across oceans. In the chapters that follow, I will examine how widespread practices of skill-selective immigration policies may demean low-skilled migrants who have not yet entered the receiving state.

PART II

WRONGFUL DISCRIMINATION AND SKILL-SELECTIVE IMMIGRATION POLICIES

3
Selecting Immigrants by Skill I
Wrongful Direct Discrimination

1. Introduction

Assuming that states are obliged to uphold the social equality of migrants, what implications does this have for present-day immigration policy? Noncitizens' right to social equality would unequivocally rule out many cruel practices that are already in place: separating children from their parents, containing detainees in squalid conditions, and deporting long-time residents. All these, I think, would be required by a minimally decent immigration policy. However, I turn to a different question: quite apart from how states *enforce* the exclusion of migrants, in what way (if at all) must their *selection* of migrants be constrained by social equality? Questions about selection are, in a way, prior to questions about enforcement. We cannot fully assess the permissibility of a particular enforcement policy without reflecting on *who* will be subject to it. Suppose that the uses of coercive measures like detention and deportation were only restricted to a small class of highly dangerous criminals who are picked out for exclusion. The argument in favor of such mechanisms, in this example, would seem much stronger than if they were targeted exclusively at migrants of a particular racial or ethnic group. Certain enforcement measures, just like family separation and detention in inhumane living conditions, may go beyond the pale *regardless* of who they are applied to, simply because they violate basic human rights that everyone is entitled to as a matter of equal respect. That said, there are at least some enforcement policies that do not, in themselves, cross this threshold. In such cases, their permissibility will turn on *who* they are used to exclude. For example, a relatively "soft" mode of immigration enforcement, like a small fine for crossing the border without authorization, can seem pernicious if it is used explicitly or disproportionately on persons of a particular race. Regardless of its severity, the fine *demeans* members of the targeted group.

Immigration and Social Equality. Désirée Lim, Oxford University Press. © Oxford University Press 2023.
DOI: 10.1093/oso/9780197658093.003.0004

On what basis, then, may states permissibly select migrants for admission, keeping in mind that the act of selection typically necessitates the forcible exclusion of others? Many theorists accept, during the process of selection, that states have no right to directly discriminate against would-be immigrants on grounds of race or sex. This antidiscrimination principle must hold even assuming that states have a right to exclude noncitizens. However, while the discourse on cases of wrongful discrimination has largely focused on discrimination on grounds of gender, race, and sexual orientation, states frequently engage in discrimination of a different kind when it comes to admissions and naturalization policies: the preference of highly skilled over low-skilled migrants. As Ayelet Shachar and Ran Hirschl note, governments pick winners "through fast-tracked, strategic grants of citizenship for those with exceptional skills and extraordinary talent, while at the same time holding other categories of immigration applicants to ever stricter admission and permission-to-stay requirements" (2013, 71). It is assumed that the antidiscrimination principle does not include such cases of skill-based discrimination, and that these fall well within the rights of states. While I acknowledge that it is not necessarily wrong to select immigrants on the basis of their having particular skills, I suggest, to the contrary, that states' broad preference for highly skilled migrants in the present context constitutes a form of wrongful discrimination. To be clear, though I will argue that skill-based selection is presumptively wrongful in social contexts that resemble our own, it would not be wrongful under emergency circumstances where the preference for specific skills doesn't result from demeaning beliefs about low-skilled migrants.

In Section 2, with reference to Deborah Hellman's expressive theory of discrimination, which particularly resonates with the notion of social equality, I explain what is wrongful about particular forms of state discrimination between would-be migrants. Next, in Section 3, I tackle the issue of immigrant selection on grounds of talent, which I refer to as "skill-based selection." Unlike gender or race-based selection, it is generally not regarded as *wrongful* discrimination, for the reason that it does not express disrespect in the same way that sexist or racist selection criteria does. I argue that this assumption is mistaken, as skill-based discrimination *does* involve the expression of disrespect. In the existing social context, and in its current form, it has the expressive effect of reproducing demeaning stereotypes about low-skilled migrants. Finally, in Section 4, I anticipate three objections to my conclusion.

2. What is wrongful discrimination?

a. Wrongful discrimination and immigration

Many agree that immigration policies that directly discriminate between candidates for admission on the basis of gender or race are wrongful. For example, David Miller regards "discrimination on grounds of race, sex, or, in most instances, religion" to be indefensible under any circumstance, because it is insulting for would-be immigrants to be told that they belong to the wrong race or sex, or have the wrong color, given how "these features do not connect to anything of real significance to the society they want to join" (2013, 217). However, Miller's explanation of why such discrimination is wrong is unsatisfying in three serious ways.

First, he cannot mean that discrimination is wrong insofar as would-be migrants *feel* insulted. I might feel extremely offended, were I told that the people of the United States do not need my highly specific and well-honed furniture-testing skill. Yet this is not, in itself, a compelling reason to think that I have been wrongfully discriminated against. Or imagine that the potential migrants who are rejected for wrongfully discriminatory reasons take the news in good stride; it is no skin off their noses. But the fact they are not offended does not seem to neutralize the wrongfulness of the immigration policy in question. Overall, it seems that the insult in the immigration policy must operate *independently* of the discriminatees' subjective responses.

Second, it is unclear what Miller means by race, sex, or religion not connecting to anything of *real significance* for the society in question. Could a racist state not insist that maintaining a homogeneous racial identity is extremely important for members of its society? An Australian minister of immigration, for example, claimed that nobody could reasonably object to Australians, as a whole, seeking to create a racially homogeneous nation (Carens 1988, 165). But another way of interpreting "real significance" is to say that gender and race are objectively irrelevant grounds for immigrant selection, regardless of how existing members of the state feel. Even if I strongly desire to award an essay prize to the most attractive philosopher, and it is of enormous significance for *me* that I do that, good looks are an entirely irrelevant reason for awarding someone an essay prize. However, *why* is race an objectively irrelevant criterion for selecting immigrants? Certainly, good looks have nothing to do with how rigorous one's philosophical writing is, but it begs the question against a "White Australia" advocate to say that race is irrelevant to the goal of securing Australia's national identity and culture.

Finally, in line with my conclusions in Chapter One, pointing out their irrelevance does not seem to fully explain why we think some forms of discrimination are so wrong. For example, the Chinese Exclusion Acts, which barred entry to Chinese immigrants, were founded on the belief that Chinese people were fundamentally strange, inassimilable, and ultimately incapable of comprehending republican values (Volpp 2005, 459–470). Locating wrongfulness in its use of "irrelevant" or "unimportant" criteria makes it sound as though those behind US border policy merely used arbitrary or irrational criteria about who to take in, like if I were to select my marriage partner based on how round their head is, or how many pairs of purple socks they have. But this is hardly the full story. As Chapter One has argued, disrespectful behavior is not limited to morally arbitrary treatment. Rather, a big part of why the Chinese Exclusion Acts were morally egregious is that they were primarily driven by beliefs in the innate inferiority of Chinese people, and an attitude of profound contempt toward them. In this sense, they were not, strictly speaking, arbitrary or irrational; instead, they were based on a set of widely shared racist views that seemed perfectly rational to hold at the time. Similarly, racially segregated public toilets for Black and white people are not morally objectionable because one's race is irrelevant to which toilet he or she uses, or because it is irrational to separate toilets on such grounds. Rather, they are wrongful because they reflect the belief that Black people are *inferior* to white people, and therefore ought not to share the same facilities as them. Simply shrugging these cases off as applications of objectively irrelevant criteria means stopping short of morally evaluating *why* such criteria were used in the first place, and confronting the racist attitudes that underpinned them.

b. The status-harm theory of discrimination

A promising alternative to the arguments above, which directly relates to the imperative of social equality, can be found in Owen Fiss's account of wrongful discrimination. Fiss argues that discrimination is wrong when it results in "status-harm" to members of a specially disadvantaged group who suffer from socioeconomic and political disadvantage (1976, 155). According to this view, discrimination is wrong because it *worsens* the social position of an already marginalized group. For example, as Peter Higgins writes, virtually all past or ongoing exclusions on the basis of perceived race, religion, and sexual preference are plainly unjust because denial of their admission avoidably harms unjustly disadvantaged groups, including members of the same or similar groups who are already present in the receiving country (2013, 208). This is because "such policies intimate an official belief in the inferiority of members of excluded groups, and thereby make domestic members of excluded groups (more) vulnerable to discrimination and oppression" (208). The "status-harm" account could do well in answering the concerns I outlined above. First, it gives those who are excluded on the basis of their gender or race an *objective* reason for feeling insulted, if their already disadvantaged position in society would be worsened as a result. On top of this, it would give us a prima facie reason to criticize the White Australia policy, even if race were of special significance to Australians. It would not matter that race *does* connect to something of 'real significance'; what matters is whether or not it will worsen the status of an already disadvantaged group. Finally, it would also help to complete our account of why the Chinese Exclusion Acts were wrong; they did not merely involve the employment of arbitrary or irrational criteria, but criteria that worsened the position of a disadvantaged group.

However, this suggestion suffers from two major limitations. To understand why, it is necessary to take a closer look at what counts as a "status-harm." According to Fiss, in the realm of discriminatory employment criteria, a full theory of status-harm could have to include an assessment of the status or prestige of the job itself, the public visibility of the position, how diffuse the exclusionary impact is, and how strongly the criterion can be justified (Fiss 1976, 158–159). To extrapolate from this, the wrongfulness of a discriminatory immigration policy could well be assessed according to factors like the global status of the state in question (e.g., exclusion from a rich superpower could be much worse for a marginalized group's status than exclusion from a relatively small and poor one), or the visibility of the exclusion (e.g., the status of a marginalized group would be more severely harmed if their exclusion from the state was made official, thus enshrining the state's belief in the group's inferiority in a highly visible way, as opposed to if strenuous efforts were made to conceal the discrimination taking place). Yet this seems odd. For example, it does not seem less wrongful for a less globally powerful state like Burkina Faso to racially discriminate against a particular group than for a wealthy superpower like the United States, even if exclusion from the latter would affect the group's status on a grander scale. At the same time, it seems that a racist exclusion policy remains seriously wrong, even if it is relatively "invisible," because it is quietly and stealthily undertaken. To sum up, the wrongfulness of a racist immigration policy does not seem to vary in accordance with the scale of its disadvantageous impact.

Furthermore, suppose that the exclusion of a racial group would have the unexpected effect of further *improving* the status of group members who are present in the receiving state, because members of the dominant race are satisfied that they are unlikely to be present in large enough numbers to take over the country, and thus no longer constitute a threat, or perhaps even because group members tend to favor certain occupations, and there will be less competition for prestigious positions within those occupations than if more members of the group were to enter the receiving state. But as the status-harm view locates the wrongfulness of discrimination in how it worsens disadvantage, discrimination that confers unexpected advantage cannot be wrongful on its account. We may respond to this objection in two ways. One is to maintain that discrimination could still be wrong even if it has the surprising consequence of improving the group's status, except for reasons on other grounds. This would not necessarily impugn the widespread applicability or appeal of the status-harm view. Another is to concede that discrimination is *not* wrong when it has the effect of improving group status. Both these options, I believe, seem unattractive. First, if the status-harm view cannot, on its own, explain the wrongfulness of discrimination that *improves* group status, why not prefer other accounts of wrongful discrimination that can readily offer an explanation? I will argue that at least one such account is available. On the other hand, conceding that exclusion would not be wrongful if it improves the status of the group in question seems to misrepresent how we generally view discrimination. Peculiar or unforeseen circumstances could plausibly lead to situations where discriminatory policies we normally consider wrongful end up improving the position of a disadvantaged group. But it would be very unappealing for the wrongfulness of a discriminatory policy to depend in part on the contingent circumstances that materialize after its implementation.

c. The expressive theory of disrespect

I now turn to Deborah Hellman's account of wrongful discrimination, which I believe can successfully explain why sexist or racist immigration policies violate social equality *even if* they have the accidental consequence of "improving" the status of a group or fail to worsen it in the sense that Fiss explains. For Hellman, racist immigration policies would be wrong because they *express disrespect* for the forbidden group. There would be no need to demonstrate that the group in question suffers a material status-harm. Instead, an instance of discrimination is wrongful if it "distinguish[es] among people on the basis of an attribute when doing so *demeans* any of the people affected" (Hellman 2011, 7–8). As Hellman observes,

> the point of prohibiting discrimination is not to forbid distinguishing between people—differentiation is important and even necessary in some instances. Neither is it to ensure that we always act efficiently and sensibly. Stupid or careless judgment, without more, is not of particular concern from the perspective of equality. Rather the point of equality is to treat one another as equals, and thus the wrong of discrimination is to fail to treat people as equals. We do that when we differentiate among people in a manner that ranks some as less morally worthy than others. This is the concern that fuels our worries about classification and differentiation. (2011, 204)

Demeaning also need not be intentional or explicit. After all, only a select number of wrongful discrimination cases occur because discriminators *intentionally* wish to mark discriminatees out as unequals. Those accused of wrongfully discriminatory practices are often very quick to assure their detractors that they *do* afford the affected parties equal respect. For example, a racist state may deny that they see potential immigrants of certain races as socially subordinate; they may simply claim that they prefer mixing with their own race, just as Jim Crow laws claimed to leave Black people "separate but equal." For this reason, it is sufficient that the act is *expressive* of disrespect. In the same vein as my discussion of social meanings in the book's introduction, Hellman holds that "[i]t is our common history and culture and its conventions and social understandings that determine which actions express a rejection of the equal humanity of others" (2011, 35).

Consequently, there are no objective criteria for what constitutes a demeaning act; the question of whether or not something is demeaning will have to be decided with reference to the relevant historical or cultural context. In some cases, this will prove no easy task, but I do not regard potential difficulties as a theoretical flaw. Disrespect is often frustratingly complex. As the writer Toni Morrison aptly observed, expressions of hateful prejudice have "mysterious definitions but clear meanings." The slurs themselves may lack offensive dictionary definitions, but it is often *obvious* to their targets that they are demeaning. The same can be said of discrimination. It may not be immediately apparent *why* an act of discrimination demeans, and it will take time to tease out a cultural analysis—tell a story, as it were—about why the selection or differential treatment in question is loaded with disrespect. Take, for example, how Black prisoners in apartheid South Africa were made to wear shorts, while white prisoners wore pants (Hellman 2011, 5). This form of discrimination was not self-evidently demeaning to the Black prisoners. They may even have felt more comfortable in the sweltering heat. But to understand what made this act of discrimination wrong, we need to look to the sartorial culture of the postcolonial regime, and how it viewed shorts as infantilizing (5). It is only then that we can understand how this different uniform symbolically reflected the Black prisoners' disrespected status.

In summary, to decide on whether or not an act of discrimination is wrongful, we must refer to our existing social conventions and understandings to see if the differential treatment is charged with particular disrespectful meanings. I will now go on to explain what skill-based selection is, and how it passes both these tests.

3. Talent and wrongful discrimination

a. Skill-based selection

In this section, I take stock of current trends in skill-selective immigration policy that extend preferential treatment to highly skilled migrants, like myself, over low-skilled migrants. Shachar observes that "a growing number of well-off countries [are vying] to attract and retain skilled migrants with abundant talent" (2011, 2088). This occurs amid increasing pressure on competing nations to transform citizenship into a tradable good that will help them recruit the world's "best and brightest" (2088). The practice of making immigration and naturalization accessible to "talented" people has been termed "Olympic citizenship" by Shachar and Hirschl, in reference to governments attempting to attract accomplished athletes to represent them in the Olympic games by fast-tracking their citizenship, although it now applies to the business of attracting many different types of Olympians, not just the athletically skilled. As Shachar and Hirschl write,

> Just as they introduce restrictions on most other categories of entrants, governments are proactively "picking winners" who are fast-tracked to citizenship based on their skills, innovation, and potential contribution to the country's stature, economic growth, and international reputation. From the wealthy and highly educated, to top scientists, elite athletes, world-class artists, and successful entrepreneurs and innovators, a citizenship-for-talent exchange—what we might call *Olympic citizenship*—is on the rise. (2013, 73)

It is tempting to see skill-based selection as applying only to exceptionally talented individuals, in a number of extraordinary cases that do not bear much on the selection patterns. For example, Anna Netrebko, a Russian-born opera star soprano singer, was granted fast-tracked Austrian citizenship due to her status as one of the world's most distinguished singers—in the process evading the nationality test that most applicants would have to take (Shachar and Hirschl 2014, 238). However, as I have alluded in the Introduction, the basic machinery of states' immigration bureaucracy routinely scrutinizes the talent levels of ordinary applicants and ranks them accordingly. Presently, Canada has separate immigration programs for highly skilled and low-skilled workers (Law Library of Congress). For example, under the Express Entry system, skilled workers are admitted under a point-system selection matrix called the Comprehensive Ranking System, which "assesses applicants by assigning them a score based on combined factors such as level of education, professional experience in high-demand occupations, age, linguistic ability, and adaptability (with bonus points increasingly awarded for job offers as well)" (Shachar and Hirschl 2014, 238).

Those who receive at least the minimum number of points will be ranked against other applicants, after which the highest-ranking candidates will be invited to apply for permanent residence (Government of Canada 2015). On the other hand, low-skilled workers are not assessed through a point system, but primarily enter through specific guest worker programs (The Low Skilled Worker Pilot, the Live-In Caregiver Program, and the Seasonal Agricultural Worker Program), which normally deny them the right to apply for citizenship (Lenard and Straehle 2011, 213). Similarly, while Australia utilizes a points-based skilled migration system whose purpose is to "help select skilled migrants who offer the best in terms of economic benefit to Australia," low-skilled migrants may only enter and work through temporary guest worker programs (the Seasonal Worker Program and Working Holiday Programs), which also prevent them from applying for further visas while on the territory (Law Library of Congress). In the chapters that follow, I also discuss skill-selective immigration policies in the United Kingdom and United States in far more detail; for the time being, it suffices to note this broad pattern of selection across wealthy Western states.

While Shachar and Hirschl have not framed Olympic citizenship in these terms, it clearly constitutes a case of discrimination. Although these point-based systems sometimes do discriminate between highly skilled migrants (e.g., there may be highly skilled migrants who do not meet the minimum points threshold because they lack the relevant language skills), I will focus exclusively on a broad trend of discrimination against low-skilled migrants while demonstrating an overall preference for highly skilled migrants. Countries are sharply indicating that they desire to bring in those with specialized skills and talents, and extending attractive admission offers to high-skilled migrants while creating higher and higher legal walls to prevent the entry of those deemed "unwanted" or "too different" (Shachar and Hirschl 2014, 236). On top of low-skilled migrants finding themselves subjected to unfavorable terms of entry, or facing the closure of low-skilled categories as avenues to entry, those seeking admission on the basis of family ties or humanitarian causes are also becoming the targets of increased scrutiny and control (236). A question that arises, then, is whether or not skill-based selection involves *wrongful* discrimination, in a way that makes it comparable to a sexist or racist immigration policy. I suggest, according to the criteria I have sketched out, that it can be shown to be an example of wrongful discrimination.

b. Is skill-based discrimination disrespectful?

As we have seen in Section 2, in order for skill-based discrimination to qualify as wrongful discrimination, it must be demeaning. As a starting point, we must first identify the relevant group who are being wrongfully discriminated against. I believe that the group of people, in this case, are low-skilled migrants. Defining who should count as "low-skilled" or "highly skilled" can be contentious, as definitions vary over time to reflect changes in the economic and labor market structures of national and global economies (Batalova and Lowell 2006, 86). However, for the purposes of this chapter, I will use the definitions and groupings adopted by the United Kingdom's Migration Advisory Committee, which generally fits with common intuitions about who low-skilled migrants are. According to them, low-skilled work involves "competence associated with a general education, usually acquired by the time compulsory education is complete," and does not require long periods of on-the-job training. These include people typically employed as waiters, construction workers, and cleaners. In contrast, we may understand highly skilled workers as those who work in "management, business/finance operations, information technology, math science and engineering, architecture and engineering, life and physical sciences," etc.

Here, two important concerns may be raised. First, why should we focus on low-skilled migrants as a group, instead of talking about migrants *in general*? The answer is straightforward: skill-based selection benefits highly skilled migrants at the expense of wrongfully discriminating against low-skilled migrants, rather than wrongfully discriminating against *all* foreigners. At the same time, we have good reason to think of low-skilled migrants as a distinct category. As I have already suggested, the particular experience of being perceived as a low-skilled migrant, and how this perception determines how one is treated in multiple contexts, is not reducible to one that migrants *at large* endure. It is well-established that hierarchical social distinctions are frequently drawn between different categories of migrants. For example, while a Migration Observatory survey found in 2011, among UK respondents, that there was majority support for reducing immigration of low-skilled workers (64%), there was minority support for reducing immigration of highly skilled workers (32%). The survey results also indicated that low-skilled workers were also among the most popular targets for reductions to immigration. Jens Hainmueller and Daniel Hopkins also found, in the US context, that "the preferred immigrant—one who is well educated and in a high-status occupation, with plans to work, good English skills, and no prior unauthorized entries—hardly varies based on respondent characteristics including age, income, labour market position, partisanship, ethnocentrism, and self-monitoring" (2014, 17). This is not to say that that highly skilled migrants do not ever face xenophobia. The point is simply that we should avoid a broad-brush approach while performing an analysis of xenophobia, as some categories of foreigners suffer their own strain of xenophobic stigma that others do not.

Now that we have identified the group of people who are demeaned, I turn to the question of *why* skill-based discrimination is demeaning. At first glance, it looks starkly different from the other types of discrimination I discussed in Section 2. In fact, it might even be said to be the *antithesis* of gender or race-discriminatory immigration policies, because it is technically blind to those traits. It is theoretically open to everyone, regardless of race, gender, religion, etc., so long as they display the necessary talent, and belong to the "best and the brightest." As Iris Marion Young puts it, with meritocracy, "the unjust hierarchy of caste is to be replaced by a 'natural' hierarchy of intellect and skill" (1990, 200).

On what grounds, then, can skill-based selection be accused of disrespecting low-skilled migrants? It will help, as a starting point, to understand why highly skilled migrants are commonly preferred. While there may be several reasons why low-skilled migrants are undesirable in comparison, from a receiving state's point of view, I will briefly outline two familiar arguments. It has been argued that low-skilled and poorly educated migrants are bad for the economy, and that they might also place a heavy strain on welfare systems. These claims have been raised in both the economic literature and, even more frequently, in the mainstream media. For example, George Borjas and Lawrence Katz's study of the effects of low-skilled Mexican immigrants on the American economy purported to show that the large influx, in recent decades, "widened the U.S. wage structure by adversely affecting the earnings of less-educated native workers," and "[lowered] the prices of non-traded goods and services that are low-skill labour intensive" (2007, 53). Steven Camarota also concludes that immigrants are "creating a significant burden on public coffers," and that by using welfare programs, they may "strain public resources, harming taxpayers, and making it more difficult to assist the low-income population already in the country" (2015, 3).

Notably, both these claims are highly contested. David Card has argued, for example, that the wages of native dropouts, relative to native high school graduates have remained almost constant since 1980, despite pressures from immigration inflows (2004, 23), while Leighton Ku and Brian Bruen found that low-income noncitizen children and adults utilize American welfare benefits at generally lower rates than comparable low-income, native-born citizen children and adults, and that "the average value of public benefits received per person is generally lower for non-citizens than for natives" (2014, 1). The belief that low-skilled migrants disproportionately use welfare benefits in the United Kingdom continues, despite the fact that a large proportion of immigrants are not permitted access to public funds, and others have restricted access to them. To be sure, my goal is not to claim that we have *decisive* evidence that these popular rationales for excluding low-skilled migrants are false. New studies may prove these wrong, and these issues may remain controversial for years to come. Rather, what I find interesting is the pervasive currency of these ideas in mainstream immigration discourse, even if they rest on relatively shaky ground. For instance, the majority of people in a 2013 British Social Attitudes survey believed that immigration was bad for the economy. Furthermore, as one UK newspaper report claims, "[t]ens of thousands are expected to flock to the UK—in part due to our generous welfare system. Under current rules, they would only have to live here for three months before claiming benefits" (Balch and Balabanova 2016, 9).

These beliefs are often firmly held, I think, not because empirical data has clearly demonstrated that low-skilled migrants have particular effects on the economy, but because citizens believe these immigrants to be *particular kinds of undesirable people*. That is, the preponderance of these beliefs is less attributable to well-grounded fears about the economic effects of low-skilled migrants entering the country, than to their holding prejudiced stereotypes about low-skilled migrants. I am suggesting, here, that the opposition to low-skilled migrants is a product of *xenophobia*. Citizens are not inhospitable to low-skilled migrants because of demonstrable economic concerns, but rather, because they are widely perceived as harmful, threatening, and deserving of civic ostracism in order to avert such dangers.

It may be asked, however, why highly skilled migrants are not ostracized in the same way. After all, aren't they "foreign" as well? My suspicion is that low-skilled migrants are perceived as *more* "foreign" or "alien" than highly skilled migrants because they do not have as much economic, social, or cultural capital to guide their successful conformity to the society's dominant social mores. Secondly, "foreignness" and "alienage" are *classed* and *racialized* concepts that tend to be associated far more strongly with low-skilled migrants.[1] One can certainly be culturally *different*, but not "alien" in the above sense. Think, for example, of a white French poet who is considered highly glamorous and exotic in the United States. She may be perceived as different, but her difference is *celebrated* or *admired* rather than considered threatening. (I will have more to say about the relationship between class, race, and skill in Chapter Six.) Thirdly, highly skilled migrants may be tolerated despite their strangeness because of their perceived ability to contribute to society. In the eyes of the public, however, low-skilled migrants only have *bad* things to contribute. They *want* to steal jobs and lower our wages, grab benefits from the poor, and take hard-earned money from citizens if they can, primarily because they are greedy, unscrupulous, and exploitative by nature. The only appropriate response is for the state to neutralize these dangers by designing immigration policy to *keep out* low-skilled migrants.[2]

Two questions arise at this point. First, it might be protested that these beliefs about low-skilled migrants are rude, unfair, or unpleasant, but not *demeaning*. After all, you can call someone untrustworthy or money-grubbing without also claiming that they have a lower moral status. But this response ignores the *expressive* dimension of disrespect. Insults that are not *objectively* demeaning on some universal standard may nevertheless be demeaning relative to the sociocultural context. For example, sexist comments about women might take the form of comments that women are "liars" or "too emotional." These are ascriptions of negative personal traits that need not have anything to do with the denial of equal status. But they are demeaning, in this case, because they have been employed to reduce women to two-dimensional stereotypes that are repeatedly used to deny them basic rights or entitlements. The same can be said of low-skilled migrants, whose equal status is denied precisely because they are only allowed to exist as unflattering caricatures, hungry for jobs and benefits. Instead of possessing unique histories, personalities, and life-goals, with their own specific reasons for migration, they are assumed to be uniformly morally dubious, with the singular agenda of worsening the lives of citizens and snatching up public resources to which they are not entitled. In a particularly repugnant example that portrays low-skilled migrants as society's "vermin," one columnist has written, "Some of our towns are festering sores, plagued by swarms of migrants and asylum seekers, shelling out benefits like Monopoly money," while also likening them to "cockroaches" (Usbourne 2015).

Secondly, what does the subordination of low-skilled migrants have to do with skill-based selection? An objection might look like this: if states were to introduce policies directly aimed at stemming the flow of low-skilled workers, much as the United Kingdom placed a ban in 2007 on unskilled workers from outside European Union territories, we *might* be able to make the case that those policies are demeaning. Admittedly, they send the message that low-skilled workers are unwanted. But could states not simply *prefer* talented foreigners? Certainly, in theory, a state might have a predominantly talent-focused admission policy that is not at all connected to such disrespectful beliefs; its appreciation for the benefits of taking in highly skilled migrants *need not* imply animosity toward low-skilled migrants, in the manner I have described. In this vein, Douglas MacKay has suggested that the public endorsement of skill as a favorable factor is "no more objectionable than state policies promoting adult enrolment in post-secondary education, or state employers' favouring of skilled citizens when hiring" (2016, 135).

However, I believe that it is no coincidence that skill-based selection is practiced *alongside* the greater policing of noncitizens seeking family reunification or asylum. The preference for highly skilled migrants, in the nonideal circumstances at hand, cannot be conceptually disentangled from popularly expressed demeaning views on low-skilled migrants. Think, for example, of the myth of the "model minority," which refers to minority groups that have "ostensibly achieved a high level of success," such as Asian Americans in US society, and how it serves to fuel stigma against other ethnic groups (Bodenhausen 2011, 173). On the face of it, there is nothing wrong with holding up a particular minority group who are especially prosperous and well-educated, with low crime rates. We may say, following MacKay's argument, that the public endorsement of model minorities' success on these grounds is no more objectionable than state policies that encourage educational achievement and discourage criminal behavior. However, to understand why it is problematic, we must look to the existing social context. One serious problem with the myth is that it tends to reproduce binary representations of ethnic minorities. On one hand, there are the "good minorities" who play by society's rules, work hard, and do whatever is demanded of them without protest. While they are still read as fundamentally *different*, they show that difference can be *unthreatening* to the majority's dominance. On the other, there are the "*bad* minorities," who are undisciplined, disorderly, and dangerous. The model minority is meaningfully compared against these groups to send a particular message, namely one that upholds a white-supremacist social order by pitting Asian Americans against African Americans and Latin Americans (Lee 2020, 232). In Claire Jean Kim's words, "the model minority myth has always worked in tandem with explicit constructions of Blacks as culturally deficient" (1999, 121). This is because model minorities are held up as exemplars of how the material consequences of racism can be overcome by hard work and good behavior, and that the persistently disadvantaged position of "bad minorities" is solely attributable to personal failure, which society bears no responsibility for. In line with the pattern of oppression I have sketched out, examples of "bad minority" traits include character flaws like laziness, lack of discipline, and criminal inclinations (Kim 1999, 121), which together form a negative *stereotype* about group members. Overall, the model minority myth ought not to be read as benevolent approval, but as a convenient tool to reinforce demeaning beliefs about other groups.

Significantly, the notion of the "model minority" also makes so-called model citizens vulnerable to racial injustice. To be clear, here I do not seek to make the argument that highly skilled citizens are treated unjustly by skill-selective immigration policies. I simply observe that idealizations of minority groups, positive as they may initially appear, can be profoundly bound up with social inequality. It is illustrative to look at Emily S. Lee's careful account of how the "model minority" myth oppresses Asian Americans by *overdetermining* their social identities and constraining the possibilities for who they are able to be (Lee 2014, 150). Specifically, it incorrectly associates them with middle-class status, in a way that obscures class diversity among Asian Americans and renders invisible the lives of lower-middle-class and poor Asian Americans (150). Furthermore, as Lee points out, the "model minority" stereotype rests on a false assumption: the belief that Asian Americans are particularly capable of ascending the economic ladder and availing themselves of the opportunities offered by capitalism (2014, 152). Following Karen Hossfeld's historical analysis, Lee suggests that the stereotype originated from "changes in immigration laws reflecting the United States' need for skilled laborers" (2014, 151).

During the late 1960s, Asian immigrants arrived "educated and skilled"; they predominantly originated from middle-class families who maintained their original class, rather than actually scaling the economic ladder (151). This myth, as I've mentioned above, is used to blame other minority groups for failing to achieve the economic success that has been inaccurately attributed to Asian Americans. Yet it also hurts Asian Americans by tying their identity to economic mobility, which typically requires cultural assimilation to bourgeois white norms and the relative neglect of one's original culture, while simultaneously faulting less economically mobile Asian Americans for engaging in "insular, isolationist practices" (Lee 2014, 152–153). Particularly in light of the rash of high-profile violent attacks on Asians and Asian Americans in 2020 and beyond, it is clear that the "model minority" stereotype fails to secure social equality for Asian Americans—arguably, it directly contributes to their social subordination alongside that of other racial groups.

Something very similar is going on, I think, in the case of skill-based selection. Why do states proudly declare their desire to admit the "best and the brightest," while practicing increased surveillance and regulation of other categories of noncitizens? Just as how praise for "model minorities" serves to express disrespectful stereotypes about other ethnic groups, the privileging of highly skilled immigrants, in the current social context, also expresses contempt for *other* categories of foreigners: the ones who are known to heedlessly threaten the receiving society by worsening their economic prospects and stealing their welfare benefits. To quote Bridget Anderson, "[t]he kinds of people wanted and not wanted are described in graphic and value-laden terms: 'bogus' asylum seekers, 'sham' marriages, 'low-skilled' workers versus 'genuine refugees', 'genuine and subsisting marriages', 'the brightest and the best' "(2013, 69). This tendency is exemplified in a quote by the British Home Secretary about newly implemented restrictions on immigration: "The new rules will see us exercising control, ensuring that only the best and the brightest remain in Britain permanently" (Waldron and Ali 2015). This is tantamount to saying that we only want the *good* foreigners, and we will use whatever measure we can to keep out the *bad*.

Here, an important clarification must be made. I do not claim that it is *never* appropriate, in principle, for states to admit people on the basis of particular skills—as skill-based admittance is not intrinsically disrespectful, it can be permissible on the expressive theory of discrimination. Suppose that a state has suffered a serious drought that seriously threatens crop production, and workers with the relevant know-how are specifically required to improve matters. The preference for workers with this skill set seems benign, simply because there are no demeaning stereotypes about noncitizens who do not have technical knowledge about drought management. However, for reasons I have explained above, the strongly expressed preference for highly skilled workers in the existing social context is inextricable from the (relative) cultural elevation of highly skilled migrants, and the contemptuous devaluation of low-skilled migrants. Thus, the thrust of my argument is not that the possession of particular skill sets can never be a permissible reason to favor one potential immigrant over another, but to draw attention to the demeaning expressive effect of the widespread preference for highly skilled workers. Much like how the admiration of "model minorities" is inextricably connected to the expression of disrespect toward so-called bad minorities, the welcoming of highly skilled migrants cannot be conceptually detached from the reviled status of low-skilled migrants. Furthermore, while developed countries may retort that they are selecting for skills that are genuinely scarce amongst their citizenry, this response does not necessarily let them off the hook. If the lack of such skill can be traced back to foreseeable consequences of policy decisions that were actively made, such as a pointed lack of investment in medical training or care work that outsources this task to immigrants from developing countries, this does not seem too different from employers making business decisions that will, in the future, justify the explicit selection of workers with specific skill sets that are foreseeably exclusionary toward applicants of color.

As a whole, I have sought to illustrate how skill-based selection, much like the model minority myth, should not be interpreted as the mere approval, or preference of a group with particular positive traits. Rather, it is intimately bound up with binary representations of "good" and "bad" foreigners' that demean low-skilled migrants by reducing them to ugly caricatures, out to destroy the lives of citizens. As I have shown, highly skilled migrants are presented as the polar opposite of low-skilled migrants. They are hard-working assets to society and will help to *improve* it, in contrast to how low-skilled migrants will threaten and undermine society. The immigration practices that privilege the former cannot be understood without also referring to the pathological desire to keep out the latter.

4. Objections

Why should we assume that states' immigration policies must never violate the antidiscrimination norm I have described? Contrary to this, it might be argued that states reserve the *right* to wrongfully discriminate, even if we acknowledge that they would violate equal respect. According to Christopher Heath Wellman, for example, autonomous individuals and legitimate states both have rights to autonomy, occupying morally privileged positions of control over their own affairs, and the freedom of association is just one component of the exercise of autonomy (2008, 110). This is why Wellman believes in states' pro tanto right to exercise discretion over whom it allows entry to, even if they employ criteria that he acknowledges as wrongfully discriminatory. Citizens' right to associate, or not associate with whomever they choose (even if we morally disapprove of the criteria in question) fully entitles them to discriminate against certain groups of potential migrants, whether by race or by perceived levels of "skill."

Importantly, Wellman does not disagree that the antidiscrimination principle ought to hold in some cases, like in the state's dealings with its citizens. However, recall that he simply denies that duties of nondiscrimination—that is, duties to treat people as if they are moral equals—are things that we owe to *noncitizens*. Racial discrimination in immigration policy is only wrong when states institute an immigration policy that excludes entry to members of a given group, and in the process disrespects *citizens* who fall into the dispreferred category (2008, 139). This is because we have a "special duty to respect our fellow citizens as equal partners in the political cooperative," a responsibility that we do not equally owe to foreigners (139). By extension, it seems that the Chinese Exclusion Acts, for example, would only be off the table for states if there were *already* immigrants of Chinese descent who had become citizens prior, who would be impermissibly disrespected by it.

As I have already stated in Chapter Two, I think this argument is ultimately implausible. First, antidiscrimination norms are *not* secondarily derived from our duties to respect fellow citizens as equal partners. Rather, as I have argued in the previous chapter, they are derived from the *universal* entitlement to social equality. Second, the state cannot be assumed to have the same right of freedom of association as private individuals. Wellman's argument appeals to the claim that, if "racist individuals cannot permissibly be forced to marry someone (or adopt a child) outside of their race," because their freedom of association entitles them to racially discriminate during the process of choosing a suitable marriage partner, the freedom of association *should* also entitle racist citizens to exclude immigrants based on racial criteria at least insofar as it does not disrespect existing citizens (2008, 138). It might be said that the state should commit itself to upholding social equality wherever possible, but this obligation is trumped by the important right to freedom of association. Likewise, even if it might be protested that skill-based selection is wrongfully discriminatory, this complaint is overruled by the state's freedom to associate with talented migrants.

This, however, is a misleading picture. According to Michael Blake, the problem with Wellman's account of the freedom of association is that it is falsely characterized as a "simple, deontic trump right" (Blake 2012, 750). That is, "[i]f we have a right to freedom of association, then anyone who forces an unwanted association upon us wrongs us—a conclusion which does not fail simply because the one who is being forced upon us is in circumstances of dire need" (750). In contrast, on Blake's account, freedom of association should be understood as part of a complex set of political rights, each of which is derived from the basic moral norm that governments should treat all those impacted by their policies with equal concern and respect (2012, 751). While none of these political rights can be sacrificed for a greater quantity of well-being, there can be serious tensions between them, and it becomes a matter of judgment and argument as to which right ought to take precedence in particular cases (751). In other words, the right to freedom of association is certainly an important one that, in line with Wellman's view, cannot be trumped by consequentialist considerations (e.g., states cannot force people into marriage in the hopes of boosting population growth, as doing so would violate their right to freedom of association). But it can be defeated by another right that is part of the complex set, if the two come into conflict, if it is successfully demonstrated that favoring the competing right would *better express* the norm of equal respect that they are both derived from.

Overall, we do not have a straightforwardly simple, trump-like right to not associate with unwanted others. Wellman presents the freedom of association as freestanding, and in competition with equal respect *itself*, rather than with other political rights: in this case, the right to not face wrongful discrimination. However, for Blake, we cannot suspend our obligation to uphold equal respect; as I have mentioned, it is *constitutive* of the liberal ethos, rather than a mere guideline or consideration. For the state, what the freedom of association must be measured against are *other* norms that better accord with equal respect. It seems that our understanding of freedom of association within the domestic context fits Blake's model, rather than Wellman's construction. For one, it does a good job of explaining why private golf clubs, for example, do not have the right to wrongfully discriminate in selecting their members, even if individuals do in choosing their marriage partners. The key difference between marriage and golf clubs is that one's desire to marry another does not fall within the scope of justice, even if their life may be affected by the other party's decision not to marry them. As individuals have a basic interest in being able to determine who they have intimate relationships with, the special character of marriage demands that the best way to treat individuals with equal concern and respect is *not* for the state to interfere in such choices. We recognize that it is deeply disrespectful to force people to marry or have sex with others against their will. For example, Article 16(2) of the Universal Declaration of Human Rights states that "[f]orced marriage is a violation of internationally recognized human rights standards. Marriage shall be entered into only with the free and full consent of the intending spouses." This holds in spite of whether one's marriage choices may negatively affect the lives of other people. As Robert Nozick rightly notes, if four men propose marriage to a woman, even if "her decision about whom, if any of them, to marry importantly affects each of the lives of those four persons, her own life, and the lives of any other persons wishing to marry one of these four men, and so on," nobody would propose a democratic solution to the issue (1974, 269). Likewise, even if a decision not to marry someone is rooted in discriminatory beliefs, the state ought not to interfere.

But marriage presents a unique case. We may have strong preferences about who we share our favored golf course with, but it is not generally recognized that we should enjoy a "morally privileged position of dominion" over who we associate with in *this* realm, unlike in the marital one (Wellman 2008, 110). Having to play golf in the same vicinity as a person we do not like simply does not harm our fundamental interests in the same way that forced marriage would, and it does not disrespect us to force us to do so. Antidiscrimination norms kick in because the large impact of social marginalization on the self-constitution of the marginalized individuals has far more moral significance than the relatively superficial annoyance of playing golf with people we dislike (Blake 2012, 757). Thus, in contrast, the racist members of a golf club may have to admit people they would rather avoid on grounds of antidiscrimination. Given the similar character of immigration, the same criticism can be made of wrongfully discriminatory immigration policies. Arguably, the serious impact of disrespect on the demeaned group trumps the state's right to freedom of association.

a. Disrespect and qualifying standards

It might be objected that some jobs establish qualifying standards that are necessary for the legitimate purposes of the job to be achieved, and that these standards are distinct from their engaging in wrongful discrimination. For example, in the sphere of employment, government and for-profit employers have a legitimate purpose in offering particular types of goods and services (Mackay 2016, 132). While it is wrong for them to select employees on the basis of religion, as neither government nor for-profit employers have a legitimate purpose in promoting certain religious identities, it is nonetheless permissible for them to select employees on the basis of skill (132). In contrast, religious employers may do so, as the promotion and practice of a particular religious faith is a legitimate purpose of religious institutions (132). Overall, it seems that as long as skill-based selection can be shown to serve some "legitimate purpose" of the state, it is morally permissible.

However, there are two remaining problems with this objection. The first, obvious issue is that, on the account I have argued for, discrimination is not wrongful when it fails to serve some "legitimate purpose," but is wrong when it *demeans* the discriminatees. In line with Mackay's observations, it is not generally wrong for governmental or for-profit offices to hire employees on the basis of particular skills, because these do not usually express a belief in the inferiority of particular groups, while selecting employees on the basis of religion *would* demean members of the excluded religious groups. We need not say that such religious discrimination amounts to pursuing the illegitimate goal of promoting a particular religious identity, when we can simply point to how it would convey demeaning messages about the unreliability, untrustworthiness, or incapacity of members of those religious groups.

But matters are not always so cut-and-dried. Leaving aside the concept of "legitimate purposes"—what if some skill-based qualifying standards express demeaning beliefs about particular groups, even if they seem truly necessary for employers' ability to offer socially valuable goods and services? Ought those standards be eliminated entirely, in the name of combating wrongful discrimination, even if they result in great social costs? While I am sympathetic to this view, it bears mentioning that our perspective on which qualifying standards are "necessary" for the employer to continue offering important goods and services may be distorted by existing stereotypes and prejudices that are not obvious to us. For example, while the possession of an undergraduate degree is still widely regarded as a minimum academic qualification for many jobs, several prominent companies have recently taken the lead in no longer requiring candidates for jobs to have a university degree, and acknowledging that degree-holding is not strictly "necessary" for meeting the demands of the job. Similarly, fire services often only employ firefighters who are not overweight, as they believe that firefighters must be sufficiently fit. However, it is not obvious that overweight people cannot satisfyingly perform firefighting duties, as weight requirements may not track fitness accurately. Many overweight people are perfectly fit and able to perform demanding physical tasks. Likewise, many still believe that it is inappropriate for the military to hire women, because they are thought to be physically incapable of performing the necessary tasks, or enduring physical hardship that men can. Calls to exclude women from the military often involve the suggestion that *only* men can properly perform military jobs, effectively repackaging sexist beliefs in the language of a legitimate rationale for exclusion. Thus, while I accept that respect is not the only value, and that there may be job requirements that are nevertheless genuinely *important* for important goals to be met, the potential to express disrespect places a particularly heavy burden of proof on the discriminators. They must fully demonstrate that these criteria *must* be met for the job to be effectively performed, and that they are not actually motivated by spurious stereotypic beliefs. As I noted in the previous section, I do not believe that this has been sufficiently shown in the case of immigrant selection: it remains an open question whether low-skilled migrants are *genuinely* bad for countries.

Even more importantly, a second issue is that the comparison between job discrimination and immigration discrimination seems to be false. Jobs are purely *instrumental* in nature; each job has a specific function, designed to allow the employer to fulfill its aims. For this reason, it is of paramount importance that the applicant is equipped to perform the tasks that the job demands. But being a *member* of the state, whether as a temporary resident or a fully fledged citizen, is not at all like being given a job. It would be strange to say that residency is like occupying an instrumental role that applicants must be sufficiently equipped for, such as having the necessary know-how to contribute to the economy. This functional view of membership would certainly exclude many existing citizens from "qualifying."[3] Furthermore, as I have mentioned earlier, states already by-and-large recognize *other* reasons for admitting people; not everyone is admitted to perform an instrumental function. Asylum seekers and refugees are admitted not because of their potential contributions (even though it may be hoped that they will contribute), but because of the right to asylum and the principle of nonrefoulement. Similarly, people are admitted on the basis of family reunification because the state recognizes the value and importance of being able to live with one's family.

b. Economic interests

Another possible objection could be that skill-based selection is fundamentally different from other wrongfully discriminatory policies, not because it does not demean, but because it is *necessary* for the legitimate economic interests of the state, such as the achievement of a desired level of economic prosperity. For example, Caleb Yong observes that states are permitted to design labor immigration policies led by the aim of generating a higher level of economic resources, as "greater access to economic resources generally facilitates the pursuit of various personal ends," hence allowing states to promote their citizens' autonomy.[4] Put differently, economic success "can be reasonably expected to facilitate the realization of states' legitimate purposes in securing and promoting the freedom, health, and well-being of their citizens" (2016, 827). These domestic considerations should take precedence over any demeaning effect skill-based selection might have. The claim I want to consider is not that skill-based selection is not *wrongful* discrimination, but that it is a necessary evil.

One drawback of this view, however, is that almost every other kind of wrongful immigration-related discrimination can be reformulated in a way that makes them seem necessary for the fulfillment of legitimate state interests. Indeed, this is already true of current practice. As Sarah Fine observes, "[o]ften, the clear targeting of particular groups is thinly veiled behind what states see as more legitimate, 'acceptable' policy objectives, such as securing their borders from foreign terror threats, or from large numbers of undocumented migrants, or for the protection of the migrants themselves" (2016, 6). One salient example is the British government's proposal to impose a £3000 "migrant bond" on short-term visitors to the country, which would be forfeited if visitors were to overstay their visas. These bonds were specifically targeted at people from so-called high risk countries like India, Bangladesh, Ghana, Pakistan, Nigeria, and Sri Lanka, whose nationals were purported to have a tendency to overstay (6). At first glance, there is nothing ostensibly illegitimate about this policy; it is a legitimate state objective to crack down on visa overstaying, and to create deterrents by imposing significant costs on those who engage in such behavior. But a quick glance at the groups it directly affects—citizens of relatively poor Commonwealth countries who would be unlikely to afford an upfront payment of £3,000—will suggest that the *actual* purpose of the "migrant bond" is to discourage their *entry* to the United Kingdom, not just cases of overstaying. This seems to be another way of expressing the demeaning belief that there are uniformly "good" and "bad immigrants," and that people from those countries neatly fall into the "bad" category.

In response, it might be pointed out that there is a significant difference between the "migrant bond" and skill-based selection. The problem with the "migrant bond" is that it utilizes an unnecessary and inappropriate measure, under the pretense of fulfilling a legitimate aim. There could be other ways to discourage overstaying that do not unfairly impede the opportunities of particular groups to enter the United Kingdom. In contrast, skill-based selection may be a genuinely effective means of ensuring economic success. Suppose that, with the use of a high-tech algorithm, states could select migrants who are likely to be of maximal economic benefit in the future. If disrespectful attitudes or intent disappear from the picture, do we have reason to object to the algorithm? The potential algorithm I have described above would be troubling, I think, for as long as we are committed to antidiscrimination norms. Though high-tech algorithms are not the kind of entity that can harbor a demeaning attitude toward marginalized social groups (at least not for now), under nonideal circumstances with deeply entrenched inequalities in respect and esteem, the decisions of such an algorithm are almost certainly bound to be ableist and ageist, if not obviously racist and sexist. More deeply, I do not think that insisting on the economic benefits of skill-based selection is particularly helpful, when part of the force of antidiscrimination norms is that they cannot be defeated by the positive consequences that noncompliance might engender. Even if it is true that eschewing antidiscrimination norms in general would be to the state's enormous economic benefit, we do not recognize economic benefit as an appropriate consideration that counts in favor of permitting wrongful discrimination. Instead, conflicting political rights should overall be assessed in terms of how well they express the state's commitment to equal respect and concern. Insisting that wrongful discrimination might sometimes be necessary, simply by dint of the material benefits it accords, certainly runs counter to this.

5. Conclusion

I have sought to argue that states' practice of skill-based selection should be viewed as an instance of wrongful discrimination, that is thoroughly incompatible with liberal states' supposed commitment to equal respect for the people its policies affect. First, I identified the expressive theory of wrongful discrimination as the one that convincingly explains why we consider some discriminatory immigration policies to be unacceptable: racist, sexist, or homophobic immigration policies are wrong because they *demean* people of those groups. However, this picture has an interesting implication. It seems that an apparently benign form of immigration-related discrimination, skill-based selection, is wrong by the same token: it has the expressive effect of demeaning low-skilled migrants. If it turns out that Hellman's account of discrimination correctly diagnoses what is wrongful about other discriminatory immigration policies, we must think twice about allowing skill-based selection to form a significant part of immigration policy. Even assuming that states have the right to exclude, immigration policy must be carefully reined in by the concern for social equality, instead of allowing these concerns to be overshadowed and dictated by the drive for economic success. Potential economic benefits do not justify the use of demeaning or subordinating practices. Along these lines, there is a further worry that skill-selective immigration policies may also be troubling from the perspective of *gender* equality. I turn to this issue in the next chapter.

4

Selecting Immigrants by Skill II

Wrongful Indirect Discrimination

1. Introduction

The previous chapter argued for the ethical impermissibility of a form of *direct* immigration discrimination: the exclusion of low-skilled migrants through skill-selective immigration policies. While direct discrimination is typically captured in acts or policies that explicitly single out members of a particular group for (wrongful) differential treatment, indirect discrimination is typically captured in acts or policies that disparately affect members of a particular group without explicitly singling them out. In those cases, the "differential treatment" is located in the *indirect* consequences of a particular act or policy that seem group-neutral in theory, bearing no direct reference to a particular group identity. In this chapter, I argue that there is another sense in which skill-selective immigration policies are wrongfully discriminatory. Notably, while skill-based selection only directly discriminates against low-skilled workers in theory, it may have the effect of indirectly discriminating against *women*. Evidence shows that, even if women are not explicitly excluded from admission, they are considerably less likely to meet skill-based entry requirements than men. Consequently, they tend to be admitted as family dependents rather than economic migrants. I contend that the disparate impact on women is wrongful because it reflects *negligence* on the part of immigration policymakers: they have breached their duty of care to avoid worsening disrespectful norms and beliefs about women, who constitute a socially subordinated group in their society. Specifically, skill-based selection worsens existing beliefs about the inferiority of women's capacity as workers, as well as women's status as passive or helpless dependents who only achieve their ends by leaning on men. For these reasons, skill-selective immigration policy should be viewed as a form of wrongful indirect discrimination against women that is incompatible with equal respect.

Immigration and Social Equality. Désirée Lim, Oxford University Press.
DOI: 10.1093/oso/9780197658093.003.0005

My argument proceeds in three stages. In Section 2, I begin by offering a short survey of empirical evidence that skill-based selection may indirectly discriminate against women. Next, Section 3 provides the conceptual groundwork for why we should regard skill-based selection as wrongful indirect discrimination. In particular, I argue that indirect discrimination is wrongful when it negligently *worsens* existing disrespect toward a socially subordinated group. Put differently, bringing about particular kinds of disparate impact breaches the preexisting duty *not* to reinforce inferiorizing social norms that relate to those groups. Section 4 shows how skill-based discrimination can be said to worsen existing disrespect against women, thus giving us a pro tanto reason to object to skill-based immigration selection. Finally, before concluding, Section 5 responds to two possible objections.

2. Gender and skilled migration

As I described in Chapter Three, many states have drawn sharper distinctions between skilled foreigners who are welcomed, at least on a temporary basis, and low-skilled foreigners who are viewed as problematic (Kofman and Raghuram 2006, 295). To recap, it is helpful to return to Ayelet Shachar and Ran Hirschl's description: "Whereas the 'unwanted' are pejoratively presented as exhibiting immutable differences that make them unassimilable, quintessential 'Others,' skilled migration is treated functionally and technocratically as a measure to advance the country's economic, reputational, and scientific advantage" (2014, 241). While privileged migrants have more destination countries they may choose from, with each offering its own set of benefits and incentives (Shachar and Hirschl 2014, 232), "unwanted" migrants find themselves blocked by the implementation of new obstacles that make it increasingly harder for them to enter (Shachar and Hirschl 2014, 235). To illustrate this phenomenon more vividly, I want to focus on the United Kingdom's points-based admission system. Previously, the United Kingdom separated prospective immigrants into five "tiers." Tiers 4 and 5 were intended to admit noncitizens on a more "temporary" basis. While Tier 4 allowed international students to be territorially present for the duration of their study, Tier 5 admitted temporary workers for the purposes of work experience or training, and therefore only allows them to remain for a relatively short period of time (up to twelve or twenty-four months). For the purposes of my chapter, Tiers 1–3 are of greater interest. Those who enter under Tier 1 ("business people, investors, and those with exceptional talent") and Tier 2 (highly skilled workers) were allowed to take on permanent jobs, remain for a significantly longer period of time (a maximum of five years and fourteen days), and were eligible to apply for settlement. Tier 2, in particular, admitted the greatest number of immigrants; in 2014, 44 percent of immigrants entered through Tier 2 visas (Blinder 2016). Tellingly, in contrast, Tier 3, the category originally intended for low-skilled workers outside of the EU, was never operational and formally discontinued in 2013.

Following the United Kingdom's departure from the European Union and the formal loss of EU citizens' right of free movement to the United Kingdom, the logic of the points-based system is likely to become even more deeply entrenched. A revised version of the tiered system was formally announced in February 2020. According to this new statement on immigration policy, the British government planned to "reduce overall levels of migration and give top priority to those with the highest skills and the greatest talents: scientists, engineers, academics and other highly-skilled workers" (Gov.uk 2020). Following the recommendations of the Migration Advisory Committee, skilled workers from anywhere in the world, including EU states, must earn a minimum salary of £25,600 (lower than the current £30,000 for non-EU migrants) and need to be sponsored by an employer (BBC News 2020). Most strikingly of all, the statement declared that "[The United Kingdom] will not introduce a general low-skilled or temporary work route. We need to shift the focus of our economy away from a reliance on cheap labor from Europe and instead concentrate on investment in technology and automation. Employers will need to adjust." While the last British government had planned a post-Brexit scheme for lower-skilled workers to enter the United Kingdom on visas limited to a twelve-month period, the announcement effectively dissolved all hope that low-skilled EU citizens might still have a pathway for entry. Many prospective EU workers who perform essential work in the United Kingdom, such as low-paid care workers who assist older and disabled adults, would easily fall short of the new immigration requirements (BBC News 2020). The news, while devastating to many, was somewhat unsurprising. Leading up to the announcement, the interior minister Priti Patel had written pointedly that the new immigration system would "turn off the tap of cheap, foreign low-skilled labour.... From next year, all skilled workers will need to earn enough points to work in the

United Kingdom. They will need to speak English, have a firm job offer, and meet the salary requirements" (Reuters 2020). In stark contrast, the former Prime Minister Boris Johnson announced an uncapped "global talent" visa that would replace the "exceptional talent" route (BBC News 2020).

In the social context described above, the hostility toward low-skilled migrants is plain to see. Shachar and Hirschl's analysis could not resonate any more strongly. Leaving aside the problematically demeaning attitudes toward low-skilled migrants, I want to focus on an indirect consequence that the large-scale exclusion of low-skilled migrants may have: specifically, its disparate impact on women's prospects for admission as economic migrants. I will use the phrases "disparate impact" and "indirect discrimination" interchangeably. As Alasdair Murray reported on the old points-based system,

> One major side effect of the structure of the points-based system is that it appears to be admitting far more men than women. In Tier 1, two thirds of applicants are male, a figure rising to 78 per cent in Tier 2 (where applicants require a job offer) even though women now form a small majority in the UK workforce as a whole. This has led to concerns that it is structured in a manner which is biased against working women and may not reflect changing UK labour demand. (2011, 39)

The "bias" against women that Murray identifies in this passage is far from anomalous. Dating back to 1991, the majority of labor migrants admitted yearly to the United Kingdom have been young and male, including 63 percent in 2014, compared to the family pathway, which predominantly admits women, many of whom are work dependents (Blinder 2016). While I will continue to focus more narrowly on the British context, it is important to note that this phenomenon does not seem confined to the United Kingdom alone, although the claim is not that it *always* generalizes. In both North America and western Europe, where "family reunification" is an important mode of entry, migrant workers often enter as wives and dependents of men, and have their admission sponsored by them (Piper 2005, 2). For example, in 2012, 73,312 men obtained legal permanent resident status in the United States under employment-based categories compared to 70,684 women, a figure already inclusive of many women who were derivatives of principal male visa holders (American Immigration Council 2014). Similarly, in 2015, Canada admitted 36,816 male permanent residents through their status as skilled workers, in comparison to 33,328 women; on the other hand, 27,113 women gained permanent residency as sponsored spouses or partners, in comparison with 19,237 men (Government of Canada 2015). A more extreme example is that of Australia, which granted 32,165 skilled visas to men in 2015/2016, compared to 13,229 of the same visas to women. Overall, women accounted for only 29 percent of primary applicants to enter Australia, but 64 percent of secondary applicants who were granted such visas (Wright et al. 2016). Overall, as we can glean from this data, there are noticeable differences in the numbers of men and women who are directly admitted under skilled categories, as opposed to *dependents* of skilled migrants.

What, then, could account for the fewer numbers of skilled migrants who are women? Leaving open the possibility that the causal factors may vary depending on the country in question, I now focus on four possible reasons that apply in the British case:

a. The majority of sectors that hire "talented" migrants under the UK points-based system are male-dominated (Murray 2011, 40). For example, although skilled jobs must normally be advertised to local workers before they can be offered to a Tier 2 worker, the United Kingdom has published a yearly list of "shortage occupations" which can be directly offered to noncitizens. Jobs on the 2015 list include "production managers and directors in mining and energy," "physical scientists," "civil engineers," "IT specialist managers," and "medical practitioners" (Gov.uk 2015). These "skilled" occupations that are especially welcomed by the United Kingdom and receiving states in general—that is, those in science, engineering and computing—tend to be heavily male (Iredale 2005). While such occupational segregation may be attributable to gendered preferences, a substantial body of social science research has suggested that "socialization in relation to gender norms continues to influence men's and women's average preferences and behavior" (Hegeswisch et al. 2010, 1). Moreover, "much of these reflect barriers to entry to occupations, ranging from lack of information about alternative job options to active discouragement and harassment" (Hegeswisch et al. 2010, 2).
b. Societal interpretations of what counts as "skilled" or "unskilled" labor, for the purposes of migration categories, may already favor

male-dominated professions, or those involving work that is perceived as traditionally "male." There seems to be no objective method of establishing standards of complexity across different types of skills, and historical studies have shown that employers have neither defined women's work as skilled nor compensated it in accordance with its occupational content (Steinberg 1990, 452). Instead, "the evaluation of skill is shaped by and confounded with a worker's sex" (452), and "saturated with sexual bias" (Phillips and Taylor 1980, 79). Thus, the problem is not only that women find it challenging to enter "skilled occupations"; a deeper issue is that particular jobs are viewed as low-skilled or unskilled simply because *women* are more likely to perform it. In light of the difficulty in defining what "skill" amounts to, Bridget Anderson points out that the centrality of skill categorization to labor migration policy overlooks the ways in which work and jobs are "socially constructed, imagined as suitable for different races and genders" (2013, 59).

c. Even if male-dominated occupations are not given the highest weightings in point systems, generic skill categories that use years of labor market experience and income levels to allocate points are also likely to place women at a disadvantage, because they are more likely to take career breaks, earn lower salaries, and experience difficulties in breaking through the glass ceiling (Kofman et al. 2000 [cited in Kofman and Raghuram 2006, 293]). Consider the United Kingdom's minimum salary requirements for Tier 2 visas. Tier 2 (General) visa holders presently require a minimum salary of £25,000, and Tier 2 intracompany transfer visa holders require a greater threshold of £30,000. These conditions tend to disadvantage applicants who are women, as women are paid less even when they work in the same sector. For example, according to a 2016 report, women in India (the top non-EU sending country of migrants in the United Kingdom) earned an average of 27 percent less than men (*Business Standard* 2016).
d. Social factors aside, the high costs of *migration* itself have an important role to play. The United Kingdom expects skilled migrants to be able to pay "petitioning fees," which applicants must pay to process applications, as well as other entry-related fees. On top of an immigration health surcharge that is supposed to cover the costs of their healthcare, most prospective Tier 2 immigrants must pay a minimum of

£437 to process their own applications, and the same amount for each dependent. These fees may have the effect of deterring *women* from initiating migration attempts. As Monica Boyd and Deanna Pikkov put it, "[s]ince gender hierarchies in source countries are usually associated with low earnings of women compared with men, women who seek to immigrate as principal applicants or as autonomous migrants bear a higher relative financial burden than their male counterparts" (2005, 11).

In summary, the use of skill-based selection disparately disadvantages women for myriad reasons that connect to persistent gender inequalities in society. Under skill-based regimes, women experience significantly more difficulty than men in gaining admission under economic immigration categories, and are far more likely to enter as family migrants. Consequently, in line with the definition of indirect discrimination I utilize above, we can understand skill-based selection as indirectly discriminatory toward would-be immigrants who are women.

Before proceeding to my analysis of whether such indirect discrimination is *wrongful*, an important clarification should be made. My argument does not rest on the suggestion that woman migrants are *overall* disadvantaged by present-day immigration policies. It may be well the case that *more* migrants who are women, generally speaking, are admitted than men; for example, in 2015, 52 percent of international migrants in Europe and North America were women (Birchall 2016, 11). Rather, I have drawn attention to how, under skill-selective programs, there is a pattern where *men* are predominantly admitted as primary migrants, and *women* as their dependents. It is not simply the sheer *numbers* of woman migrants admitted that matters morally; the main *pathways* through which they are admitted is equally salient. Firstly, it is worth emphasizing that an individual's immigration pathway exacts consequences on their prospects. As family dependents, women can experience serious disadvantage as a result of rules that govern how and when the primary migrant is allowed to sponsor their partner. For example, it was proposed in 2015 that the dependents of Tier 2 visa holders ought to be prevented from working. While the government proposal did not go through, owing to tremendous support for the continued right of Tier 2 dependents to work, it remains a grim reminder of the persistent precarity of dependents' labor rights, in comparison to that of the principal visa-holder's.

We might also worry about the prospect of women being enclosed in dominating or abusive relationships for fear of losing their visa status. These issues aside, women's tendency to enter as dependents, as opposed to skilled migrants, may be troubling for a *third* reason relating to their resonance with *demeaning social perceptions* of women. The remainder of my chapter will focus on exploring this notion.

3. Indirect discrimination and disrespect

a. What's wrong with disparate impact?

I now turn to *why* skill-based selection may be considered a form of wrongful discrimination, assuming it gives rise to the immigration patterns I have described. Importantly, the question of whether a policy indirectly discriminates can be disentangled from whether it indirectly discriminates *wrongfully*. The fact that a particular group suffers disparate impact of some sort, as the result of an action or policy, does not seem to show in itself that they have been wronged. Take, for example, the minimal leg room encountered in economy-class aeroplane seats. This no doubt has a disparate impact on long-legged individuals, who find themselves considerably more prone to discomfort and cramping during plane rides. But it seems we need a *further* explanation for why the structure of economy-class seating wrongs long-legged individuals in particular, and it is not obvious that any such explanation is available in this case. Consider, however, Susan Okin's description of the labor market's demands:

> The constraints placed on wives as workers are strengthened by the fact that many full-time employers assume, in innumerable ways, that someone is at home at least part-time during the day to assume primary responsibility for children. The traditional or quasi-traditional division of labor is clearly assumed in the vast discrepancy between normal full-time working hours and children's school hours and vacations. It is assumed by the high degree of geographical mobility required by many higher-level management positions. It is also implicit in the structure of the professions, in which the greatest demands are placed on workers at the very peak of the child-rearing years. Academia and the law are two clear

> examples; both tenure and partnership decisions are typically made for a person between the ages of thirty and thirty-five, with *obvious discriminatory implications* for the professional parent (almost always a woman) who does not have a partner willing to assume the major responsibility for children. (Okin 1991, 155–156, my emphasis)

It is clear, I think, that Okin is not simply making a descriptive claim about the disparate impact that commonplace job demands have on women, given that they often assume the role of primary caregiver. Rather, in pointing to how they disadvantage women, she is making a *normative* claim about the objectionable nature of those demands. But what, then, separates wrongful indirect discrimination from morally neutral indirect discrimination?

One initial answer is that we can distinguish between *intended* and *unintended* disparate impact. To illustrate this point, consider the *Griggs* case, where a public utility corporation required its employees to possess a high school diploma, or to pass intelligence tests, in order to take on higher-ranked positions. These requirements had the effect of "disqualifying" Black applicants at a "substantially higher rate than white applicants" (*Griggs v. Duke Power Co.*) and trapping them in low-ranked laborer positions, due to their poorer levels of education resulting from poverty and segregation. Thus, even though race *itself* was not a criterion for employment, and the tests had to be taken by all would-be employees, they disparately impacted Black applicants. The tests were hence described as "operat[ing] invidiously to discriminate on the basis of race" (*Griggs v. Duke Power Co.*). Significantly, the judgment on the *Griggs* case seemed to be motivated by the sense that the education tests were in fact a poorly masked *intentional* attempt to exclude Black employees. As Michael Selmi observes, "[t]he timing of the company's implementation of the new practices—literally the day after the [1964 Civil Rights Act, which prohibited racial discrimination]—has always aroused suspicions that the company's intent was to keep its African-American employees on the lowest rung of jobs . . . there was [also] another fact that pointed towards an intent to discriminate, namely [that] all of the incumbent white employees were exempted from the new requirements" (2013, 252–253). One test for whether a case of indirect discrimination is wrongful, then, is to ask if it was invidiously *intended*.

I think this answer is unsatisfying. While Okin, in the above passage, explicitly names the constraints women face as examples of indirect discrimination, the policies that exclude women from the workforce do not seem *intentionally* designed to keep women out of it. It is safe, I think, to assume that the requirement of geographical mobility was in *most* cases not contrived to make sure that women continued to be unemployed, but sincerely considered a necessary part of the scope of higher-level management positions. Similarly, I do not think the wrongfulness of the disparate effect that skill-based selection has on women turns on the presence of malicious *intent* to exclude migrants who are women. In the following section, I provide an alternative explanation for *why* these cases of gender-based indirect discrimination are ethically problematic.

b. Negligence and disparate impact

One promising account of wrongful indirect discrimination is that it constitutes a kind of *negligence*, understood in tort law as unreasonably imposing a risk on someone else (Moreau 2013, 135). Sophia Moreau proposes that discrimination is negligent when the discriminator *unreasonably* fails to accommodate the discriminatee, thus allowing them to be disadvantaged or excluded because of a feature such as their race, gender, or disability (2013, 138). The test for unreasonableness, Moreau believes, is quite straightforward: if the discriminator's other interests at stake are more important than the discriminatee's interest in not being disadvantaged, requiring them to adjust their policies would amount to undue hardship (Moreau 2013, 139). However, if the discriminatee's interest in not being disadvantaged outweighs the discriminator's interests, it would be unreasonable for the discriminator not to accommodate them. In sum, indirect discrimination is an "act that excludes someone in circumstances where there is some reasonable way of accommodating this person short of undue hardship" (Moreau 2013, 134).

To illustrate Moreau's theory in practice, consider a scenario where a visually impaired person, who requires her guide-dog's presence at all times, attempts to have lunch at a local café. The café shuns her because they have a strict policy that no animals are to be allowed on the premises, because allowing so would cheapen the café's ambience (Moreau 2013, 133). This would constitute wrongful indirect discrimination, as "it seems unreasonable of the restaurant to refuse to serve this client when doing so would not materially harm the premises or substantially interfere with the running of the restaurant" (133). On the other hand, if the café staff are religiously motivated, and ban dogs from the premises because they believe that coming into contact with a dog would render them ritually impure and require them to cleanse themselves repeatedly after, it would be substantially difficult for a waiter to have to cleanse himself frequently due to his encounters with the guide-dog. As this would truly result in undue hardship for the café, the staff's refusal to serve her does not amount to indirect discrimination (Moreau 2013, 134). Indeed, a similar judgment was also ruled with regard to the *Griggs* case. Duke Power Company was found to be guilty of indirect discrimination because it failed to show that the required tests were "job-related and governed by principles of business necessity" (Hunter 2014, 113). In short, they were *unreasonable* because they disadvantaged Black applicants on the basis of an insufficiently important interest. Significantly, this would have held true *regardless* of whether Duke Power Company harbored the invidious intent to exclude Black applicants.

However, the "reasonableness" test for negligence suffers from at least three shortfalls. Firstly, it tends to lead to indeterminate results that rely too much on our answers to more fundamental questions about *how* to weigh various interests. For Moreau, acting reasonably entails *correctly* weighing the discriminator's interests against the discriminatee's. In other words, discriminators fail to act reasonably when they obstruct important interests on the discriminatee's part in pursuit of less important interests of their own. We may say, for example, that firms *unreasonably* fail to accommodate women, as the interests that women have in not being excluded from employment outweigh the firms' interests at stake. Returning to Okin's comments, it seems highly plausible that women have a very strong fundamental interest in seeking employment and achieving financial autonomy. On this view, perhaps their interest cannot be outweighed by any number of economic gains that accrue to the firms in question, or the economy at large, and we may conclude that firms' failure to respond to this interest is unreasonable. However, the waters are considerably muddier in the immigration case. Presumably, the competing interests at stake are noncitizen women's interests in admission, and the state's interest in admitting highly skilled migrants, or being able to dictate the terms of their admission policies. How, exactly, do we adjudicate between them? It seems that our views about the comparative weightiness of these interests rest on our views about more fundamental questions.

For example, we may hold that noncitizen women have very strong interests in admission, given how it may significantly enhance or equalize their life-prospects, and that these are more important than the state interests at stake. Or we may go in another direction and hold that the state interests enumerated above outweigh the interests of noncitizen women. The point, here, is not that there is no objective way to weigh up the interests in question, but that the "unreasonableness test" brings up *more* questions than it offers answers. When asking whether a case of disparate impact is wrongful, we do not want the verdict to hinge excessively on how we resolve other complex and intractable issues.

Secondly, even if we could successfully determine which interests are weightier than others, it is not obvious that disparate impact is *only* wrongful when the disadvantage faced by the discriminatee can be described in terms of interests fundamental enough to outweigh the discriminator's. Consider the case of *G v. St Gregory's Catholic Science College*, where a young boy of Afro-Caribbean ethnicity took his school to court to challenge its ban on boys wearing their hair in cornrows. The school only permitted a conservative "short back and sides" hairstyle for boys, with an explicit ban on "braids," along with a more general prohibition on "peculiar and bizarre styles," which the school was concerned would encourage the proliferation of "gang culture." "G" protested the school's strict policy on the grounds that he wore his hair in cornrows as part of a family tradition, and that it was "of great importance to his cultural and racial identity." In response, the judge rejected the school's submission that it needed to be shown that a practice was of "exceptional importance" to the person alleging disadvantage. Rather, the relevant question was simply whether or not "G" had faced a particular *group* disadvantage—that is, a disadvantage affecting Afro-Caribbeans—and it seemed that the school had imposed one on him by restricting his family and social customs. Consequently, the school's ban on cornrows was eventually ruled as a case of wrongful indirect racial discrimination, in spite of the judge's acceptance that the school's aim, in only permitting conservative male haircuts, was to "make the school a place where children are first and foremost safe and valued equally," and keep them safe from the influence of gang culture. Significantly, the judge's decision did not appear to be grounded in the assertion that the school had acted *unreasonably*; that is, how "G" 's interest in retaining his cornrows ultimately *outweighed* its interest in keeping its students safe from negative influences.

Finally, defining the phenomenon of wrongful indirect discrimination as unreasonable interest-weighing seems to miss out on an important dimension of what makes wrongful discrimination normatively and politically significant. Everyone, of course, ought to have their interests weighed reasonably; nobody's fundamental interests should be disregarded in favor of more trivial ones. This seems to be a good guideline on how to treat persons *in general*. But we are not usually worried about just *anyone* facing indirect discrimination; we are typically primarily concerned about indirect discrimination against historically marginalized groups, like women, ethnic minorities, and non-able-bodied persons. In fact, there certainly seem to be cases of unreasonable interest-weighing that we would not consider to be wrongful indirect discrimination. Returning to an example discussed at the beginning of this section, it could be unreasonable for airlines to subject tall people to uncomfortable aeroplane seats because tall persons' interest in leg circulation outweighs their interest in high profit margins, but we do not think of that example as constituting wrongful indirect discrimination, even if it is wrong *qua* unreasonableness. Instead, wrongful indirect discrimination, at least in ordinary parlance, seems to be almost exclusively the domain of historically marginalized groups. Moreau's account, on its own, does not seem to be able to explain why we focus specially on those groups and not unreasonable interest-weighing writ large. One possible reply is that these groups are *especially* prone to having their interests weighed unreasonably, because of a history of subordination, and this is why they merit special concern. Yet this seems to place the cart before the horse. Why do we require a story about unreasonable interest-weighing when *the* distinctively bad thing about wrongful indirect discrimination could simply be that it worsens the status of subordinated groups? I will take up this approach in the next section by drawing a lesson from some of the literature on direct discrimination.

c. Negligence as the failure to discharge a duty of care

As I noted in the previous chapter, it has been argued that direct discrimination is wrongful because it expresses disrespect for members of the group that they treat differentially. Starting from the assumption that all persons are entitled to equal respect, discrimination is wrongful when it "distinguish[es] among people on the basis of an attribute when doing so demeans any of the people affected" (Hellman 2011, 6). Put differently, discrimination is wrong when it expresses a belief in the *inferiority* of discriminatees and thus fails to accord them equal respect. For example, a white-only swimming pool wrongfully discriminates against nonwhites because it expresses the demeaning belief that they are dangerous or unsavory to the extent that they should not be permitted to enter white territory. While it is not within the scope of my chapter to fully flesh out or defend Hellman's account of wrongful discrimination, I believe that this sense of *treating-as-inferior* is central to the concept of wrongful discrimination, and we may draw on it for a novel account of wrongful indirect discrimination.

I will now suggest an amendment to Moreau's view that allows us to preserve the useful idea of negligence and incorporate Hellman's insights, while avoiding the shortfalls I identified. We can look to another available meaning of negligence: *the failure to discharge a duty of care*. Normally, in order to legally determine negligence, a three-part test must be satisfied. It must be established that a person is owed a duty of care; that the duty of care has been breached; and that as a result of that breach, harm has been caused (Bryden and Storey 2011, 124). Consider a case where an elderly person, who has been admitted to a hospital, dies of sepsis because a serious bedsore has gone untreated, due to his doctors failing to perform a routine bedsore check. Here, the hospital staff owe him a duty of care; "it has been argued by medical law academics that any patient [doctors] come across in our professional environment is owed a duty of care, not only by the doctors the patient comes into contact with, but also by those who are employed . . . to deliver patient care" (Bryden and Storey 2011, 125). At the same time, the doctors' duty of care has been breached because they failed to adhere to the "standard of comparable professional practice" (125). Finally, the patient suffered harm precisely *because* the doctors failed to perform the routine check; he would not have died otherwise.

I propose that wrongful indirect discrimination is structurally similar to negligence because it involves the failure to discharge a duty of care. Agents owe a duty of care to socially subordinated groups, to examine the expressive significance of their actions, and avoid worsening demeaning social beliefs about those groups. When an agent fails to observe the social impact of their actions, they can be understood as breaching this duty of care. Furthermore, harm—in this case, "disparate impact" that carries a particular social meaning—ensues as a result of the breach. Returning to Okin's complaint, we may say that the labor market's indirect gender discrimination is wrongful, because it involves *negligence* on the part of firms; their failure to consciously observe the social meaning of their actions worsens demeaning beliefs about women's labor. By failing to accommodate those with caregiving responsibilities, firms send the message that the realm of employment and the realm of caregiving duties are wholly irreconcilable. To pursue a career, a woman must avail herself of the roles that impose such duties, particularly that of motherhood. (Perhaps a closely related case of discrimination is when women have their job applications thrown aside because of the suspicion that they may soon become pregnant.) This is a familiar trope in film and fiction; women are often depicted as having to give up their hopes of having children, or shunting their children to one side, if they want to be taken seriously as *real* career persons. In the popular television series *Mad Men*, the character Peggy Olson gives up her child for adoption in order to focus on her demanding career as an advertising executive. This hard-nosed dichotomy between home and work life reveals a *contempt* for the feminine, through the rejection of features that are typically associated with women, such as possessing the desire to, or finding value in, caring and nurturing. Similarly, we might say that St Gregory's negligently failed to avoid worsening demeaning social beliefs about Black people. This is because the school rules, in failing to distinguish between cornrows and "gang-related hairstyles" inadvertently reinforces existing demeaning stereotypes about Black culture: for example, that it primarily revolves around violent gang activities and criminal mindsets, and distinctively Black hairstyles like dreadlocks mark out one's participation in such aberrant behavior.

One initial worry may be that the "duty of care" owed to socially subordinated groups is potentially infantilizing toward them. It marks them out as helpless, weak, and in need of coddling by those who are stronger and more powerful. However, the term is a purely technical one that need not contain such implications. That I owe a duty of care to my employees does not mean, for example, that I have such an orientation toward them. Similarly, the fact that my favorite manufacturer of spaghetti sauce owes me a duty of care to produce uncontaminated jars of sauce need not imply that it treats me in an infantilizing way.

It may also be argued, at this point, that I have ignored a clear disanalogy between indirect discrimination and medical negligence. Doctors *acquire* a professional duty of care when a patient, for example, is admitted to hospital; by virtue of their role, they begin to stand in a particular relation to the patient. But where does the duty of care to socially subordinated groups stem from? This is where the idea of equal respect comes in. Because we have a basic duty to treat all persons with equal respect—that is, as social equals—we have a secondarily derived duty of care to avoid *exacerbating* disrespectful social meanings about subordinated groups. While we must refrain from directly expressing disrespect, as in the case of direct discrimination, we must also avoid indirectly exacerbating existing subordination. Before I extend this analysis to the case of skill-based selection, the argument I have made thus far must be fine-tuned.

Firstly, by "agents," I refer both to individual and collective agents, including institutions and corporations. Secondly, it must be noted, again, that this is not a straightforward status-harm view, where indirect discrimination will be wrong when its disparate effect *worsens* the position of a historically disadvantaged group. But I want to argue that it is insufficient that their position is *worsened*; rather, it must be worsened in a particular way. The disparate effect must have the additional impact of *reinforcing demeaning and inferiorizing social norms* about those groups, in a manner irreducible to material harm. Thirdly, while we determine whether doctors have breached their duty of care according to current professional standards, the "professional standard" for discrimination is our existing knowledge of harmful social norms pertaining to socially subordinated groups. Doctors cannot escape charges of negligence by claiming ignorance of how they should have acted (unless, of course, the relevant fact is extremely obscure); the retort is that they *should* be aware of standard medical practice. Likewise, agents cannot insist that they have not breached their duty of care because they were ignorant of a particular strain of demeaning beliefs, when they should have taken the necessary steps to educate themselves. Fourthly, the disparate impact must be *foreseeable*. It remains possible that a very well-deliberated policy, where the agents dutifully took existing social meanings into account, might somehow have the completely unexpected effect of excluding a socially subordinated group in a way that worsened demeaning stereotypes. I grant that such cases will not count as instances of negligent behavior. While the agents remain obliged to amend or replace the exclusionary policy, and may be held responsible for failing to do so after the problem has been identified, they have not wronged the socially subordinated group by implementing it—although they may commit wrong if they do not make the necessary changes afterward.

Lastly, it bears mentioning that, on this account of wrongful indirect discrimination, the idea of *reasonableness* still has a significant role to play. After all, it seems that a plausible duty of care ought not to impose an unreasonable cost or burden on the persons who bear the duty. Suppose that a parent has a duty of care toward her child, but that their child can only be kept alive if they donate a vital organ to it, thus sacrificing their own life. The child's resulting death, though regrettable, could not be understood as stemming from *negligence* on the parent's part, compared to a case where a child dies because its parent forgets to buy infant formula, where the purchase of infant formula *would not* have imposed an unreasonable burden on the parent. Likewise, there may be a number of instances where the cost of discharging the duty of care would be so unreasonably onerous that the failure to do so would not count as negligent, and therefore, *not* as wrongful indirect discrimination.

Take, for example, the requirement of a doctorate for lectureship positions. Suppose that this requirement is far less likely to be met by people from a minority ethnic group because of past injustice and historic barriers to entry, thus resulting in a disparate impact on their ability to enter the academic profession. Furthermore, suppose that this impact *does* worsen demeaning stereotypes about the group in question, e.g., that they are uneducated and of inferior intellect. The costs of waiving the requirement, however, would potentially be immense: students would find their courses taught by insufficiently qualified people, and the quality of research at the university might seriously suffer. In this case, the doctorate requirement *does not* amount to universities' failure to discharge a duty of care, as the relevant costs of doing so would be too high. To be sure, however, the role that unreasonableness plays in my account remains very different from the role it plays in Moreau's. Recall that, for Moreau, disparate impact is wrong when it is *unreasonable*; unreasonable behavior is *constitutive* of wrongful indirect discrimination. On the other hand, according to my proposed alternative, indirect discrimination is wrongful when it involves the negligent failure to discharge the duty of care to avoid worsening existing disrespect toward socially subordinated groups. Here, the failure to discharge one's duty of care is *only* negligent if it does not involve unreasonable costs to the agent in question.

4. The British points-based system, revisited

Now that I have laid out my alternative explanation for when indirect discrimination is disrespectful, I will examine its implications for skill-based selection. To reiterate, indirect discrimination is wrongful when the discriminator neglects to pay attention to the social significance of their actions, and fails to avoid reinforcing demeaning social norms about a socially subordinated group. Vis-à-vis the UK points-based system, we might say that immigration policymakers negligently failed to consider the foreseeable disparate impact on women who wish to migrate and its downstream effects on social meanings: the reinforcement of demeaning beliefs about women that already exist in the United Kingdom. To justify this claim, I will now expand on the content of those social meanings and how they are buttressed by the effects of the points-based system.

Recall that, under the points-based immigration system, women face particular difficulty in entering as *workers*, due to the United Kingdom's strong demonstration of its preference for "skilled workers"—a loaded category that women are excluded from consequent on reasons attached to entrenched gender inequality. Certainly, as I have already mentioned, the very structure of the system tends to frustrate women's opportunities to migrate with an independent visa status that offers them prized prospects like the ability to reside in the United Kingdom on a long-term basis, or eventually qualify for citizenship, without those being contingent on another person's visa status or potentially unstable rules about the rights of dependents. But, more than its tangible effects on women's prospects, we should look to how the exclusion of women on this front contributes to their existing social subordination. In the United Kingdom, and indeed many other Western receiving states, the labor of women is already traditionally considered to be inferior to that of men, and women *themselves* also tend to be regarded as less competent or valuable workers, particularly in fields where the labor in question does not conform to stereotypically feminine forms. Rather than operating in a vacuum, the exclusion of women from the United Kingdom's pool of foreign workers acquires a particular resonance in this social context. It serves as one more nail in the coffin for the equal valuing of women's work in the United Kingdom, as on top of women's exclusion from highly ranked jobs and positions within the domestic labor market, the state *also* signals its lack of interest in bringing in women workers from overseas, reinforcing the demeaning social belief that they are undesirable and inferior to male workers.

At the same time, it is not only the fact of women's exclusion that matters; we must also look at *how* they are entering. Recall that under the UK points-based system, when women *do* enter, they end up most frequently admitted as dependents of male migrants. Given that their right to remain and work in the United Kingdom is contingent upon their male partners, as well as potentially open to removal by the authorities, these women are undoubtedly placed in a precarious position. But more than this, their dependency on men has a charged meaning in the United Kingdom's social context. Women are *already* widely viewed as passive or helpless beings; under the ideology of protective paternalism, they require male protection and help (Wakefield et al. 2012, 1). On one hand, this leads to benevolent sexism, where men provide unrequested assistance to women in unequal "helping transactions" that position one individual as capable and the other as reliant on them, therefore conveying the power and authority of men (1) and the weakness of women. On the other hand, these social norms are also used to justify outright misogyny: chiefly, the denigration of women as lazy and useless, and only capable of achieving their ends by manipulating men into doing their work. In this climate, the fact that noncitizen women are frequently granted admission as dependents of men who have been granted entry to work in the receiving state, rather than as workers in their own right, inadvertently contributes to the disrespectful belief that women as a group are inherently reliant on men, constantly seeking to improve their lot through men's achievements, rather than through their own efforts.

It may be said, then, that United Kingdom immigration policymakers disrespect women through *negligently* failing to consider the social significance of women's exclusion from the "skilled" category, which reproduces preexisting sexist norms in British society—assuming, of course, that those norms are present. Furthermore, the indirect discrimination of skill-based selection wrongs *women* in general and not just the *foreign* women who are excluded, as the same disrespectful stereotypes apply to women at large, even if on an intersectional analysis, they have a more serious impact on the lived experience of some sub-groups, due to their country of origin, race, or class. In making this assertion, my account does not depart from other theories that understand wrongful discrimination as wronging a *group* on top *of* the individual wrong it does to particular members of the group.

Importantly, my claim is not contingent on the assumption that home countries have a special responsibility to remedy distributive injustice abroad. The relevant wrong I have identified is *not* that skill-based selection contributes to patterns of existing distributive gender injustice in other countries (although it may certainly do so), but that it worsens demeaning *social norms and beliefs* about women in the receiving state.[1] Furthermore, it should be noted that *admissions* themselves, and not just *exclusion*, can wrongfully worsen stereotypes. For example, the Philippines is well-known for incentivizing Filipino women to perform caregiving jobs in wealthier states like Singapore, Hong Kong, and Saudi Arabia. Here, the admission of women specifically to perform care work might reproduce the social belief, in receiving states, that caregiving is essentially "women's work," and not something that can be performed by both genders. The argument I have sketched out is alive to this possibility, even if it would not be appropriate to describe such cases as instances of wrongful indirect discrimination, as they involve the wrongful *preferential* admission of women (and not exclusion). Up to this point, I have sought to emphasize that the gender justice of immigration policies does not merely rest on women being admitted as frequently as men. Instead, we ought to think about the *avenues* through which women are gaining admission, and what those say about social perceptions of women and their role in society. This concern is reflected in my acknowledgment that women's frequent *admission* as dependents may be morally amiss. Clearly, a scenario where a particular number of women enter the receiving state as skilled migrants is normatively different from a scenario where the same number of women enter as family dependents, or specifically to perform care work. I now turn to two objections to my analysis.

5. Objections

a. A cultural solution to a cultural problem?

I have primarily framed wrongful indirect indiscrimination as a problem of social subordination. However, if discrimination is a cultural problem at its core, due to the norms and values expressed in patriarchal cultures, does this not imply that it can be remedied with a purely cultural *solution*?

Return to the case of women facing indirect discrimination in the workforce. Assuming that my theory is correct, states wrong women because they risk reinforcing the demeaning beliefs that stereotypically feminine forms of labor are unwanted and lack value, and that women are passively reliant on men. Instead of doing our best to avoid indirectly discriminatory practices, why not resolve this problem by *elevating* "women's work" in popular culture? If a project of revaluation succeeded, caregiving roles might become *more* socially valued than "men's work," rather than perceived as inferior, and women would no longer be socially subordinated. Consequently, their disparate exclusion from skilled immigration categories would no longer count as wrongful indirect discrimination. That we would rightly regard this solution as inadequate seems to strongly indicate that indirect discrimination, or possibly discrimination as a whole, is not primarily a cultural problem.

However, the fact that we cannot reduce social subordination to material harm does not mean that the two are not closely linked. For example, the material consequences of an indirectly discriminatory policy, like Black people being disparately prevented from gaining employment in respected jobs like academia and legal professions, can nevertheless play a salient role in perpetuating demeaning norms about Black people, as there is a component of racist stereotypes that relates strongly to their poor economic status, and how they are particularly suited for low-ranked forms of work. At the same time, even if *some* educational campaigns might have some degree of success in changing social beliefs, culture is only one dimension. Consider the ongoing Black Lives Matter campaign that underscores the equal worth of Black people's lives in the face of police brutality. It calls for both cultural and material change because it is difficult to imagine how Black lives *could* come to be equally valued and respected, even if attitudes toward them changed, if Black people continued to be disparately subjected to police profiling, violence, and incarceration. Furthermore, while campaigns about the importance and value of domestic labor and caregiving occupations might play some role in shifting the cultural consciousness, ham-fisted campaigns might even risk being *more* disrespectful to women by promoting stereotypical or essentializing beliefs about them. For example, an advertisement praising women's ability to cope with difficult domestic work might inadvertently reinforce the notion that they are more naturally suited to such activities. In sum, it is simply not true that a "cultural solution" is a sufficient response to discrimination, even if it is primarily identified as a cultural problem.

b. Why should individual agents pay the cost of a structural problem?

A second objection might relate to a fundamental difference between direct and indirect discrimination, and why they create responsibilities on the part of agents. As Selmi suggests, while direct discrimination typically implies some element of individual fault, disparate impact theory shifts away from "issues of fault to distributive remedial concerns" (2013, 250). In his words,

> Indirect discrimination focuses on results, an issue of equality, and requires employers to justify their employment practices that disparately affect groups that are protected by anti-discrimination laws. Implicit in this theory is that neither the employer or the employees (or applicants) have acted wrongfully but there is instead a social inequity that collectively we have determined should be addressed or justified. (Selmi 2013, 253)

If we accept this distinction between direct and indirect discrimination, the absence of liability has serious consequences for the issue of responsibility; in particular, the duty to compensate the victims of wrongful discrimination. While I have preferred to focus on demeaning social beliefs, rather than distributive equality, Selmi's criticism still applies. Suppose that an employer directly discriminates against its Black employees on the basis of race, giving them a significantly lower salary than white employees despite their having the same job titles and duties. Here, we might say that the employer has committed a *fault*; it is liable for compensation to its Black employees because it demeaned them. But suppose that, in another case, an employer award significant year-end bonuses to full-time employees, and not to part-time employees, even if the latter have worked for the same number of hours. This indirectly discriminates against women, because women are disparately employed part-time due to their caregiving responsibilities. But why should the *employer* be responsible for compensating those women? After all, unlike in the previous case, disparate impact only occurs *because* of preexisting demeaning beliefs about women, not through the employer's fault. In other words, it is unclear why employers should pay the cost of those accommodations, since they have little to do with *creating* those societal presumptions (Selmi 2013, 260).

I believe that my theory of indirect discrimination shows how we can resolve this issue. To start with, it is not true that we cannot bear responsibility to other agents, in the form of compensatory duties or otherwise, if our actions only harm them *because* of some preexisting conditions that we played no part in creating. Imagine that I am a strict gym teacher. As part of my syllabus, all my students must warm up by doing a vigorous set of jumping jacks at the beginning of every class. I forget that one of my students has a serious knee injury that he sustained many years ago. The intense jumping jacks aggravate the knee injury and he must undergo further surgery. In this case, it seems likely that the school *is* responsible for the aggravated knee injury, and ought to pay some degree of compensation to the unfortunate student, *even* if the student's predicament only arose because of a preexisting condition that I played no role in creating. Denying this possibility means that we might be able to absolve many agents of responsibility by simply reframing instances of harm, so as to trace their origin to a preexisting condition ("I am not responsible for breaking your heart, given how fragile it was even before I met you"). In fact, this may even apply to cases of direct discrimination. An employer liable for racial discrimination—for example, by racially segregating their cafeteria—may retort by insisting that they played no role in creating the social meanings that make the act of racial segregation demeaning.

Keeping this in mind, we can understand how agents may be liable for wrongful indirect discrimination, even if they did not bring about the social conditions that lead to disparate impact. As I have argued, agents are liable because they act *negligently* by failing to discharge their duty of care to socially subordinated groups. While they are not responsible for the background of cultural subordination, they are responsible for negligence in the same way that a gym teacher may be responsible for negligence, even if they are not responsible for causing a student's prior knee injury. Furthermore, it is highly misleading to suggest that there is a one-way relation between the context of demeaning social norms and the present actions of agents, where inferiorizing social meanings affect the consequences of agents' actions, but remains static regardless of how agents behave. As my account of indirect discrimination has underscored, the actions and omissions of agents, especially those who are powerful and influential, continue to breathe life into disrespectful social meanings.

6. Conclusion

I have sought to provide an account of wrongful indirect discrimination that is complementary to the disrespect-oriented theory of direct discrimination I introduced in the previous chapter. I have argued that indirect discrimination is wrongful when agents negligently breach their duty of care to members of socially subordinated groups, to examine the social meaning of their actions and avoid worsening demeaning beliefs about them. This duty of care is derived from our basic duty to treat all persons as social equals; while we must refrain from directly demeaning behavior, we must also avoid indirectly worsening social subordination. I then applied my account of indirect discrimination to the case of skill-based selection, explaining how it leads us to the troubling conclusion that skill-based selection is a form of wrongful indirect discrimination, because immigration policymakers have *neglected* to avoid worsening existing demeaning social beliefs about women that relate to their capacities and the value of their work, in comparison to men's. If philosophers regard direct immigration discrimination against women as wrongful, they should also be concerned about skill-based selection and its potential for gender-based indirect discrimination.

PART III
IMMIGRATION AND INJUSTICE

5
Decolonial Justice and Immigration Policy

1. Introduction

One of the central aims of my book, as outlined in Chapter Two, has been to show that noncitizens have a right to be treated as social equals, under a principle of social equality, and that the state's right to exclude must be constrained by this weighty consideration. In Chapters Three and Four, I argued that skill-based selection violates this right; the preference for highly skilled migrants can generally be understood as a form of direct *and* indirect wrongful discrimination. The principle of social equality I have defended, however, has an even broader application: chiefly, how should we design immigration policy within a social context that is already structured by profound and entrenched social inequalities: that is, a world tainted by an extensive history of colonial injustice? For this reason, in this chapter, I examine the implications of colonialism for present-day immigration policy. In particular, I focus on the racial exploitation that took place under colonial injustice and the unequal social relationships that were constitutive of it. A properly *decolonial* orientation toward immigration justice in the present day might require us not only to provide redress to the groups who were subjected to racial exploitation but also to *refrain* from engaging in practices that produce (or reproduce) such colonial relationships between persons. The aims of decolonial justice, as I have just defined it, are no easy task when some states, such as the United States, are responsible for multiple acts of colonialism; consequently, they may owe redress to members of *several* groups, not just one, and it may be difficult in practice to provide redress to one without detracting from the other. For example, under conditions of scarcity, attending to the historical injustices that the United States perpetrated against El Salvador may significantly take away from its ability to attend to injustices committed against the Navajo nation and Black Americans. For

Immigration and Social Equality. Désirée Lim, Oxford University Press. © Oxford University Press 2023.
DOI: 10.1093/oso/9780197658093.003.0006

the purposes of my chapter, however, I will focus on providing an analysis of how the United States' present-day treatments of Latino/a/x migrants follows a distinctively colonial pattern of injustice that warrants redress. Such an analysis, I believe, is valuable in its own right, and certainly shouldn't be taken as a suggestion that justice for Latino/a/x migrants should be prioritized over and above other potential duties of redress to other groups.

To be sure, one might agree that decolonial projects are a moral imperative, but insist that they can be carried out *without* any consequences for how states decide on which noncitizens enter, reside in, or become members of their political communities. Certainly, in theory, decolonial justice may not require us to alter the shape of immigration policy. For example, the United Kingdom might uphold agreements to transfer reparative funds to Malaysia, but this doesn't require them to admit Malaysian would-be immigrants. Refusing to extend the scope of decolonial justice to immigration policy, however, seems counterintuitive—particularly because of the historically salient patterns of migration between colonizing powers and ex-colonies. As Phillip Cole observes, migratory movements tend to arise from the existence of prior links between sending and receiving countries, colonialism included—for example, the leading sources of migration to the United Kingdom are India, Pakistan, and Bangladesh, three of its former colonies (Cole 2000, 29). We can also see similar movements from Martinique to France, Surinam to the Netherlands, and Algeria to France (29). Before I continue, it's worth mentioning three possible reasons behind these patterns.

Firstly, colonial subjects were sometimes given the right to migrate to the colonizing power for limited periods. Take, for example, the British Nationality Act of 1948, which redefined members of British colonies as "British subjects" and gave them the right to settle in the United Kingdom—until the Commonwealth Immigrants Act of 1962, which subjected those not born in the United Kingdom, or already holding a British passport, to new immigration controls. Secondly, it was not at all unusual for colonial subjects to migrate to the colonial center for the purposes of work, either voluntarily (troops from British India who worked for the Allies during the two World Wars) or nonvoluntarily (e.g., African slaves who accompanied their master back to Europe and retained their slave status while in Europe).[1] Thirdly, even after formal decolonization, there remain strong economic and cultural reasons for citizens of ex-colonies to choose to migrate to the previous colonial center over other receiving states—for example, because they are fluent in the language, or because moving there for work or study remains very prestigious (e.g., a "British education" may be admired and regarded as a status-marker for the most wealthy members of ex-colonies, as is the case in Singapore). Overall, the historical movement of persons has been so influenced by colonial relationships that it would be misguided to treat immigration policy as off-limits. This chapter, then, examines the question of what a decolonial ethics of migration would look like.

My analysis will proceed in this order. In Section 2, I examine two existing proposals for a decolonial ethics of immigration that relate specifically to would-be migrants from former colonies: firstly, Alasia Nuti and Sara Amighetti's argument that well-known justifications for the "right to exclude" may not actually apply to such migrants, and secondly, Suketu Mehta's suggestion that that inclusion in the polity could serve as a vital form of colonial reparation. I argue that, while highly promising, these proposals do not exhaust the scope of a decolonial ethics of immigration—especially if we understand the wrong of colonialism to lie in racial exploitation. In Section 3, focusing on the case of the United States, I show how its racial exploitation of low-skilled Latino/a/x migrants points toward a problematic relation of *coloniality* between such migrants and the state, which can result in serious harms for those subject to such exploitation. The pursuit of decolonial justice, then, would require serious reforms to immigration policy that can be motivated by unequal social relationships in the present-day that (to some extent) stand independently of past colonial relationships, even if it may not call for open borders tout court. Section 4 addresses three objections to this claim.

2. Migrants from former colonies

As this chapter argues, a decolonial ethics of migration may have strong implications for how states ought to exercise their right to exclude vis-à-vis migrants from countries all over the world, particularly with regard to *low-skilled migrants*. However, I start by focusing more closely on would-be migrants from former colonies. Chiefly, do colonizing powers have the right to exclude members of former colonies? If not, what are the relevant properties of members of former colonies that distinguish them from other noncitizens? In this section, I explicate and defend two claims: firstly, that justifications for the right to exclude may simply not apply to citizens of ex-colonies, and secondly, that decolonial duties of justice may require colonizing states to admit them.

a. Grounds for the right to exclude

To begin with, some familiar justifications for the right to exclude may simply not be applicable to members of former colonies because of the special relationships they have with colonizing powers. One well-known argument, which I have covered in Chapter One, appeals to the strong interest that states have in maintaining a particular cultural identity (Miller 2013, 200). To recap, in David Miller's words, "the public culture of their country is something that people have an interest in controlling: they want to shape the way that their nation develops, including the values that are contained in the public culture" (200). Consequently, states would be justified in limiting immigration or sharply differentiating among immigrants who are perceived as sharing the public culture and those who do not. Against this, Sara Amighetti and Alasia Nuti point out that Miller's argument fails to justify the exclusion of members of previous colonies. Because of the "intertwined histories" between colonizers and the colonized, where colonies played a significant role in shaping the self-conceptions of colonizing states, members of ex-colonies share in the national identity of colonizing states *even if* they may be popularly judged as unassimilable or hostile to national values, as in the case of France and Algerian immigrants (Amighetti and Nuti 2016, 553).

Though Amighetti and Nuti focus specifically on culture as a justification for exclusion, their argument sets a precedent that may easily apply to other rationales. Take, for example, Ryan Pevnick's claim that citizens' ownership over their collective institutions supplies them with a presumptive claim to make decisions about who gets to share in those institutions (2011, 33). If "collective institutions" were partly built through the *forced labor and contributions* of colonial subjects, then it seems plausible that members of ex-colonies also have a claim to joint ownership that overrides the colonizing state's right to exclude them. Here, it might be tempting to claim that the present-day citizens of past colonies are *not* shared owners because they did not *personally* contribute to the building of collective institutions. However, this view is clearly mistaken when Pevnick's view does not rest on the *actual* contributions of present-day citizens; he explicitly states that collectively owned goods or institutions can plausibly be passed down to future generations (2011, 35). If it's true that colonial subjects had rightful claims over the fruits of their labor, which was instrumentalized to enrich the metropole under conditions of slavery and exploitation, then it is not clear why current members of ex-colonies could not also have "inherited" ownership rights.

In defense of their right to exclude, it could be argued that colonizing powers' right to exclude members of ex-colonies could still be justified by other considerations. The appeal to culture or joint ownership are not the only arguments that may ground a robust right to exclude. One other candidate might be Christopher Heath Wellman's contention that the right to exclude is grounded in the state's freedom of association (2008). If Wellman's theory is correct, citizens' right to choose not to associate with members of past colonies may ultimately still prevail. It is worth reiterating, however, that I have already considered some persuasive objections against Wellman's justifications for the right to exclude in Chapter Three. In light of the problems with Wellman's argument, let's suppose that, at the conceptual level, there is some other plausible justification for the right to exclude that remains unaffected by colonial histories.[2] It is possible, however, to supplement our rethinking of the basis of states' right to exclude with a stronger argument: that states may have a duty to *admit* members of past colonies, as a vital mode of corrective justice.

b. Inclusion as a form of corrective justice

As I have suggested above, a decolonial ethics of migration might include a corrective justice-based requirement for colonizing states to allow the free movement of persons originating from ex-colonies into their territory. One version of this argument has been made by Suketu Mehta, who argues that "[i]mmigration quotas should be based on how much the host country has ruined other countries" (2019). In his words, the United States and Europe has run up a "far bigger bill" than the considerable reparations the United States owes its African American citizens for slavery: they owe other countries reparations for "their colonial adventures, for the wars they imposed on them, [and] for the inequality they have built into the world order" (Mehta 2019). While reparations might be paid back in the form of financial compensation, Mehta asks instead "for the borders of the rich countries to be opened to goods and people, to Indian textiles as well as Nigerian doctors" (2019). The right to migrate, itself, could be treated as a form of reparations for past colonial injustice. Under this system, immigration quotas could be based on the *extent* to which the colonizing power has perpetuated injustice:[3]

> A vast majority of migrants move from a poor to a less poor country, not a rich one. Immigration quotas should be based on how much the host country has ruined other countries. Britain should have quotas for Indians and Nigerians; France for Malians and Tunisians; Belgium for very large numbers of Congolese. (Mehta 2019)

Mehta's argument may sound provocative, but it does not argue for anything radically different from what has already been suggested or considered in the philosophical literature. As I covered in Chapter One, theorists like Joseph Carens have argued that, as a matter of global justice, migrants from poorer countries should have the right to migrate to richer ones as a means of equalizing their opportunities. In theory, these demands of justice might apply to would-be migrants from any country whose citizens experience diminished prospects. One serious objection to this claim, which I previously considered in Chapter One, is that states have a *special relationship* with their own citizens—one that they do not share with just any other people in the world.

Yet, much like what we have just seen in Amighetti and Nuti's argument, colonizing states *do* share special relationships with members of ex-colonies. We cannot afford to ignore the enormous impact that colonial histories have had on the life-prospects of persons today, and Mehta's argument helps to situate the rather general argument from "global justice" in a historically specific context where the global north is not wealthy *simpliciter*, but *in virtue of* its shameful history of racial exploitation. It is no accident that colonizing states tend to command a disproportionate share of the world's wealth. While this does not necessarily mean that citizens of ex-colonies are entitled to justice in the sense of "equal opportunities," they are (on Mehta's view) *at least* entitled to some degree of corrective justice. A policy of inclusion in the past colonial metropole would give members of past colonies the vital opportunity to benefit from state coffers that been substantially enriched by colonial injustice. We might also think that the right to migrate, as a means of reparation, is especially fitting given the fact that migration and mobility have historically been used as a means of creating and preserving the disproportionate power of the global north. In Phillip Cole's words, "European nations controlled a migration regime in which they had the power to travel the world and exploit resources and people, and to determine the flow of resources and people to particular places to further their own interests" (Cole 221, 2011). If migration has indeed been used as a tool of furthering colonial interests, perhaps it can now be used to benefit the lives of the populations who have been seriously disadvantaged by the global order.

In sum, to the extent that inequalities of opportunity experienced by members of past colonies can (at least to a significant degree) be traced back to colonial injustice, colonizing states might have a duty to *correct* it—and one way could be fixing immigration quotas for the victims of historical injustice today. One serious objection, at this stage, is that decolonial justice need not take the form of inclusion in the polity. Why can't colonizing states just focus on other strategies like developmental assistance or fund transfers, which could be accomplished from a distance?[4] Leaving aside the thorny empirical question of how effective those measures have been in practice, there are two possible responses to this question.

Firstly, certain valuable life-opportunities are nonsubstitutable; they are each distinct enough that they cannot replace each other. Even if fund transfers go some way in creating attractive new opportunities for citizens in ex-colonies, those opportunities cannot replace the ones located in the colonizing state. Suppose that a member of a past colony wishes to work as a software engineer at a prestigious technological firm, or as a professor at a prestigious academic institution. Developmental assistance or other fund transfers cannot easily create equivalent opportunities. It could be argued, in response, that citizens of ex-colonies are entitled to *better* opportunities, not *particular* ones. Having entitlement to better opportunities overall doesn't mean being entitled to the job of your dreams. However, I think this reply fails to take seriously the structural causes behind inequalities in opportunity between states. Ex-colonies may be devoid of such opportunities for their citizens exactly because of unjust legacies of exploitation and expropriation that have long-running consequences for their economic development. Insofar as the absence of such desirable jobs are (at least in part) traceable to colonial injustice, corrective justice seems to require that citizens of ex-colonies be granted access to them.

A second criticism may go like this: we have good reasons to avoid framing the right to migrate to colonizing states as the most appropriate mode of reparation. One basic desideratum of a method of corrective justice is that it should not make the persons in question worse off than they would otherwise be *without* implementing the measure (e.g., if it is demonstrably true that affirmative action policies for African Americans make the group worse-off as a whole). Furthermore, if there are *other* available methods of corrective justice that make those persons better-off *in comparison*, without imposing heavier costs, we ought to prefer those methods (e.g., if direct fund transfers, for example, make African Americans better-off than affirmative action policies). Keeping these considerations in mind, Gillian Brock has warned of the negative consequences of "brain drain": the "movement of talented (and often expensively trained) people from developing nations to developed ones" (Brock and Blake 2015, 2).[5] Brain drain tends to result from a "shared history of colonialism and violence," wherein the large-scale migration of skilled workers from past colonies "seems poised to perpetuate the inequality in life-chances between developing and developed countries" (Brock 2015, 3). Put differently, we may worry that the migration of workers vital for development (e.g., doctors, nurses, engineers, construction workers) may worsen the prospects of those left behind, even if individual migrants may certainly benefit from the right to move.

There is a real worry, then, that admissions-as-reparations might make members of past colonies worse off *on the whole* than other methods of corrective justice, taking into consideration the basic needs of those "left behind." Unless we can persuasively show that large-scale migration would not have this result, other modes of reparation may be preferable. Note, again, that I am not saying that citizens of ex-colonies *must be excluded* by colonizing states in order to protect their countries against the harms of brain drain, or even that sending states should place limitations on their ability to migrate.[6] But I take it that there is a nontrivial difference between merely allowing the admission of such citizens, should they decide to migrate, and framing such migration as a means of righting past wrongs—particularly when it may worsen the circumstances of those left behind. What if the "Nigerian doctors" that Mehti speaks of need to be around to provide medical care for fellow Nigerians?

I think that we should take this objection seriously, but there are two ways of responding to it. Firstly, it is worth underscoring that immigration-as-reparations does not *require* a particular number of citizens of past colonies to migrate. It simply allows the space for them to do so, if this is the decision that they wish to make. Assuming the harms of "brain drain," it might be morally wrong for a Nigerian doctor to leave his home country in pursuit of better opportunities in the United Kingdom, but this is consistent with receiving states preserving his *right* to do so.[7] Quite similarly, people receiving cash transfers as reparations might choose to do harmful or otherwise immoral things with the money they receive. It is not the authority of a colonizing power to decide on what is wrong or right for members of ex-colonies to do. The focus here, then, would be on respecting the autonomy of would-be migrants. Secondly, for those who are unmoved by the argument from autonomy, it is possible to make immigration-as-reparations sensitive to worries relating to brain drain. Over time, immigration quotas could be adjusted in light of evidence that the right to migrate is seriously hurting the sending state in question, or the criteria for eligibility could be more clearly specified (e.g., places could be reserved specifically for would-be migrants below a certain income level, or for would-be migrants whose remittances tend to confer the greatest socioeconomic benefits on their fellow citizens). While neither of these are perfect solutions, and this issue certainly needs to be examined in considerably more detail than my chapter can allow, the point is that immigration-as-reparations *can* take the risk of brain drain into account.

3. Low-skilled migrants and decolonial justice

There is a deeper concern about devoting our attention to members of ex-colonies alone, even if they may merit special concern. We risk having too little to say about migration as a whole when many citizens of the global south wish to migrate to states that they have no prior historical relationship with. As I have already pointed out, even if colonizing powers agreed that all citizens of their past colonies had the right to be included, this would be compatible with a world where they continue to enforce harsh exclusion policies against every other person. In fact, states might target other noncitizens even more aggressively because of the widespread perception that migration quotas have already been filled by members of ex-colonies. A decolonial ethics of migration, I believe, may require states to rethink their treatment of *low-skilled migrants* as a whole. This is because certain forms of immigration exclusion, by dint of their *racial exploitation* of noncitizens, may constitute a form of ongoing colonial injustice. States' treatment of low-skilled migrant workers often fits the structure of colonial injustice; that is, through its *racial exploitation* of low-skilled migrants. Furthermore, as we will see, such exploitation can be deeply harmful to migrants, and it is morally wrong for states to maintain a legal apparatus built on differentiation that directly contributes to such harms. A decolonial ethics of migration, then, would require us to significantly rethink skill-selective immigration practices.

In this section, I make my case by paying closer attention to the structure of racial exploitation and analyzing how the United States, as a case study in point, uses immigration policy to racially exploit low-skilled Latino/a/x migrants in the present day. First, I reconstruct Charles Mills's account of racial exploitation. Next, I explain how racial exploitation underpinned the relationship between colonizing powers and colonial subjects. Thirdly, I show how the United States racially exploits noncitizens and therefore reproduces colonial injustice. In particular, under skill-selective immigration policies, low-skilled Latino/a/x migrants are routinely subject to skewed or disadvantageous transactions *on the basis of their race.* These transactions, as I will show, are economically beneficial to the state and (at least some of) its citizens. If it is true that racial exploitation lies at the heart of colonialism, we must treat skill-based exclusion as a distinctively colonial injustice.

a. Racial exploitation

Colonial injustice was characterized by a particular type of unequal social relationship: *racial exploitation* of colonial subjects. To be sure, rather than something that was unique to colonialism and only happened in the past, we have good reason to believe that racially exploitative relationships continue to obtain between various groups today: a point I will expand on in the next section. Here, I focus on clarifying and expanding on the definition of racial exploitation.

It is helpful to begin from Charles Mills's account of racial exploitation. Mills primarily uses the concept to describe the socioeconomic relations between white Americans and other racial groups in the United States, but he also suggests that relationships between colonizers and the colonized had a similar character (2006, 248). Though the word "exploitation" is strongly associated with Marx's notion of the "transfer of surplus value from the workers to the capitalists" (Mills 2006, 242), Mills forcefully develops the concept of a particularly *racial* mode of exploitation and its manifold dimensions (2006, 236). On Mills's account, racial exploitation differs from Marxist class exploitation in three ways. First of all, he observes that racial exploitation is "just one variety of exploitation, and if it is a necessary condition that races be involved in the transaction, it is not a sufficient one": an exploitative relationship between Black workers and a white employer may simply be a standard capitalist one if "race plays no role in the establishment or particular character or reproduction of the relations of exploitation" (Mills 2006, 246). After all, the Black workers may simply be exploited *qua* worker if they are forced to sell their labor for less than the full value of the goods they produce at the same rate as (equally exploited) white workers in the same firm. What Mills has in mind are instances where, when R1 exploits R2, "*the relations of race* [my emphasis] play a role in the nature and degree of the exploitation itself" (246). As he writes,

> I suggest the paradigm case of racial exploitation is one in which the moral/ontological/civic status of the subordinate race makes possible the transaction in the first place (that is, the transaction would have been morally or legally prohibited had the R2s been R1s) or makes the terms significantly worse than they would have been (the R2s get a much poorer deal than if they had been R1s). (Mills 2006, 247)

As Mills posits, the rationale for R2s getting a "poorer deal" would be their subordinate status relative to whites: "[w]hat justifies African slavery and colonial forced labor, for example, is the lesser moral status of the people involved—they are not seen as full humans in the first place" (Mills 2006, 248).

Secondly, in another departure from the Marxist view of exploitation, the "transactions" that Mills has in mind go above and beyond proletarian wage labor. Mills notes that "[s]ociety is characterized by economic transactions of all kinds, and if race becomes a normative dividing line running through all or most of these transactions, then racial exploitation can pervade the whole economic order" (Mills 2006, 249–250). On this view, racially exploitative wages, where persons of color are pervasively more poorly remunerated for the same labor than white persons *because* of their race (or not remunerated at all), are one instance of a broader phenomenon. While racial exploitation brings about *bad* economic transactions for persons of color (e.g., the undervaluing of their property or their having to sign contracts on worse terms than white persons), it can also result in *exclusion* from certain transactions altogether (247). The latter might include being promoted at differential rates and to lower levels than white persons with comparable credentials, being turned down for a job in favor of a white candidate, or perhaps even lacking the chance to compete for certain jobs because one is excluded from racially exclusionary word-of-mouth networks (252–253).

Thirdly, a crucial component of Mills's theory is that whites (or, more generally, dominant racial groups) *benefit* from racial exploitation. While some white persons benefit from directly bringing about racially exploitative transactions (e.g., the white employer who intentionally discriminates against employees of color), many also do so *indirectly*. Due to their whiteness, they are able to engage in transactions that persons of color are disproportionately excluded from, or participate in transactions with far more favorable terms and therefore enjoy higher levels of advantage from "being the privileged race in a system of social subordination" (Mills 2006, 255). So, racial exploitation is not just about bad transactions or the lack of opportunity to engage in transactions for persons of color, but the ability of dominant groups to illicitly *benefit* at their expense.

b. Racial exploitation and colonial injustice

It is abundantly clear that colonialism involved the large-scale subordination of colonized populations, in ways that are encapsulated by Mills's definition of racial exploitation. The relations between conquering and conquered populations were codified by *race*, a new sociohistorical category at the time (Quijano 2000, 216). Following Spain's conquest, people in today's Latin America were classed as "Spanish" (and eventually "Whites and "Europeans") who ruled over "Indians," "Negroes," and "Mestizos." In turn, such classification was "associated with the nature of roles and places in the division of labor and in the control of resources of production" (216). Specifically, throughout the entire period of colonial domination, being categorized as white was associated almost exclusively with being paid a salary (e.g., through work as an independent merchant, artisan, peasant, or commodity producer or trader) and alternatively, qualifying to occupy the commanding posts of colonial administration (217). The control of capital and the right of salary was thus reserved for "Whites" alone.

I believe that we should think of racial exploitation as one of the central injustices of colonialism; that is, it was one of the main things that *made colonialism unjust*. In Chapter Two, I described colonialism as a clear-cut example of states' violation of noncitizens' social equality: colonizing powers commonly sought to destroy and undermine colonial subjects' sense of self. To this end, aside from racial exploitation, colonialism may also have included many other forms of injustice that merit harsh condemnation. For example, as Daniel Butt characterizes it, colonialism "involved multiple instances of genocide, slavery, rape, and sexual enslavement, murder, torture, displacement, and the misappropriation and destruction of property, alongside many other serious moral transgressions" (2013, 229). Among those transgressions might also be "the denial of self-determination, the imposition of an economic order on a people, and the supplanting of its culture and language" (Tan 2007, 282). After the United Nations' Declaration on the Granting of Independence to Colonial Countries and Peoples in 1960, which "affirmed the right of all people to self-determination and proclaimed that colonialism should be brought to a speedy and unconditional end" (United Nations), a sweeping wave of decolonization and national independence ensured that many of these injustices could no longer be inflicted upon colonized peoples. I have already suggested in Section 2 that colonizing powers may remain on the hook for reparations, and that reparations could be one powerful means of disbursing reparations. At the same time, however, there are residual forms of colonial injustice that must be attended to—we must recognize that colonialism is not just a phenomenon of the past. Specifically, colonizing powers may be responsible for perpetuating colonial injustice in the *present* by continuing to racially exploit noncitizens; in particular, low-skilled Latino/a/x migrants. As I've noted in the Introduction, the intersection between racial identity and perceived skill-level, as well as the marginalization and oppression that accompanies one's being read as a low-skilled racial Other, is extremely pronounced in the case of Latino/a/x migrants in the United States. I explain why below.

c. Racial exploitation and low-skilled Latino/a/x migrants

I have noted that colonial rule was strongly characterized by the *racial segmentation of labor*. Powerful positions, or even the ability to command a salary, was generally reserved for whites, while back-breaking (and often unpaid) labor fell to persons of color. Unfortunately, a hierarchical division of labor, organized by racial designations, is still alive and well. Iris Marion Young notes the continued existence of a "segmented labor market that tends to reserve skilled, high-paying, unionized jobs for whites" (1990, 51), while menial labor (which Young uses to refer to "servile, unskilled, low-paying work") tends to be designated for persons of color (1990, 52). We have reason to believe, however, that the labor market is *doubly* segmented. It is not just citizens of color, but predominantly low-skilled Latino/a/x migrants who disproportionately perform (and are assumed to perform) menial forms of labor.

We often hear the claim that immigrants "take the jobs that citizens don't want to do." The implication, here, is not so much that citizens *literally* reject jobs that migrants take on, but that the work associated with migrants is widely considered to be low-status and undesirable. The existing empirical data on migrant labor in the United States seems to confirm this. A 2017 survey by the Bureau of Labor Statistics (2018) showed that foreign-born workers were considerably more likely than the native-born to be employed in low-status occupations, including service, construction, and transportation, as opposed to higher-status occupations like managerial or professional positions. The division of labor between citizens and noncitizens is also reflected in US employers' heavy reliance on unauthorized migrants in many low-skilled occupations, including fields like construction, agriculture, accommodation, and food services (Sumption and Papademetriou 1, 2013).

Yet there is much more to the picture. It is not just immigrants in general, but predominantly Latino/a/x migrants and other immigrants of color who are employed in such occupations. The racial demographics of migrant workers by industry is revealing. According to the Bureau of Labor Statistics (2013), the vast majority of foreign-born *whites* worked in managerial or professional positions. In stark contrast, the majority of foreign-born persons of Latin American origin were concentrated in low-status industries like service, construction, and maintenance. Similarly, foreign-born care workers are overwhelmingly nonwhite (Hartmann et al. 2018). More generally, approximately half of low-skilled immigrants in the United States are from Mexico and another one-quarter originate from Latin American and Caribbean countries (Hanson et al. 2017).

Indeed, there is evidence to show that even native and immigrant workers with similar educational backgrounds are likely to perform different kinds of work. According to Maria Enchautegui, the most common occupations for immigrant workers are maids and house cleaners, cooks, and miscellaneous agricultural workers, while native workers are most likely to be cashiers, truck drivers, and janitors and building cleaners (2015). Enchautegui argues that the differences are theoretically significant: "[l]ess-educated native workers are over-represented in occupations that interact with the public and coworkers and that have supervising responsibilities, licensing requirements, and demanding mechanical and computer operations." On the other hand, immigrants "dominate manual jobs, occupations that are more physically demanding, and jobs where interactions with the public happen in more controlled settings" (2013). In short, the sphere of low-skilled labor *itself* contains hierarchical racial divisions that reserve relatively powerful and autonomous roles for whites.

The double segmentation of labor (where labor is segmented on the basis of race *and* immigration status) I have just described is part and parcel of a *racially exploitative* economic order that strongly resembles the colonial division of labor. It forms part of an existing social structure under which noncitizens—in this case, low-skilled Latino/a/x *migrants*—are treated as servants of dominant groups in the receiving state, taking their orders instead of exercising their own autonomy (Young 1990, 52). They are assumed to be responsible for the kind of dull, simple, rote work that is suitable for those with supposedly less developed rational capacities, who must rely on the command of their superiors. One familiar rejoinder might be that there is nothing inherently bad about a labor market that is segmented by race and immigration status. It just happens that there is demand for occupations that many citizens *prefer* not to perform, creating the opportunity for migrant workers to voluntarily fill them. Call this the "mere preference" argument. The problem with the "mere preference" argument, however, is that it naturalizes the double segmentation of menial work by failing to interrogate why such jobs are relatively unattractive to citizens. Much like in the colonial division of labor, there is a well-known sense that certain forms of menial work are better "suited" or "intended" for Latino/a/x migrants. The belief that certain jobs are the remit of low-skilled Latino/a/x migrants has serious implications for their terms and conditions, which in turn makes them extremely unattractive to citizens. I submit that, just like in Mills's "paradigm case" of racial exploitation, the *socially inferior status of Latino/a/x migrants* directly affects the wages they are paid and the working conditions they must endure, which can be very harmful, if not downright dangerous.

Take, for example, the relatively low wages of farmworkers. Many farmworkers are low-skilled Latino/a/x migrants who have been admitted under the H-2A temporary work visa scheme, which is specifically intended for the temporary agricultural employment of foreign workers. According to Daniel Costa,

> Farmworkers in general are paid very low wages—in 2019 they earned $13.99 per hour, which is only three-fifths of what production and non-supervisory workers outside of agriculture earned, and they earned less than what workers with lowest levels of education in the US labor market earned. (2020)

Furthermore, as Costa notes elsewhere, "[r]esearch shows that guestworkers are often paid lower wages than similarly situated US workers, and earn wages similar to those of undocumented immigrant workers" (2017). The laws and regulations that oversee the H-2B temporary worker program, under which nonagricultural workers like landscaping and groundskeeping workers and forest and conservation workers are admitted, allow employers to pay low-skilled Latino/a/x workers much less than the local average wage for the jobs they fill (Costa 2016). Relatively low wages aside, there is good evidence that thousands of migrant workers are frequently injured at work or become exposed to dangerous chemicals or conditions that can result in serious illness and disease; the US Census of Fatal Occupational Injuries found that, between 2003 to 2016, migrant workers were 15 percent more likely to be fatally injured on the job than native-born workers (Underwood 2018). One reason for this is that the highest percentages of migrant workers are employed in the most hazardous industries, such as agriculture and construction. Importantly, however, even when performing the same work, Latino construction workers experience more fatalities at work when compared to non-Latinos (2018). On the whole, it seems that *being a Latino/a/x migrant* in the context of low-skilled labor itself predisposes individuals to "differential and inferior treatment" (Mills 2006, 247) that occurs *qua* their socially subordinated status as Latino/a/x migrants.[8]

The racial exploitation of low-skilled Latino/a/x migrants is actively reproduced and maintained by the United States' skill-selective immigration policies. In Chapters Three and Four, I have noted how the United States (and other wealthy Western states) have an expressed preference for highly skilled migrants over low-skilled migrants. States are therefore only willing to admit relatively few numbers of low-skilled migrants on very restrictive terms, and the United States is no exception to this rule. The dispreference for low-skilled migrants affects the social standing of Latino/a/x migrants and exacerbates their racial exploitation in at least two ways, which I will now elaborate on.

i. Structure of existing guest worker programs

The structure of existing low-skilled guest worker programs, which are targeted toward Latino/a/x migrants, heavily contributes to the state's ability to racially exploit them. Patti Lenard and Christine Straehle note some well-known contributing factors in their analysis of guest worker exploitation. To be sure, a number of these are external to guest worker programs. For example, exploitation may partly stem from the unwillingness or inability of host countries to protect workers from violations of the labor contracts they have signed; while the contracts seem to be legitimate, they are frequently violated (Lenard and Straehle 2010, 285). States could technically preserve the legal framework of guest worker programs while making sure that guest workers are more reliably protected. However, other factors are *internal* to the guest worker programs: they are defining characteristics of "guest work." For example, unlike permanent residents who are eligible to apply for any job of their choice, guest workers are "often denied the right to change employers (and job loss frequently results in near immediate deportation)." At the same time, they are also often denied the right to join unions and strike (Lenard and Straehle 2010, 288).[9]

The impact of guest workers' inability to switch employers cannot be overstated. Because they are effectively tied to one employer, this endows the employer with the power to own and control their visa status, leading to a form of indentured servitude (Costa 2017). The specter of retaliation and deportation looms over workers who "speak up about wage theft, workplace abuses, or other working conditions like substandard health and safety procedures on the job" (2019). For instance, when workers attempt to recover wages owed to them, employers may threaten to report the workers as having "abandoned" their work and therefore give immigration enforcement officers license to detain and deport them (Apgar 2015). Even if employers do not fire guest workers for speaking out about workplace abuses, they can still punish them by refusing to rehire them the following year or getting recruiters in their countries of origin to blacklist them from future job opportunities in the United States (Costa 2019). All in all, as Michael Walzer succinctly puts it,

> [Guest workers] experience the state as a pervasive and frightening power that shapes their lives and regulates their every move—and never asks their opinion. Departure is only a formal option; deportation, a continuous practical threat. As a group, they constitute a disenfranchised class. (1983, 59)

ii. Undocumented immigrants

So far, I have focused on low-skilled Latino/a/x migrants who are legally authorized to work in the United States. It is equally important to note, however, that many of them also lack legal authorization. Based on data from 2012–2016, there are an estimated 11.3 million undocumented workers in the United States who primarily originate from Latin American countries like Mexico, El Salvador, Guatemala, and Honduras.[10] Undocumented workers tend to cluster in farming, construction, and service occupations—exactly those that I have shown to be characteristic of low-skilled migrant workers. Significantly, low-skilled Latino/a/x migrants tend to enter without authorization because immigration laws are "misaligned with the reality of migrant flows and labor needs" (Golash-Boza 2009, 297). The United States continues to admit much smaller numbers of low-skilled workers than are actually required by key industries like service, construction, and agriculture, leading these industries to rely heavily on an undocumented workforce (Sumption and Papademetriou 2013). By placing significant restrictions on the number of low-skilled migrants who are authorized to work, the system has effectively sustained a socially subordinated workforce composed of unauthorized Latino/a/x migrants.

While the threat of deportation looms over low-skilled migrants who are legally authorized, unauthorized migrants are even more vulnerable to immigration enforcement. It is unsurprising, then, that unauthorized migrants often find themselves in the same bind as guest workers: they are unable to complain about low or unpaid wages, as well as substandard or abusive working conditions, out of fear of retaliation by employers who can easily report them to immigration authorities. It is similarly difficult for them to join unions and participate in collective forms of organization (Costa 2019). On the whole, being an unauthorized worker means that one's work is all the more likely to be "dirty, difficult and dangerous" (Carens 2015, 141). Returning to Mills's point that racial exploitation may entail a diverse range of unfavorable transactions outside of wage labor, unauthorized migrants may find themselves stuck with "poorer deals" in other social contexts. For example, landlords can evict tenants, raise rents, or silence complaints about poor living conditions by threatening to report them to ICE.[11]

Saliently, low-skilled Latino/a/x migrants with legal authorization to work may experience similar forms of disadvantageous treatment to undocumented migrants, lending further credence to the theory that their exploitation is fueled by *race* and its close intersections with class and immigration status. Regardless of their immigration status, many low-skilled migrants routinely experience demeaning treatment, harassment by the police and immigration enforcement, and dominating treatment in worksites that we typically associate with undocumented migrant labor (Reed-Sandoval 2019, 49). As Amy Reed-Sandoval has recently argued, persons can be understood as "socially undocumented" when they are "presumed to be undocumented on the mere basis of their appearance and subject to demeaning, immigration-related constraints on that basis" (2019, 61).[12] Persons are perceived as "socially undocumented" on the basis of "visible race and class markers" (Reed-Sandoval 2019, 85): reading as Latino/a/x *and* working-class. For example, Reed-Sandoval points to an ethnography by Mary Romero, *Maid in the USA*, which investigates how many Latina legal residents in the United States who are employed as domestic workers often work under the same conditions as Latina domestic workers who are legally undocumented (2019, 54). It has also been observed that "Mexican temporary foreign workers' employment outcomes are as poor as, or even worse than, those experienced by unauthorized Mexican immigrants" (Apgar 2015). Interestingly, the line between being a "documented" and "undocumented" worker can also be blurry. It is possible for certain migrants (such as those who were victims of workplace crimes) to receive an initial certification from a federal agency that they qualify for visas, while simultaneously being criminally prosecuted or put in deportation proceedings for obtaining work through false identification documents (Morrison 2017, 301).

iii. Benefits for the receiving state

The racial exploitation of low-skilled Latino/a/x migrants has had obvious economic benefits for the United States. The failure of US immigration laws to fit with the country's labor needs and migrant flows can be explained by a profit motive. Employers naturally gain from their capacity to underpay migrant workers. At the same time, however, the receiving state itself does not have to provide low-skilled Latino/a/x migrants with the package of rights and protections that citizens would typically be entitled to, such as access to public pension and social welfare programs. As a result, labor in essential industries like caregiving and fruit-picking is much cheaper for the receiving state than it would be if low-skilled Latino/a/x migrants were granted those rights. This bears a striking resemblance to colonizing powers' racial exploitation of colonial subjects, whose provision of cheap labor was vital to the wealth and success of colonizing powers.

But the racial exploitation of low-skilled Latino/a/x goes beyond their provision of cheap essential labor. Consider, also, the growth of the immigration industrial complex, which refers to the "confluence of public and private sector interests in the criminalization of undocumented migration, immigration law enforcement, and the promotion of 'anti-illegal' rhetoric" (Golash-Boza 2009). Here, we see another answer to the question of why the United States chooses to restrict low-skilled migration despite existing labor demands; namely that the United States also profits tremendously from the *enforcement* of immigration laws against low-skilled migrants. Since 2006, the United States' policy toward apprehended unauthorized migrants has been to "catch and detain" them (Douglas and Sáenz 206, 2013). Recently, detention centers have come under fire for their uninhabitable living conditions, coupled with the separation of immigrant children from their parents. While it is not clear that detention has successfully lowered the rate of unauthorized migration, it has other upsides: it offers private prison entrepreneurs an optimal growth market (Douglas and Sáenz 2013, 208) and creates more jobs in public agencies. As of fiscal year 2019, the budget for

ICE grew to $6.7 billion, with most of the funding going to detention centers around the country. At the same time, the number of government-employed agents tasked with apprehending, removing, and prosecuting unauthorized migrants has skyrocketed (American Immigration Council 2014). For example, since 1993, the number of US Border Patrol agents has grown from 4,139 agents to 23,645 (American Immigration Council 2014).

On the whole, in order to refrain from perpetrating colonial injustice in the present day through their racial exploitation of low-skilled Latino/a/x migrants, the United States' skill-selective immigration policies stand in need of serious reform. Put differently, the United States can perpetuate colonial injustice against Latino/a/x migrants in the present day even though it was not responsible for colonizing their countries of origin in the past. To "decolonize" its immigration policy, the United States should lift quotas on the flow of low-skilled migrants from sending states like Mexico, El Salvador, Guatemala, and Honduras. Naturally, this should be accompanied by freeing the undocumented migrants who remain imprisoned in detention centers, reuniting parents and children who have been separated, and giving undocumented migrants a definite path to legal residency. For the purposes of my chapter, however, I focus on the lifting of quotas on low-skilled migration from particular regions that supply the United States with essential labor.

Before responding to objections in the next section, I want to make three important clarifications. First of all, again, I am not necessarily arguing for a system of open borders. It would be consistent with my claims to hold that states may exclude migrants for other reasons (e.g., quotas on highly skilled workers who originate from other parts of the global north), or even to have a system of preference for family members of existing citizens/residents. As far as *decolonial justice* goes, however, it is clear that the United States' ongoing policy of excluding low-skilled migrants wrongfully perpetuates racial exploitation. Secondly, although I have focused particularly on the plight of low-skilled Latino/a/x migrants in the United States, I do not mean to suggest that other groups in other wealthy countries cannot also be the targets of ongoing racial exploitation. Thirdly, my intention is not to blame skill-selective immigration policy *alone* for the racial exploitation I have identified. Rather, as I have explained, skill-selective immigration policies *coordinate* and *combine* with punitive enforcement mechanisms to uphold racial exploitation. It must be noted, however, that the state's purported right to control the skill levels of its migrant population is currently a major component of the public justification for heavy-handed immigration enforcement.

4. Objections

a. Overinclusion

One objection to the above claim is that my definition of colonial injustice is overly broad. There are other instances of racial exploitation that we would not ordinarily describe as "colonial injustice." Take, for example, the past and present racial exploitation of African Americans in the United States. This includes (but is not limited to) over two hundred years of slavery, as well as the ongoing phenomenon of mass incarceration, which enables public and private actors to profit from their large-scale imprisonment. In fact, the country's ability to profit from mass incarceration seems to have served as the model for immigrant detention. If African Americans are not appropriately understood as the victims of *colonial* injustice, perhaps the distinctive wrong of colonialism is not actually captured in racial exploitation. An account of colonial injustice like Lea Ypi's (2013), which mainly locates the wrong of colonialism in unequal and nonreciprocal interactions between political cooperatives, would neatly exclude slavery and mass incarceration from the category. If skill-selective immigration policies perpetrate colonial injustice at all, it would have to be for a different reason.

On one possible view, assuming that the relevant political collective is the state, the racial exploitation of fellow citizens, who are members of the same political collective, will not count as "colonial." This doesn't mean that the racial exploitation of fellow citizens is *less bad*; it is just a different kind of injustice. That said, it is not always possible to draw a sharp boundary between those who are "internal" or "external" to the collective. An individual can be formally included as a member, but nevertheless be persistently treated as alien or other. Although immigration enforcement is supposed to target low-skilled noncitizens, it also directly affects Latino/a/x citizens who are coded as "socially undocumented." In such cases, I think it makes sense to say that a state has adopted a colonial attitude toward people who are its own citizens because it treats them as economically exploitable racial inferiors. If, as Robert Blauner has suggested, white-Black relations in the United States are "those of colonizer and colonized" (1969), there doesn't have to be a contradiction in the claim that a state has subjected some of its own citizens to colonial injustice.

For this reason, it is not necessarily a sign of weakness that my definition of colonial injustice implicates relations of racial exploitation between fellow citizens, even if the conclusion may seem counterintuitive at first blush. On an ameliorative view of language, such as the one espoused by Sally Haslanger (2005), the conceptual definition we should adopt is the one that would be most effective in achieving a set of goals. If the overarching goal is to end racial exploitation, it is most helpful to think of *internal* racial exploitation as not fundamentally different in kind to *external* racial exploitation, but conterminous with it. This is consistent with how many instances of *internal* racial exploitation, such as slavery in the United States, originate from colonial modes of organization. Although we can expect racially exploitative practices to evolve over time and take on a localized character, we should expect some degree of "coloniality," which constructs nonwhites as the biological and structural inferiors of whites (Quijano 2000, 171), to be inherent in most (if not all) instances of racial exploitation.

b. Lack of feasibility

A second objection is that, even granted the commitment to decolonial justice, it is simply not *practically feasible* to expect states to dismantle their skill-selective practices and implement a system of open borders. Decolonial justice cannot be pursued at all costs—it is simply one consideration among many, and we must not neglect competing considerations. Under nonideal conditions, a policy of open borders would be too difficult for states to undertake without fervent opposition.

This objection assumes that, for a philosophical argument to be plausible, it must contain proposals that can be implemented in society with ease. However, this seems false. We can distinguish between theories that are intended to serve as a yardstick for measuring how much a society is failing in comparison to a fully ideal one, and others that are trying to design prescriptions that are likely to be effective given feasibility constraints (Valentini 2012, 8). Performing a diagnosis of how a society is currently failing does not necessarily require us to make effective proposals for changing it. We can also distinguish between theories that set out a long-term goal for institutional reform, in comparison to theories that explore how this long-term goal may be gradually achieved in incremental steps (8). In many cases, the long-term goal may appear out of reach simply because we are constrained by unjust circumstances that *could* be changed, if only we are willing to try.

Secondly, I am skeptical of any tendency to dismiss arguments simply because they do not offer up obviously "feasible" solutions, particularly when applied to the issue of low-skilled immigration. As I have emphasized in Chapter One, attention to the nonideal and engagement with political realities does not mean throwing out ideals altogether. In this case, while feasibility can refer to the likelihood that a particular policy will be implemented in the here and now, it can also refer to the effectiveness or success of the current policy *itself*. I assume that a policy is not "feasible" when it fails to accomplish its stated goals or can only do so with very harmful consequences for certain groups. Focusing on the second sense of feasibility, it is odd that the opponent of racially exploitative immigration policies is under a disproportionate burden to prove that their claims are "feasible" when the *existing policies themselves* are not "working" in accordance with how they have been justified to the public. For example, rather than effectively preventing the entry of low-skilled migrants, we have seen that the United States' policy of skill-selective immigration has instead created serious social problems, including labor shortages, a large underclass of undocumented workers who must resort to extreme measures to minimally function in a society that needs them, and a glut of immigration detainees who are presently enduring horrific conditions.[13] Our theorizing about immigration justice must be anchored in *this* reality. If anything, it is perhaps more "practical" and "feasible" to acknowledge that states' present-day exercise of their right to exclude has generally failed to deter entry, while simultaneously leading to extremely negative consequences for migrants *and* host societies.

c. Nonexploitative skill-selective immigration policy?

A final rejoinder may be that skill-selective immigration practices that prefer highly skilled migrants over low-skilled migrants can be kept mostly intact while taking care to remove the core elements that perpetrate racial exploitation. Guest worker programs could undergo a series of reforms that entitle guest workers to a much larger bundle of rights. Guest workers could be eligible for citizenship after a minimum period of residence. They could also be granted full access to the labor market, so that their right to stay does not depend on the will of their employers. Similarly, immigration enforcement could be significantly relaxed. While the use of force (such as through detention and deportation) could be reserved for a far smaller class of unauthorized migrants, like those who have committed serious crimes, instead of targeting low-skilled migrants as a whole. If these changes were implemented, the racial exploitation of low-skilled migrants might be dramatically reduced. All things considered, it may not be necessary to change the underlying structure of skill-based discrimination by admitting more low-skilled migrants.

This perspective sounds appealing at first blush. However, it faces a serious dilemma. On one horn of the dilemma, the restrictions on low-skilled migrants are so permissive as to be trivially different from my proposal that we lift restrictions on low-skilled migrants entirely. The freedom of low-skilled migrants to enter the United States does not mean the automatic granting of citizenship or a completely unregulated system of entry, but it *does* at the very least bestow upon migrants the legal right to enter the country in search of work, and in turn, the right to be protected from demeaning enforcement policies. At the same time, neither does the freedom of movement mean that genuinely dangerous noncitizens cannot, by definition, be banned from the territory. The difference between "unrestricted low-skilled migration" and "substantially reformed immigration restrictions on low-skilled immigration," then, seems to be merely semantic.

Against this, it might be argued that reformed skill-selective immigration policies would, in practice, *still* be substantially different from lifting quotas on low-skilled migrants. Even if low-skilled migrants are granted more favorable terms of residence, they would still need to apply for approval in order to legally enter. Furthermore, unauthorized migration could still remain a civil offense that would (at least in some cases) warrant removal from the territory. Unfortunately, on the other horn of the dilemma, continuing to uphold skill-selective immigration policies in this fashion would threaten to perpetrate the same forms of racial exploitation that we are worried about. It is very likely that the number of persons who are legally granted entry would still be significantly smaller than the number of persons who wish to migrate. This numerical gap leaves room for a sizable class of undocumented migrants who are particularly vulnerable to racial exploitation and its related harms. Relatedly, so long as noncitizens lack the right to enter, the state is permitted to *use force against them.* It is difficult to see how undocumented migrants could be removed at all without engaging in the same old practices of detention or deportation, which would still be rife with the possibility of abuse. One alternative would be for states to focus on regulating immigration through "soft," rather than "hard" measures. For example, instead of relying on detention and deportation, states could use financial incentives to persuade unauthorized migrants to leave, but the choice would ultimately lie with the migrants themselves. Importantly, however, the use of "soft" power is prima facie compatible with lifting quotas on certain low-skilled migrants—and so we return to the first horn of the dilemma, according to which the defender of skill-based selection is not actually suggesting anything meaningfully different from what I have proposed.

5. Conclusion

In the last four chapters, I have tried to show that there are at least two principled reasons for states to reform existing skill-selective immigration policies, rather than simply taking them as a desirable and legitimate component of states' right to exclude. Both these reasons are undergirded by the value and importance of preserving equal relationships between citizens and noncitizens. Chapter Three and Four appealed to the presumptive shared commitment to *antidiscrimination norms.* Given the expressive and disparate harms of skill-based selection, we ought to treat it as a form of wrongful discrimination, which states ought not to engage in. This chapter built a complementary case against skill-based selection. If—as I have claimed—it is true that colonial injustice has often manifested itself in the form of racial exploitation, the pursuit of decolonial justice would require us to refrain from engaging in similar practices. Skill-selective immigration policies, as they stand in the here and now, clearly constitute a set of racially exploitative practices. At least in the US context (and perhaps in a host of other wealthy Western countries), the commitment to decolonial justice would also require us to rethink states' right to select highly skilled migrants over lower-skilled ones.

In the final chapter, I proceed with a somewhat different aim in mind. Suppose that I am correct that current immigration policy is deeply unjust, and also about what states ought to do to remedy the injustice. We do know, however, that it is very unlikely for states to reverse their stance on skilled migration anytime soon, the same way that other kinds of injustice do not simply go away overnight. How should migrants and would-be migrants respond in the meantime, as persons who are routinely subject to unjust immigration law? Must they continue to respect immigration laws that are, as I have argued, wrongfully discriminatory and colonial in character, or do they have the right to disobey them? As we will see in Chapter Six, we can make the philosophical case for would-be migrants' right to disobey.

6
Migratorial Disobedience and Immigration Justice

1. Introduction

We have established that at least some immigration laws, as they stand in the real world, are unjust. Often, they are unjust by dint of their tendency to worsen social inequality between citizens and noncitizens. Are migrants obliged to obey such laws? Despite widespread "migratorial disobedience" by individual and collective agents (e.g., the "migrant van" from Central America that intends to enter US territory)[1] this question has received relatively scant philosophical attention. This final chapter aims to further the philosophical discussion about migratorial disobedience by primarily addressing and building on two established views. Javier Hidalgo has proposed that individual migrants may permissibly disobey unjust immigration laws in order to protect themselves against threats to their basic rights. For example, a refugee may evade, deceive, or even use force against government agents in order to enter the receiving state (Hidalgo 2015, 451). Individual migrants who face such threats, then, have no moral duty to obey unjust immigration laws. I call this the permissive view of migratorial disobedience. In contrast, Caleb Yong argues that such disobedience is permissible only if the laws in question are *egregiously* unjust.[2] Immigration laws meet the threshold for egregious injustice when they directly violate the human rights of noncitizens or allow states to shirk their required share of the international responsibility for noncitizens' human rights (Yong 2018, 470). In this way, migrants can still have moral duties to obey unjust immigration laws. I call this the restrictive view of migratorial disobedience. Against the restrictive view, I contend that migrants may permissibly disobey a much wider range of unjust immigration laws than his account suggests. Firstly, structurally unjust immigration laws may *indirectly* violate human rights,

Immigration and Social Equality. Désirée Lim, Oxford University Press. © Oxford University Press 2023.
DOI: 10.1093/oso/9780197658093.003.0007

and we should object to them on that basis. At the same time, even if immigration restrictions fall short of indirectly violating human rights, the large-scale social subordination of low-skilled migrants may render migratorial disobedience *morally desirable*, not just permissible. On my view, the desirability of such disobedience is located in the politically transformative role of principled disobedience, which refers to "politically or morally motivated resorts to illegality in the opposition or refusal to conform to the system's dominant norms" (Delmas 42, 2018).[3] The view I defend can be understood as a version of the permissive view that complements Hidalgo's robust defense of migrants' individual rights.

In Section 2, I contextualize my claims by differentiating between the permissive and restrictive views on migratorial disobedience. Section 3 argues that many immigration laws can be egregiously unjust and therefore render migratorial disobedience permissible even if they do not directly violate human rights, due to their contributions to global structural injustice. Section 4 builds on this claim by suggesting that, under present circumstances, civil *and* uncivil forms of migratorial disobedience can be justified. They are vital to overcoming democratic deficits in immigration policymaking and ultimately paving the way for immigration justice. I make my argument by drawing on Candice Delmas's more inclusive account of "principled disobedience" (2018, 22), in contrast to traditional accounts of civil disobedience. I conclude in Section 5.

2. Permissive and restrictive views of migratorial disobedience

a. The permissive view of migratorial disobedience

On what I will term the "permissive view" of migratorial disobedience, migrants may permissibly engage in acts of disobedience if the receiving state's immigration laws in question are unjust. Hidalgo's account of permissible migratorial disobedience is a novel example of a permissive view, and I seek to reconstruct it in this section. Significantly, Hidalgo begins by proposing a "minimal standard" for immigration justice: namely, that states act unjustly when they refuse to admit prospective migrants whose human rights would go unprotected or be violated as a result of exclusion, and when admitting those migrants would *not* impose "significant net burdens" on the citizens of the state in question (Hidalgo 2015, 453). In short, if immigration laws fall short of the minimal standard, Hidalgo thinks that noncitizens may permissibly disobey them.

Supposing that immigration laws are unjust, what are some permissible forms of disobedience? Hidalgo offers three important suggestions (2015, 456–457). Firstly, noncitizens may permissibly *evade* border agents; for example, by cutting through border fences in an unguarded location. Secondly, they may permissibly *deceive* border agents, such as through the falsification of immigration documents. Thirdly, noncitizens may even be permitted to use defensive force against border agents, such as throwing rocks at border agents who would otherwise capture them—even if it risks lethal injury. The reasoning behind these claims is fairly straightforward. It has far less to do with immigration law itself, or noncitizens' relationships to state authority, than with basic relations between individual moral agents. Hidalgo attempts to justify his stance on migratorial disobedience by appealing to smaller-scale cases, where it seems permissible for individuals to resist the force of agents who unjustly threaten to violate their basic rights. This includes *direct threats* (e.g., if someone attempts to punch you or push you off a ledge), as well as *indirect threats* (e.g., if they expose you to a threat by forcibly preventing you from moving to a place of refuge). It is the latter case, in particular, that illustrates the moral relationship between border agents and immigrants. After all, if the agents are attempting to enforce laws that fall short of the "minimal standard," they are threatening to indirectly cause serious harm to migrants. In turn, migrants are permitted to resist the unjust threat that border agents pose.

b. The restrictive view of migratorial disobedience

On what I will call "restrictive views" of migratorial disobedience, however, migrants may not permissibly disobey unjust immigration laws, unless those laws can be shown to be *especially* unjust. This perspective is nicely captured in Yong's response to Hidalgo. To be sure, Yong evinces a similar view to Hidalgo about the "minimal standard" for unjust immigration laws. He states that "there is no conclusive duty to comply with gravely or egregiously unjust laws—laws whose injustice exceeds a certain threshold of seriousness—whatever the procedural source of those laws in question" (2018, 454–455). Furthermore, he clarifies that "egregiously unjust laws" are those that "directly violate the human rights of non-members, or even to decisions that shirk [a state's] required share of the international responsibility to act in defense of all individuals' human rights when their own states are unable or unwilling to extend adequate protection" (470). In this sense, Yong and Hidalgo seem to agree about the type of injustice that would permit migratorial disobedience. On both accounts, noncitizens may permissibly refuse to comply with an immigration law that would violate their human rights.

Recall, however, that Hidalgo's defense of permissible resistance largely relies on an individualistic view about the right to self-defense. I cannot be under a duty *to not resist you* if you pose an unjust threat to me. For Hidalgo, the case of the immigrant evading detection by border agents is analogous to that of an individual evading detection by another person who wishes harm upon them without justification. This is where Yong begs to differ. On his view, the relationship between *noncitizens* and a *state* (that presumably has the right to exclude) is not the same as that between two individuals; it is *political*, not straightforwardly interpersonal. That is, we must take into account the possibility that a "constitutional democracy's regime of primary immigration law has legitimate authority"—legitimate authority that would place noncitizens under a moral duty to obey it (Yong 2018, 464). The person facing an unjust threat from another individual agent has no analogous duty to obey them.

Importantly, there are unjust immigration laws that do not meet the threshold for moral egregiousness. They fall within the scope of injustice (e.g., because they are arbitrary, dominating, or unfair) but do not go as far as to violate human rights or allow states to shirk their duties to protect vulnerable noncitizens. Yong holds that, despite the injustice of such laws, the state's regime of primary immigration law must be evaluated *as a whole*. If the state's "procedures for enacting and applying primary immigration law satisfy the relevant conditions for (the outcomes of) such procedures to have legitimate authority over would-be migrants," migrants are obliged to comply *even if* it is true that particular laws are unjust (Yong 2018, 464).[4] The law's legitimate authority is only defeated, and noncitizens are subsequently released from their political obligations, when the regime contains laws that are *egregiously unjust*. Noncitizens are certainly not obliged to obey rights-violating immigration laws (e.g., a policy of shooting all unauthorized migrants on sight). On the other hand, suppose that a state unjustly denies long-term denizens the right to citizenship and restricts their ability to share in social welfare programs.[5] Taken on its own, this injustice *does not* permit migratorial disobedience if the regime of law is *overall* legitimate.

Yong's view raises an interesting puzzle. What, exactly, is the source of noncitizens' duty to obey the law of foreign states, given that political obligations are normally grounded in considerations that generally apply only to citizens (e.g., fair play or associative obligations)? In response, Yong suggests that we should understand "internationally legitimate" states as having a certain moral standing with regard to the rest of international society; that is, other states and their individual members (2018, 466–467). In particular, states have a *right to political independence* that "protects the rightholder state's capacity to independently formulate and implement laws and policies in central and morally acceptable domains of domestic policymaking" (467).[6] Other states and their members are bound to respect the right to political independence. They have a duty not to interfere in the right-holder state's domestic governance, regardless of the moral merits or demerits of the specific policies that the state may choose to implement (467). It follows that legitimate states can have a *right to be obeyed* even vis-à-vis laws that are unjust. This applies to immigration law particularly because of the significant impact that immigration can have on the state. As Yong writes, "[i]mmigration, especially on a large scale, will typically have a substantial impact on various aspects of the receiving state's economy and society that the state's domestic policies might reasonably seek to regulate" (467). For instance, the rate of immigration and the skill composition of migrants have a tendency to affect other domestic outcomes like the "domestic labor market, the rate of labor productivity, levels of expenditure on social services and the welfare state," etc. (467). In other words, given the serious consequences that immigration can have for the state's future interests and prospects, it may be important for noncitizens to respect the state's legitimate authority in this regard. To be sure, I don't take Yong to be arguing that states have *a right to perpetrate injustice*; this view seems implausible. Rather, their international legitimacy has authority over the actions of noncitizens *in spite* of the injustice they may perpetrate—at least to some degree. To sum up, by disobeying immigration laws, noncitizens impermissibly *interfere* with the state's domestic governance. Consequently, disobedience can be impermissible even if the relevant immigration law is unjust.

All in all, I think that Yong identifies a potential limitation of Hidalgo's individualistic justification of migratorial disobedience. Chiefly, it oversimplifies the relationship that holds between states and migrants by abstracting away from the political relationship between migrants and the receiving state, and by extension, the duties that migrants may have to obey immigration law. Assuming that noncitizens do indeed have a general duty to obey the laws of other states, it is not possible to make a case for migrants' disobedience without explicitly addressing the moral significance of political legitimacy and the duties it may impose on noncitizens.

3. Human rights and global structural injustice

Despite the strength of Yong's objections, this chapter argues that the permissive view on migratorial disobedience can be sustained through an additional justification. Beyond individual migrants' right to resist unjust threats (as Hidalgo suggests), I propose that migratorial disobedience has a crucial role to play in the large-scale political transformation of egregiously unjust immigration laws. First of all, I establish that Yong's definition of "egregious injustice" does not pay enough attention to global structural injustice and the egregiously unjust consequences it may *indirectly* generate. Recall that Yong only gives room for disobeying laws that *directly* violate human rights, or allow states to shirk their international responsibility to refugees. Yet a significant slice of egregious immigration injustice is *structural* in origin; it cannot be traced back to a single egregiously unjust law. Many migrants suffer human rights violations, or fail to have their human rights protected, through the synchronous enforcement of *multiple* laws, many of which would not be egregiously unjust in themselves. For this reason, it is not tenable to uphold the distinction between direct and indirect human rights violations. As matters stand in the nonideal world, many immigration laws that seem prima facie "neutral" or "reasonable" have the indirect effect of violating would-be migrants' human rights, and can therefore be appropriately characterized as contributing to egregious injustice. For this reason, a much wider range of immigration laws ought to be regarded as egregiously unjust, and it is permissible for migrants to disobey them.

Before I proceed, it's worth mentioning a third account of migratorial disobedience that shares similarities to my own, but nonetheless arrives at a different conclusion. Like Yong, Michael Blake acknowledges that migrants have no duty to obey immigration laws that lead to the violation of human rights. A hypothetical migrant who is subject to human rights violations in his country of origin, and has the capacity to cross the border into a rights-protecting country, has no moral duty to obey immigration laws in said country that forbid him from doing so (Blake 2020, 174). Blake's moral threshold for migratorial disobedience is considerably higher than Yong's; he accepts that migrants may also have no duty to obey exclusionary immigration laws if they are subjected to what he calls "mere tyranny" in their countries of origin—tyranny that doesn't necessarily constitute a violation of human rights. Despite these exceptions to the rule, Blake argues that impoverished migrants remain under a moral duty to obey immigration laws that exclude them from entry (176). That is, "economic migrants" from the global south who migrate to radically improve their standard of living can be correctly understood as failing to discharge a moral duty to obey the law. Unlike human rights violations and denials of basic democratic rights, global poverty and inequality are insufficient to defeat one's duty to comply with immigration laws. I will push against this view by arguing that, under certain conditions, economic migrants have no duty to obey immigration laws. All the same, I believe that Blake makes a crucial point—one that is often lost on defenders of restrictive border regimes. As he goes on to argue, the fact a migrant has failed to perform their moral duty to obey immigration laws does not mean that they should be morally blamed or condemned, or otherwise subject to negative appraisals of their moral character (180). This is because the personal costs of complying with one's moral duties can be high enough that our noncompliance is "comprehensible and predictable" (182). In Blake's words, "[w]e cannot mark others out as uniquely immoral, when their crime is one that we would expect ourselves to do, were we in their shoes" (182). An impoverished migrant's decision to disobey immigration laws to dramatically improve her life-prospects *does* violate her moral duty to obey them, but it does not make her deserving of the moral resentment that is often publicly expressed toward unauthorized migrants. We do not need to deny the existence of a moral duty, in order to hold that a person can have quite understandably and sympathetically violated it. However, I wish to go further than Blake. As I'll show, some "economic migrants" who disobey immigration laws are not just inappropriate targets of moral condemnation; they also lack moral duties to comply with such laws.

a. The egregiousness of structural injustice

At this stage, another important issue must be clarified. Specifically, it is not clear why we should assume that only *egregious injustice*, interpreted by Yong as the direct violation of human rights, can defeat noncitizens' duties to obey immigration law. To give some additional context to the discussion: disobedience has been interpreted as part and parcel of our natural duties of justice; that is, our duties to "support and comply with just institutions that exist and apply to us," as well as to "further just arrangements not yet established, at least when this can be done without too much cost to ourselves" (Rawls 1999a, 99). When "just arrangements" are indeed not yet established, as in the case of immigration justice, our natural duties of justice may permit us to disobey the law. Note, here, that it is not necessarily required that the injustice be *egregious* in the sense that it violates human rights, in order for disobedience to be justified. For example, in *A Theory of Justice*, John Rawls notes that certain modes of disobedience may be apt "in the special case of a nearly just society, one that is well-ordered for the most part but in which *some serious violations of justice* nevertheless do occur" (1999a, 319). While it is not specified what we should take to be a "serious violation of justice," Rawls does give us a sense of the contours of such violations. Earlier in the text, he states that "[w]hether noncompliance is justified depends on the extent to which laws and institutions are unjust" (309). Here, injustice may take either take the form of current arrangements departing in various degrees from publicly shared standards that are "more or less just," *or* the publicly shared standards may *themselves* be unjust because they conform to an unreasonable or otherwise poor notion of what justice is (309). Nonetheless, again, Rawls remains vague on *which departures from public standards of justice* or *which deficient standards of justice* amount to "serious injustice." This leaves open the possibility that certain kinds of immigration injustice can be serious enough to warrant migratorial disobedience even if they do not directly violate human rights.

Let's suppose, however, that Yong is right and that only egregious injustice (i.e., direct violations of human rights) can justify migratorial disobedience. It remains clear, nonetheless, that many immigration laws today are not only unjust but *egregiously* so. As I have already referenced in earlier chapters, controversy in the United States has erupted over the family separation of unauthorized migrants, and the subsequent holding of migrant children in detention centers, including those as young as five months old. Immigration detention centers, it has been said, should be recognized as "concentration camps." According to eyewitness accounts, conditions in detention centers are intolerable: they are overcrowded, unsanitary, and deny migrants basic necessities like food, water, clothing, and medical care.[7] In some cases, children have reportedly been held in fenced cages. It is clear that these immigration policies violate basic human rights that are recognized in the Universal Declaration of Human Rights, such as the "right to a standard of living adequate for the health and well-being of himself and of his family, including food, clothing, housing and medical care and necessary social services," as well as "special care and assistance" for mothers and children, which citizens are clearly entitled to. It is equally true that, under ideal conditions, other immigration laws *indirectly* bring about violations of human rights. To explain this, I reflect closely on two real-world cases. Philosophers have thought up colorful hypothetical examples of rights-violating immigration laws, such as an immigration law that immediately consigns all the immigrants who arrive to rat-infested dungeons (Miller 2017, 14). Yet it should not surprise us that present-day immigration laws, including those with a seemingly rational justification or purpose, have had egregiously rights-violating consequences.

I begin with the deaths of Óscar Alberto Martínez Ramírez and his daughter Valeria, who was nearly two years old. Originally from El Salvador, Martínez and his family had intended to seek asylum in the United States at the US-Mexico border. Due to the state's relatively new policy of "metering," which limits the number of people who can apply for asylum each day, they were turned away without any indication of how long it would take for their applications to be processed. As one journalist writes, asylum seekers end up waiting "for days or weeks or (increasingly) months: sometimes in migrant shelters whose capacity has stretched to the breaking point, sometimes huddling together on bridges, sleeping on the street, in the cold, vulnerable to the violence they hoped to escape in their home countries" (Lind 2018). To avoid this, Martínez swam across the Rio Grande with Valeria in order to apply for asylum in Brownsville, Texas, and went back to help his wife. Valeria did not understand that she was meant to wait at the riverbank for her father to return and followed him back into the Rio Grande. In the end, both of them drowned. A skeptic might argue that they were not killed by metering *itself*, but a rash decision that Martínez had willfully undertaken. He could have *chosen* not to jump into the river. Taking the circumstances into account, however, it is clear that Martínez and Valeria's lives were not lost because of a capricious or foolish decision, but one that seemed entirely reasonable considering the limited options that were available to them. As their limited options were essentially shaped by the metering policy, alongside other failures of the immigration system, it is wholly appropriate to think of their deaths as *egregiously unjust*.

Next, consider the case of Sangarapillai Balachandran, an Australian citizen of Sri Lankan Tamil origin who faced deportation from the United Kingdom (Taylor 2018). Balachandran, a highly specialized engineer, was headhunted by a British company in 2007 and moved to the United Kingdom with his family members. However, when Balachandran's work visa expired, the Home Office refused his family indefinite leave to remain (permanent residency), and everyone lost their permission to work and study in the United Kingdom as a result, even though Balachandran's son had been given a place in university and his daughter offered a job in the civil service. Although the family agreed to be repatriated to Australia, they were unable to fly because of Balachandran's health issues. Balachandran suffered three increasingly serious strokes over a period of six years, reportedly occurring during periods of stress in his dealings with the Home Office over his family's right to remain, and continues to suffer from high blood pressure. The Home Office has insisted he is fit enough to fly back to Australia, but the family maintains that his health is concerning enough that the Home Office has asked for four medics to accompany him on the flight. Unlike Martínez and Valeria, Balachandran and his family are not asylum seekers, and it is likely that he has not been categorized as a low-skilled migrant in the way that Martínez may have been—they moved to the United Kingdom for economic reasons and it seems unlikely that their human rights would be endangered if they returned to Australia. At the same time, the family have become homeless and destitute because they have used up all their savings after being denied the right to work, to the point that they asked the Home Office to lock them up in detention so they would not have to live on the streets. It is *also* appropriate, I think, to judge that Balachandran suffered egregious injustice as a result of British immigration laws.

To reiterate, the above outcomes did not directly result from any single law that is *in itself* egregiously unjust. There is no immigration law commanding that unauthorized migrants must be forcibly kept out or removed even at the cost of their lives. Nevertheless, we can agree that Martínez and Balachandran's treatment under the immigration system was egregiously unjust. I want to argue that many migrants suffer similarly egregiously unjust outcomes as the result of *global structural injustice.* These outcomes are intimately linked to the routine social subordination of low-skilled migrants that I have discussed in earlier chapters. In order to properly evaluate whether they are just, we cannot look at individual immigration laws in isolation. Rather, we need to see how they operate together in concert, as well as how they interact with the real-world circumstances that migration occurs within.

To understand this claim, it is helpful to look to a definition of global structural injustice. According to Iris Marion Young's influential view, the social structure "consists in the connections among the positions [that people stand in relation to each other] and their relationships, and the way the attributes of positions internally constitute one another through those relationships" (Young 2006, 112). To be sure, social structures are actively upheld by social actors in ongoing processes of reinforcement; they "exist only in the action and interaction of persons" (5). Following this view, we may say that structural injustice occurs when unjust outcomes are produced through the actions of multitudes behaving in accordance with accepted social norms and rules, resulting in outcomes that enable some while constraining others (5). Notably, structural injustice can occur *across borders.* In Young's words, "[s]ome structural social processes are global in scope and condition the lives of many people within diverse nation-state jurisdictions" (Young 2011, 125). What implications, then, does this have for border controls? Here, I want to suggest that immigration policymakers must take into account the preexisting unjust structures inside *and* outside of the state that may operate *in conjunction with* seemingly justifiable immigration laws to produce egregious injustice. Although this demand might sound very burdensome at first glance, there is already a general expectation that policymakers must to be sensitive to unjust social structures that may surround the implementation of a particular law or rule.[8]

At this point, it might be objected that, although policymakers may indeed be obliged to avoid perpetuating structural injustice within the domestic sphere, no such duty exists with regard to the *global* sphere, simply because it asks for too much. Arguably, global structural justice is so pervasive that it would be very difficult for a state to avoid worsening *some* form of structural injustice that is currently experienced by citizens of other countries. For example, the imposition of trade tariffs on a neighboring state, for the purposes of protecting local manufacturers, may worsen the living conditions of citizens who are *already* badly off as a result of unjust structural processes. Yet we don't believe it is *necessarily* wrong to impose such tariffs, which are a commonplace feature of global economic policy. I agree that the above objection has some force. However, we need to remember that we are talking about *egregious* injustice. While it may be tricky for a state to avoid perpetuating structural injustice altogether, the imposition of egregious injustice—that is, injustice that involves violations of human rights—is a different story. Suppose we learn that the imposition of a particular tariff would immediately plunge some citizens below the poverty line, effectively violating their human right to an adequate standard of living. In this case, the violation of human rights means that the original state in question has perpetrated *egregious structural injustice.*

On the whole, although states may have a duty to refrain from perpetrating structural injustice suffered by their citizens, they have a somewhat less demanding, but equally serious duty to refrain from perpetrating *egregious structural injustice* against citizens. Naturally, a state may be constrained by epistemic considerations. In some cases, it may be true that policymakers simply could not foresee that their decision would cause egregious structural injustice. In some other cases, it may simply be that the state cannot *avoid* doing so, because there are no reasonable alternatives that can be pursued without bringing about *even more* egregious injustice. Yet the egregious structural injustice suffered by migrants like Martínez and Balachandran does not fall into either category. We *know* that, combined with surrounding unjust structures, the border policies that led to Martínez's death and threatened Balachandran's life have egregiously unjust consequences that play out over and over again. At the same time, those border policies are certainly *avoidable.* An opponent may argue that abandoning harsh border control measures would result in worse forms of egregious injustice for citizens. However, it is not obvious what those forms of injustice would be.

Up to this point, I have suggested that some aspects of immigration law, as it is currently practiced, are already egregiously unjust. More specifically, laws that may seem neutral or rational in their goals create egregiously unjust scenarios for migrants when they interact with *one another*, as well as the underlying social structures that surround them. If global structural injustice *indirectly* threatens would-be migrants' human rights, or is exploited by states to shirk their share of human rights protection,[9] the overall legitimacy of the receiving state's law is defeated. For adherents of the "restrictive view," present-day global structural injustice ought to be sufficiently egregious as to permit migrants' disobedience.

4. Justice and migratorial disobedience

I have assumed, in the previous section, that many immigration laws are egregiously unjust even if they do not "directly" violate citizens' human rights or allow states to shirk their fair share of human rights protection. If this is true, as matters stand in the real world, it seems that many migrants (including persons in situations similar to that of Óscar Martínez and Sangarapillai Balachandran) may permissibly disobey immigration laws. However, it is far too quick to jump to the conclusion that migratorial disobedience in the sense that Hidalgo defends would be permissible. As it has been widely noted, our natural duties of justice do not give us carte blanche to disobey unjust laws in any manner we desire. Two familiar objections to disobedience roughly go like this: Firstly, there may be limitations on the *type* of disobedience that is morally permissible. In particular, acts of disobedience may only be permissible if they are performed by citizens in public settings, with the sole purpose of communicating the fact of injustice to fellow citizens. In other words, perhaps only *civil disobedience* can be justified. Secondly, disobedience can risk *worsening* injustice. It may be better for citizens to *generally* comply with immigration laws, rather than risk the injustice that may inadvertently arise from disobedience.

At first glance, both these claims appear to pose problems for migratorial disobedience. However, I think that these objections can be overcome, and the remainder of my chapter attends to this task. In this section, I argue that migratorial disobedience is not only a legitimate form of principled disobedience; it is also deeply valuable from the standpoint of justice. As I show, migratorial disobedience has comprised civil *and* uncivil disobedience with the capacity to correct "democratic deficits" in receiving states.[10] While civil disobedience by certain migrants has gained some degree of mainstream acceptance and recognition, the issue of "uncivil disobedience" by migrants remains much more contentious. Indeed, conflicting attitudes toward "uncivil disobedience" by migrants lies at the root of Hidalgo and Yong's disagreement. First, following Delmas, I distinguish between civil and uncivil disobedience, agreeing with her that uncivil disobedience can be justified as part and parcel of principled disobedience. Secondly, in this vein, I sketch out a positive argument for the value of uncivil migratorial disobedience. Chiefly, even in its uncivil forms, migratorial disobedience provides migrants with a crucial channel for democratic engagement that they would otherwise be denied—a channel that plays a necessary role in advancing immigration justice. As Grant Silva writes, "crossing a border without the permission of the federal government is an act of disobedience and defiance against the racism, jingoism, selfishness, and fundamental injustice at the heart of immigration law" (2019).

a. Civil and uncivil disobedience

Before I proceed, it is necessary to clarify the difference between civil and uncivil disobedience. Generally speaking, the philosophical literature has tended to assume that only civil disobedience can be justified. This has raised the stakes on the question of what ought to count as civil, rather than *un*civil disobedience. Some theorists prefer a narrow conception of civil disobedience. For example, while Yong allows that civil disobedience against egregiously unjust immigration can be justified, his definition of civil disobedience is limited in three ways. Firstly, he restricts the scope of civil disobedience to the activity of citizens, and citizens alone. Noncitizens are altogether excluded from his discussion of civil disobedience. Secondly, he distinguishes between "personal disobedience" and "civil disobedience." According to Yong, civil disobedience is "communicative and political," used to call other citizens' attention to particular unjust aspects of state institutions and to publicly appeal for reform (2018, 479). In contrast, personal disobedience is "essentially a private action"; a personal disobedient may simply be concerned with following the rules of their own conscience without communicating or appealing to her co-citizens (478). Thirdly, Yong worries that civil disobedience risks encouraging others to resort to disobedience in order to achieve whatever changes in law or policy they believe to be justified, consequently undermining the stability of democratic state institutions (480). Therefore, civil disobedience should only be utilized when citizens "have already gone through legal channels of democratic contestation, without success" (480).

Yong's narrow account of civil disobedience resoundingly echoes Rawls's influential view, which stresses that civil disobedience is a public, nonviolent, conscientious yet political breach of law typically done with the aim of bringing about a change in laws or government policies (1999a, 364). Accordingly, acts of disobedience that fail to meet any of these four criteria—because they are "covert, evasive, anonymous, violent, or deliberately offensive" (Delmas 2018, 17)—would be categorized as *uncivil* disobedience that cannot be justified as a response to immigration injustice. Significantly, Yong's and Rawls's views are restrictive enough that familiar forms of disobedience like citizens' covert assistance to undocumented immigrants may not even meet the threshold of civility. Consider the organization called No More Deaths or *No Mas Muertes*, whose volunteers leave food and water for undocumented migrants traveling across the Arizona desert. While the volunteers of this organization are citizens, it is not clear that their actions are intended to publicly convey a political message, nor that they have resorted to assisting undocumented migrants because their legal attempts to change immigration law have failed. Indeed, the reasoning behind assisting undocumented immigrants could be something as personal and private as a "spiritual belief" that one should help others in distress (Matalon 2019). Disobedience that is truly "civil," then, might have to be limited to citizens' public refusal to comply with their legal duties to "monitor, report, and refrain from employing, transporting, or aiding unauthorized immigrants" (Delmas 2018, 94), as a means of changing immigration laws after attempts to go through legal channels have fallen flat.

Significantly, other theorists like Kimberley Brownlee have responded to the narrow view of civil disobedience by arguing to widen its scope. For example, Brownlee has challenged the publicity requirement by noting that that publicity can actually undermine the effectiveness of civil disobedience, often because it gives opponents and legal authorities the chance to stop you (Brownlee 2012, 4). At the same time, disobedience that is covert at first is compatible with public acknowledgment and justification after the fact (4). So, at least some forms of disobedience that are "uncivil" on Yong or Rawls's views might be moved into the "civil" category.

It may be tempting to embrace a broadened view of civil disobedience that would include the covert actions of migrant-related organizations like No More Deaths. However, following Delmas, I think the theoretical disagreement over the best definition of civil and uncivil disobedience can be usefully reframed. One of Delmas's primary hypotheses, which I find persuasive, is that the pressure to differentiate between civil and uncivil disobedience rose out of a historical imperative to defend acts of disobedience against ubiquitous public accusations that disobedience necessarily created the conditions for lawlessness and violence (2018, 24). In order to morally justify disobedience at all, philosophers purposefully drew a sharp line between civil and uncivil disobedience in order to assure detractors that disobedience did not have to take the forms that were generally regarded as threatening and undesirable. Put differently, as the discourse went, there was "good" and "bad" disobedience, and disobedients were placed under a considerable burden of proof to show that they were morally committed to the "good" kind. This burden of proof rendered their political struggles highly vulnerable to being minimized or dismissed because it had slipped into the "uncivil" range. Consequently, Delmas suggests that we should not unquestioningly accept this problematic framework, which we should understand as rising out of public opposition to large-scale social change and the accompanying present-day tendency to lionize the supposed peaceful commitments of particular activists while dismissing others as dangerous or extreme. One apt example is the contrast that is often easily drawn between Martin Luther King Jr. and Malcolm X. The former is often conveniently portrayed as a "good activist" who was exclusively committed to upholding civility, and the latter as a "bad activist" who was willing to unleash mass violence and unrest, when King's decisions (like other civil disobedients) were in fact more likely to have been motivated by strategic considerations than strict moral commitments (Delmas 2018, 27). Rather than attempting to inflate the realm of "civil disobedience" to incorporate previously excluded forms of disobedience that we find to be desirable, it is better to recognize that "uncivil acts of disobedience may preserve justice and democracy just as well as civil disobedience" (10).

To be clear, the implications for our discussion are not that there is no meaningful conceptual difference between civil and uncivil disobedience. The takeaway, here, concerns my argumentative strategy: in my view, it would be unhelpful to devote our energies to defining the boundaries of civility and, from there, arguing that (most) migratorial disobedience is civil. We should simply accept that there are civil and uncivil forms of migratorial disobedience and that it can be helpful to distinguish between the two, *but* to also press the point that uncivil migratorial disobedience can also serve as a justice-correcting measure. I expand on this claim below.

b. Civil and uncivil migratorial disobedience

i. Civil migratorial disobedience

Certain forms of migratorial disobedience fall easily into the "civil" category. Before I continue, more clarity about noncitizens' capacity to engage in civil disobedience is needed. Suppose that we accept that, per Yong's definition, civil disobedience can only be performed by citizens. This would automatically exclude the possibility of noncitizens engaging in civil disobedience from the get-go. However, I think it would be severely mistaken to exclude noncitizens from the sphere of civil disobedience by definition. Let me explain.

Firstly, noncitizens may have compelling reasons to challenge unjust laws, especially when the laws in question *apply directly to them* and subject them to state coercion, or the threat of it.[11] Consider the case of unauthorized denizens, people who live on US territory (many for extended periods of time) without a visa or US citizenship. Matthew Lister notes that, in response to the US Congress's failure to pass the DREAM act, several "DREAMers"—unauthorized migrants who entered the country as children—publicly declared their status and dared the government to take action against them (2018, 15). Apart from being performed by noncitizens, these acts bear close structural similarity to classic civil disobedience. They were performed at public rallies, university- and school-sponsored events whose intention is to draw attention to an egregiously unjust law and force the population to see that the enforcement of current immigration law is morally repugnant (Lister 2018, 16). The fact that these actions were undertaken by *noncitizens* seems like an arbitrary criterion for excluding them from the category of permissible civil disobedience. This is especially significant when their *lack of citizenship* is the relevant injustice that they are protesting. By confining permissible civil disobedience to citizens, and citizens alone, we seal off the possibility that persons might ever be able to protest their unjust denial of citizenship through acts of civil disobedience.

Perhaps, however, restricting the sphere of civil disobedience to citizens is *not* arbitrary. As I have articulated in Section 2, following Yong, perhaps states (and their current members) have a right to *political independence* that precludes noncitizens from intervening in their domestic policy. Chiefly, states have the right to independently determine their own political destiny without interference from external agents. Indeed, political theorists have shared the assumption that states in general have this right. For example, in John Rawls's elaboration of the *Law of Peoples*, he explicitly includes the principle that "[p]eoples are free and independent, and their freedom and independence are to be respected by other peoples," as well as that "[p]eoples are to observe a duty of non-intervention" (1999b, 37). In this vein, noncitizens have a corresponding duty not to interfere in the domestic policy of the state, and this can be true even if their interests are negatively affected by the rules and norms it creates.

However, matters change when we think about *why* sovereign states have a right to independence in the first place. One explanation draws a direct analogy between states and individual persons. As an autonomous being, *I* and *I* alone have the right to independently determine my own conduct—short of engaging in actions that violate other agents' rights. If autonomy primarily justifies the right to individual independence, perhaps there is a simple parallel for states. As Charles Beitz frames it, "[l]ike persons, states might be conceived as moral beings which are organic wholes with the capacity to realize their nature in the choice and pursuit of ends" (1999, 76). That said, unlike persons, states "lack the unity of consciousness and the rational will that constitute the identity of persons" (Beitz 1999, 81). States are often large and messy, and comprise diverse groups; they are simply not "organic wholes" in the way that persons are. One alternative is to say that the right to independence derives from the autonomy of its *citizens*. Although the *state* itself may lack autonomy, we can speak of citizens' autonomy as a whole. Interference would thus involve the imposition of institutions and policies on *people* against their will (77).[12] This comports nicely with Yong's claim that the right to independence "protects the capacity of the *state's members* [my emphasis] to independently choose which morally permissible public policy goals they will collectively pursue, and using what means" (2018, 467).

If states have a right to independence that is based in citizens' right to choose their own political destiny, this raises a new question: *which* agents have a duty of noninterference? With regard to individuals, it seems that each person's right to independence is held against the entire world: no individual or collective agent may seek to interfere with my choices without adequate justification. Recall that, according to Yong, "the correlative duty falls on international society, that is to say, other states and their members, requiring them to refrain from interfering in the rightholder state's domestic governance" (2018, 467). Much like with individuals, this would mean that *all nonmembers*, or groups of nonmembers, are not permitted to interfere in the state's domestic governance. For this reason, perhaps the DREAMer who proudly declares their undocumented status and challenges the state to take action is engaging in "intervention" that ultimately violates the United States' right to independently formulate and implement immigration policies.

This conclusion is clearly unappealing. It assumes that "nonmembers" have no right at all to exercise their political agency, and that the right to political participation is contingent on *formal membership* in the state. We should adopt the opposite view: that noncitizens can be entitled to have a say simply because their life-circumstances tie the fulfillment of their basic rights and interests to the decisions of a particular state, which certainly seems true of many migrants and would-be migrants in very similar situations to Martínez and Balachandran. In contrast, disallowing noncitizens from political participation, on the grounds that they are engaging in "foreign intervention," commits the very wrong that the purported duty of nonintervention is meant to protect against: the imposition of institutions and policies on persons against their will. It prevents them from having a say in the very policies that may have a serious impact on their basic rights.

Finally, it might be argued that "DREAMers" constitute a special case; unlike other noncitizens, they are uniquely entitled to participate in civil disobedience. We might recognize DREAMers' actions as civil disobedience while still broadly excluding other noncitizens from participating in it. The idea, here, is that DREAMers *ought* to be citizens. Having arrived as children, DREAMers tend to have strong social connections to the receiving state; in Joseph Carens's words, "as irregular migrants become more and more settled, their membership in society grows in moral importance, and the fact that they have settled without authorization becomes correspondingly less relevant" (2015, 150). We can recognize that DREAMers ought to be treated as persons *on the path to citizenship* on the basis of their preexisting social membership; morally, they are citizens even if they legally aren't. This might grant them membership-specific rights, including the right to civil disobedience, that other noncitizens wouldn't ordinarily have.

In reply, it seems short-sighted to make the above assertion without a fleshed-out theory of citizenship that settles the question of who is entitled to citizenship. Why assume that, unlike other undocumented migrants, DREAMers are uniquely entitled to citizenship? It is highly likely that a person who moved to a country as a child and grew up there has a stronger social connection than a person who has not lived there at all, or who has done so in short bursts, like migrant workers with "circular" patterns of migration between their country of origin and the receiving state. Yet, on its own, this doesn't establish that long-term social membership is the only basis for the right to citizenship—especially when migrant workers' visas are often designed precisely to limit how long a worker can stay on the territory. Neither does it establish that citizenship is the only form of membership that noncitizens can be justly entitled to. We can recognize that someone has a claim of justice to be *present* or *included within the state*, such as the right to work or permanent residence, even if it falls short of citizenship. Relatedly, it remains unclear that one's right to engage in civil disobedience hinges on their citizenship status or the extent of their social connection to the state, rather than their being subject to a particular unjust rule. If a noncitizen is the target of pervasive injustice, it seems unfair to expect them to sit back silently and wait for citizens to petition on their behalf; rather, we ought to recognize noncitizens' political agency and, in turn, their right to disobey egregiously unjust laws.

ii. Uncivil migratorial disobedience

In contrast to the public, arguably last-resort disobedience of DREAMers, migratorial disobedience that involves evasion, deception, and the use of defensive force would not satisfy the requirements for civil disobedience. Let's return to the hypothetical case of a migrant who falsifies immigration documents and deceives a border agent so that he can pass through the border undisturbed. The migrant may not be intending to engage in public communication of the sort that is central to migratorial disobedience. He may simply be interested in entering the receiving state without interference, and is primarily motivated by that desire. It's also unlikely that the same migrant has previously attempted to change unjust immigration law through legal channels of democratic contestation, in part because such channels tend to be limited for noncitizens. To reiterate, assuming that only civil disobedience can be justified as a response to immigration injustice, migratorial disobedience is impermissible by dint of its incivility. Against this, I argue that migratorial disobedience can—and should—be viewed as a valuable aspect of principled disobedience. Like Hidalgo's, my view of migratorial disobedience can be characterized as a permissive one. However, for me, *another* primary ethical justification, on top of the protection of one's individual rights by resisting unjust threats, is migrants' collective need to resist large-scale social subordination and bring about the broader *political transformation* of laws that subject them to egregious injustice.

Why, exactly, should we regard uncivil disobedience as a permissible mode of principled disobedience? I return, now, to some ideas I have covered above. Recall that the commonplace commitment to civil disobedience originated from an unjust history where principled disobedience was widely frowned-upon, necessitating an artificial division between "good" and "bad" disobedience and a narrow conception of what the former might be. Furthermore, under a pervasive "counter-resistance ideology" that ignores and undercuts the vital contributions of radical activists (Delmas 2018, 29), one's value or desirability as a political agent is inherently unstable. The strict insistence on "good" disobedience means that political activists are vulnerable to having their causes dismissed and delegitimized, simply by portraying them as "uncivil."[13] As I have suggested, we can sustain the conceptual difference between civil and uncivil disobedience while recognizing that both have their role to play in bringing about political change.

A recent example of uncivil disobedience is the "migrant caravan" from Central America that arrived at the US border in November 2018. Originating from Honduras, it was joined by other migrants from countries like Guatemala and El Salvador. While other similar caravans have arrived in the United States in the past, this caravan contained unprecedented large numbers of persons and seemed to spring up spontaneously through word of mouth.[14] Many of the migrants stated that they intended to seek asylum in the United States, but others explicitly stated that they had an economic motive. While the primary aim of the caravan is not to "persuade" citizens to change unjust immigration laws, and some migrants may be driven by mixed motives, I believe that it is still appropriate to view the migrants as engaging in a type of desirable principled disobedience. As one commentator has put it, "Instead of trying to cross without calling attention as waves of past migrants have done, they left Honduras openly, proudly self-organized, with signs and songs, their flags raised" (Guerra 2018). Migrants openly declared their aim to engage in open insubordination against the United States' restrictive border policies. Predictably, in response, the caravan was demonized as a "foreign invasion" that warranted a national emergency.

At the same time, I believe that the unauthorized migration of individuals who enter more covertly by evading, deceiving, and defending themselves against border agents, as in the principal cases Hidalgo discusses, are *also* participating in a rich fabric of principled disobedience. Amy Reed-Sandoval draws on James Scott's account of "everyday resistance" and "weapons of the weak" to make the observation that migrants have historically participated in activities that can still be considered powerful tools for resisting oppression and reasserting one's agency, even if they fall short of "open insubordination" (2019, 140–141). Much like how anticapitalist resistance on the part of peasants included "gossip and offstage talk," as well as "individual acts of foot-dragging and evasion," migrants have challenged the unjust social order in small but significant ways. These include pooling their financial resources, communicating information about problematic employer practices, or even sharing aphorisms and songs that challenge dominant narratives about migrants (140–141). Much like how the "personal is political," I want to suggest that in cases where the agency of the individual is heavily limited by oppressive constraints, permissibility and civility are not mutually exclusive. Rather, it makes more sense to recognize a diverse fabric of principled disobedience that is fundamentally shaped by the costs and penalties that political agents face in their daily lives.

On the whole, some instances of migratorial disobedience, as in the case of the DREAMers, will fall more in line with traditional definitions of civil disobedience, insofar as they are primarily public and communicative, as well as performed as a last resort in response to a state that unjustly refuses to recognize them as equal members. In making this claim, I have argued that it is unfair to exclude noncitizens from the sphere of civil disobedience by definition. Other examples of migratorial disobedience (like the movements of the migrant caravan), can be more uncivil in the sense that they are not strictly "public, nonviolent, conscientious yet political." Yet, as I elaborate in the next section, this is not a reason in itself to disqualify them from the realm of permissibility. In fact, uncivil disobedience may have an important role to play in addressing immigration injustice.

5. Objection: Might migratorial disobedience worsen injustice?

A serious concern is that uncivil migratorial disobedience may run counter to justice, all things considered. Agreeing that less public or communicative forms of disobedience *can* be permissible is certainly not to say that they *always* are. We might still worry that uncivil disobedience would thwart overall efforts to create just arrangements "not yet established." If noncitizens do not go through proper democratic channels, the widespread disapproving attitudes of citizens toward unauthorized migration may harden their hearts, confirm xenophobic stereotypes, and make them inclined to support even *more* grievously unjust immigration laws. How can we guarantee that migratorial disobedience will not have such adverse effects?

Responding to this objection, I think, requires us to return to the basic purpose of principled disobedience. As Yong's account itself indicates, it is not true that the permissibility of civil disobedience relies on it having a particular outcome, i.e., greater *net* justice in the relevant society. For him, the permissibility of civil disobedience does not ride on its consequences, as those may be very difficult to judge ahead of time, but the fact that there are *no other options* for the affected parties to turn to; they have exhausted their legal channels. Consider the paradigm case of Martin Luther King Jr. and the foundational role he played in organizing historic instances of civil disobedience, such as the Montgomery bus boycotts of 1955 and the Birmingham campaign of 1963. On one view, King's disobedience was permissible because of its positive consequences for racial justice. Suppose, however, that his lawbreaking had the effect of *intensifying* racism in American society by stirring up the indignation of racist white citizens. Would this make King's civil disobedience impermissible? This seems unlikely. A better view, I suspect, is that his disobedience was permissible because he had *run out of legal channels* through which he could contest racial injustice.

I argue that migrants experience a similar dearth of legal channels. As I have already noted in the case of DREAMers, circumstances may dictate that many migrants are unable to find any legal channels that will help them advance their claims to immigration justice. Because migrants lack such channels, migratorial disobedience may be the *only option* through which those views can be communicated. To flesh out this claim, I turn to Daniel Markovits's articulation of "democratic deficits," under which collective choices may depart from the political arrangements that citizens would assume a "sense of authorship" of (2005, 1921).[15] According to Markovits, deficits occur as a result of institutional inertia that may arise for two reasons. Firstly, existing democratic procedures are "open to manipulation and abuse by special interests" (2005, 1922). Persons who refuse to engage with others politically can use inertial institutions and processes to block proposals that the sovereign will might choose under different arrangements (1922). Secondly, democracies can suffer from deliberative inertia; chiefly, past decisions can shape present deliberations by *excluding* some considerations from the table, with a long-term effect of "removing them from the domain of democratic deliberation and political engagement" (1926). Once a certain consideration has been excluded, it is difficult for it to return to political discourse. For these reasons, civil disobedience can be necessary to "shock" the public back into reengaging with policy options that ordinary democratic channels would neglect.

I submit that present-day immigration policy suffers from a democratic deficit. It is well-known that several political parties in democratic states have run on a xenophobic platform, exploiting false beliefs and negative stereotypes about migrants to drum up working-class support, while introducing immigration policies that are expensive, ineffective, and ultimately fail to meet the pressing economic needs of the state. Aversion to immigrants' rights has grown to a stage where it would be challenging for a political candidate to run on a pro-migrant platform.[16] This leads me to my next point: the current immigration discourse largely excludes the possibility that immigrants have a legitimate claim to be included in the state, rather than inclusion being a matter of discretion or largesse. Even more fundamentally, it excludes the possibility that at least some noncitizens may deserve a democratic say in the policies that coerce or otherwise profoundly affect them, a say that could lead to very different policy decisions had migrants been granted a voice. As I have already hinted, their absence from the formal demos is itself symptomatic of the problem that Markovits locates. The institutional inertia surrounding immigration justice gives us reason to welcome widespread and diverse forms of migratorial disobedience as a necessary method of overcoming the deficit. Put differently, migratorial disobedience enables migrants to proudly *assert* themselves in the public sphere, "shocking" citizens into engaging with a perspective that would otherwise remain in the shadows. In this sense, it can be highly desirable from the standpoint of justice. Although it may worsen xenophobic attitudes in the short run, it's difficult to see *how else* migrants might be able to challenge the institutional inertia that has more-or-less excluded their rights and interests from the agenda.

6. Conclusion

In conclusion, I have advocated a permissive view of migratorial disobedience, under which migrants' disobedience of unjust immigration laws is not only permissible, but morally desirable. Significantly, this can be true of both civil and uncivil disobedience. First, I showed that the "restrictive view" of migratorial disobedience, or at least according to how it is spelled out by Yong, neglects the fact of global structural injustice. While certain immigration laws may not *directly* violate human rights, their interaction with other laws under conditions of immigration justice have a tendency to *indirectly* violate the human rights of migrants. If many present-day immigration laws can be permissibly disobeyed, this raises a further question: can uncivil forms of disobedience also be permitted? While I acknowledge that it is valuable for migrants to engage in individual self-defense against unjust threats through acts of evasion, deception, or violence, I propose an additional collective justification to uncivil migratorial disobedience: its capacity to bring about political transformation of unjust immigration laws. Chiefly, its potential to overcome democratic inertia—by forcing public engagement with migrants' needs and interests—may play a necessary role in the ongoing quest for immigration justice and social equality.

Conclusion

1. Low-skilled migrants and immigration injustice

We have seen that low-skilled migrants, as a socially salient group, are subject to immense injustice. On a large scale, they are subjected to exclusionary treatment by states and repeatedly characterized as "bad" migrants who need to be kept out. I have sought to argue that a social egalitarian framework is especially appropriate for clarifying the nature of the injustice that they suffer. According to this framework, each and every person has a pro tanto right to be treated as a social equal and protected from subordinating treatment, even in its informal, indirect, and unintentional forms. Furthermore, low-skilled migrants' claim to social equality is systematically violated by skill-selective immigration policies.

I began by focusing on a different question from other immigration theorists. In Chapter One, I contrasted an ideal approach to the ethics of migration with a nonideal one. According to the former, we may reach conclusions about immigration policy by formulating just principles for exclusion that are meant to apply to ideal liberal states. Put differently, assuming the backdrop of a liberal state that generally complies with its duties of justice, we should engage in the business of providing migrants with rationales for exclusion that they can reasonably endorse. Immigration injustice would take place, then, if migrants are subjected to *arbitrary* forms of coercion that cannot be justified to them. So, when considering the issue of low-skilled migration, we should seek to provide low-skilled migrants with such a rationale (assuming one can be provided at all). My approach, however, begins from the unjust circumstances of the here and now. Given the world's legacy of wrongful discrimination and colonial exploitation, and how it has historically influenced immigration policy, in which ways may skill-selective immigration policies contribute toward the marginalization of low-skilled migrants?

Chapter Two focused on the pro tanto right to social equality and why it is morally objectionable for immigration policies to demean or subordinate

Immigration and Social Equality. Désirée Lim, Oxford University Press. © Oxford University Press 2023.
DOI: 10.1093/oso/9780197658093.003.0008

noncitizens. I explained why it is mistaken for social egalitarians (or anyone who sees the immense moral and political value of social equality, for that matter) to deny that noncitizens fall within the scope of social egalitarian duties. Proper appreciation of the basis of our entitlement to social equality reveals that it is a necessary condition for developing and pursuing our conception of the good. Put differently, being systematically treated as an inferior is likely to pose the threat of serious damage to our fundamental sense of self. If this is true, we ought to acknowledge that noncitizens are just as vulnerable to harms to their sense of self, and they, too, have a basic interest in not being subordinated or demeaned. As matters stand, the immigration policies of many states flagrantly violate this basic entitlement.

To see the value of the social egalitarian approach, it is worth considering two other arguments that, in some way, challenge the exclusion of low-skilled migrants. In my view, they tend to be too narrow or too broad. Take, for example, the existing literature on guest worker programs, under which low-skilled migrants are admitted on temporary visas under highly disadvantageous conditions. Guest workers are typically not eligible to apply for citizenship or permanent residency, nor are they able to bring their family members with them. It might be argued (as I have in Chapter Five) that guest worker programs, as they presently stand, are unjust. First of all, if guest workers must leave their family members behind, this often means that their dependents will have to be cared for by other persons, or simply make do with less care. As Anca Gheaus has pointed out, the global movement of parents who perform low-skilled labor overseas (especially that of women, due to the gendered division of labor) has led to a large number of frustrated care-needs in sending states (2013, 62). At the same time, theorists have claimed that it is unjust to deny guest workers the right to citizenship, which is necessary to enshrine their entitlements to certain political, economic, or social rights that would protect them from relationships of exploitation (Lenard and Straehle 2011, 212). One example might be their right to "influence the political environment in which they operate" (Lenard and Straehle 2011, 215).

Both these arguments, I think, are correct. Yet there is a tendency to evaluate the moral permissibility of guest worker programs in a way that is conceptually detached from states' *overall* approach to low-skilled migrants. The assumption, here, is that states *do* reserve the right to exclude low-skilled migrants, and the question at hand is whether it is ethically permissible for states to *include* them in this heavily qualified way. States can choose whether or not to admit low-skilled migrants, but if they do at all, they must make sure that the low-skilled migrants in question are entitled to particular goods. As I have argued in Chapter Three and Four, however, we have good reasons to object to states' exclusion of low-skilled migrants in the first place. On the contrary, if antidiscrimination norms are grounded in the duty to not demean others, we ought to view the exclusion of low-skilled migrants as a form of wrongful direct and indirect discrimination. Skill-selective immigration policies wrong low-skilled migrants because they demean them *qua* their status as low-skilled migrants. At the same time, skill selection can be said to wrong *women* as a social group, due to the widely documented disparate impact that it has on female migrants, and the demeaning social norms and beliefs that such disparate impact reinforces. The fact that it is wrong to discriminate against low-skilled migrants from the get-go can be understood *independently* of the harms or disadvantages that may arise from the structure of particular guest worker programs.

Other theorists who argue for more permissive borders, however, often have nothing specific to say about low-skilled migrants. On such theories, the exclusion of low-skilled migrants is wrong insofar as the exclusion of noncitizens *in general* is wrong. I have already addressed an influential version of this argument in Chapter One; specifically, the idea that it is *disrespectful* for states to exclude persons based on their citizenship status, because this attribute is socially contingent and thus morally arbitrary. Where we are born, or which state we become citizens of, is a matter of sheer chance or contingency. Aside from the Argument from Social Contingency, as I have termed it, we may make the case that there is a *human right* to the freedom of movement. For example, Kieran Oberman argues that all persons have a basic interest in "being free to access the full range of existing life options when they make important personal decisions," such as options relating to our "friends, family, civic associations, expressive opportunities, religions, jobs, and marriage partners" (2016, 35). If this is true, states' exclusion of low-skilled migrants violates their human rights.

Oberman's argument is powerful, but I worry that it is too blunt of a tool to be helpful in locating the specific injustice faced by low-skilled migrants. This is because it effectively places low-skilled migrants and highly skilled migrants on the same plane. It would be unjust to exclude a low-skilled migrant *for the same reasons* as it is to exclude a highly skilled migrant. I find this conclusion rather counterintuitive. The United States' exclusion of a Swede or Norwegian from taking up a prestigious software engineering job in Silicon Valley, even if unjust, seems morally distinct from its exclusion of a Mexican or Salvadoran agricultural worker. I suspect that many people will share this intuition. Part of the reason for this intuition, as I suggested in Chapter Five, is that low-skilled migrants are excluded in order to maintain *racially exploitative* labor practices. Highly skilled migrants, on the other hand, are not as likely to be exploited in this fashion (although I leave open the possibility that they may be subject to more general forms of exploitation). More than this, racially exploitative labor practices, which disproportionately target and affect low-skilled Latino/a/x migrants, should be understood as a *distinctively colonial injustice* that effectively reproduces a defining feature of colonial governance. I have assumed that those who care about social equality have a strong interest, by extension, to refrain from upholding paradigmatically "colonial" social practices. A decolonial approach to migration requires us not only to rethink the grounds of immigration exclusion (e.g., if members of past colonies can indeed be justified on the basis of cultural difference), or to provide reparations for past injustice, but also to acknowledge how immigration exclusion *itself* upholds colonial relationships in the here and now.

In sum, I have argued that low-skilled migrants are subject to serious immigration injustice. Present-day immigration practices are unjust for at least two reasons connected to social equality. We should think of skill-selective immigration policies as iterations of *wrongful discrimination* and *colonial injustice*. I also want to reinforce, if it is under any doubt at all, that low-skilled migrants are subject to systematic injustice in wealthy Western countries like the United States and United Kingdom. Theorists of migration cannot afford to idealize away these real-world circumstances, which need to be forcefully confronted, condemned, and resisted. Due to the persistent injustice of immigration laws today, I argued in Chapter Six that migratorial disobedience is not just morally permissible, but also *desirable*. I do not see how else migrants should respond. It is too much to expect the targets of severe and long-standing social injustice to comply with the fate that states decide for them. More than this, it is unreasonable to ask them to wait for citizens to speak up for their interests. States currently suffer from a democratic deficit that takes immigrants' social equality off the table, or at best, treats it like a mere afterthought. Migratorial disobedience, while "uncivil" at times because it is neither public, nonviolent, nor conscientious, may be the only option that migrants have on the table to express their basic interests in no uncertain terms. Of course, this doesn't mean that migrants alone are responsible for resisting unjust immigration policy. We all are. The point, rather, is to acknowledge and respect migrants' political agency.

2. Next steps?

I have made the strong claims that the exclusion of low-skilled workers is *both* a form of wrongful discrimination and a distinctively colonial injustice. How, exactly, should we proceed from here? Put differently—what kinds of changes to immigration policy are required in order to address the serious injustices I have described? One possible answer, which I have briefly addressed earlier in the book, is to claim that states should adopt a policy of open borders. We should simply do away with the state's policy of excluding low-skilled migrants and allow a free-flow of migration, regardless of skill level, into the state. I have intentionally refrained from explicitly arguing in favor of open borders. Rather, my claim is a very qualified one: that acknowledging the state's duty to uphold noncitizens' social equality places limitations on the right to exclude *in those areas* that I have identified. This leaves open the possibility that the state *may* continue to exercise the right to exclude, albeit in an extremely limited and qualified manner. It is certainly not intended as an *in-principle* objection to the right to exclude, as it only problematizes certain existing practices of skill-selective exclusion.

However, suppose that there is *no way* for states to effectively exercise the right to exclude *without* violating their duty to uphold social equality, as it turns out that enforcement mechanisms cannot avoid demeaning or otherwise worsening the social equality of a marginalized group. While I have not sought to make this (very strong) claim in the preceding chapters, I believe it is worth reflecting on at length. In particular, we could ask if our concern for social equality could, in fact, provide an *indirect* argument for open borders (as opposed to a more direct approach, like the claim that there is a human right to free movement). Perhaps it is far too difficult to engage in immigration exclusion without seriously violating the core rights of at least some noncitizens, including the proposed right to social equality. Relevantly, Michael Blake has drawn a comparison between a hypothetical right to prevent compatriots from reproducing, and the right to exclude (2020, 89). Both reproduction and the right to exclude may place serious demands on citizens because "[p]eople are, quite frankly, demanding, morally speaking" (89). Nonetheless, despite the significant consequences of reproduction, it is morally impermissible to prevent persons from reproducing because it would require the state's use of coercive medical interventions (89). In the case of immigration exclusion, though, "[w]e need not think, however, that anything here necessarily troubles the right to exclude adult migrants" (90). I am less confident, however, that there is nothing troubling about the state's use of coercive procedures to exercise their right to exclude. Routine measures for immigration control like detention and deportation involve the routine deployment of coercive power over migrants' bodies. For example, detention centers bear a close resemblance to prisons, including penal-like characteristics like "an internal punishment codes, including the use of solitary confinement; transport vans with bars, escorts and handcuffing of detainees travelling to other centers, to court or to receive medical attention; the heavy use of guards," etc. (Silverman and Nethery 2015, 3). These practices may also create ample opportunities for the *abuse* of coercive power. For example, a whistleblower alleged that a government-contracted doctor sterilized women in Immigration and Customs Enforcement custody without their knowledge or consent,[1] and it has also been reported that guards in an immigrant detention center in El Paso have engaged in a "pattern and practice" of sexual abuse against inmates.[2] To be sure, some instances of immigration exclusion may not be rights-violating at all, even if they may be annoying or somewhat burdensome for the would-be migrant (e.g., the wealthy, highly skilled Swede who wishes to permanently move to the United States, but cannot legally do so unless he first finds an employer in the tech industry who is willing to sponsor his green card). Yet these seemingly innocuous cases do not mean that the right to exclude is morally unproblematic. For example, we might not need to show that the right to exclude is *necessarily* rights-violating; it might simply be the case that it is too *risky* an exercise of power.

Suppose that an advocate of restricted borders is genuinely sympathetic to my social egalitarian argument, and they agree that imposing restrictions on certain groups (including low-skilled migrants), may unavoidably lead to abusive treatment and rights-violations of people from those groups. Another solution, which can be read as the diametric opposite of the open borders approach, is for a country to completely shut down its borders and exclude all migrants, regardless of race, class, or gender. If confronted about expressing demeaning attitudes toward immigrants, the country in question may retort that they are doing the very opposite: the blanket ban on immigration is intended to protect *any* and *all* immigrants from discriminatory treatment. Would this stance on immigration pass the test for social equality?

In theory, there are no immediate issues with uniformly closed borders—at least not from the stance of social equality. A small, distant worry might be that the total ban on immigration, while well-intended at the outset, might promote xenophobic attitudes in the long run. A country whose citizens are accustomed to a total ban on immigration, as opposed to regarding it as an ordinary fact of everyday life, could begin to regard noncitizens as threatening and Other, but this concern doesn't seem to be insurmountable. There are other ways that the state could continue to promote cultural diversity and provide citizens with opportunities for interacting with noncitizens. The bigger problems crop up at the level of *practice.* Let's put aside the big and obvious point that wealthy states are very unlikely to give up the benefits of immigration as a whole, and that ending immigration entirely would probably have detrimental consequences for their economies. Under nonideal conditions, the ban on immigration would disparately impact poor and low-skilled denizens who, unlike highly skilled denizens, are much less likely to have already brought in their family members and successfully navigate the naturalization process. Relatedly, as Chapter Five has highlighted, we must acknowledge long-standing relationships between certain sending and receiving states (e.g., the United States and Mexico). These historically significant relationships will not disappear overnight. The United States imposing a ban on immigration will certainly not erase Mexican citizens' desire to work in, if not move to the United States, nor will it remove the economic incentives that American employers have to employ cheap and exploitative migrant labor. Returning to our reservations about immigration enforcement tactics and how they have been used to demean and abuse noncitizens, it is difficult to see how the ban on immigration would obviate the need for the identification, detention, and expulsion of undocumented immigrants, many of whom will be poor, low-skilled, and racialized.

Having considered open borders and closed borders alike, I want to be careful about eschewing an all-or-nothing approach toward open borders. Between the severe restrictions on low-skilled migration we currently see, and the free movement of migrants from all around the globe, there are many approaches to immigration policy that we may choose to pursue. There is a risk that, as we focus our energies on championing philosophical arguments for restricted or open borders, we may end up being too inattentive to the spaces in-between. Amy Reed-Sandoval presents an excellent example of an "in-between" argument that doesn't require us to embrace the open borders position, yet may nevertheless go a long way in ameliorating the social inequality of low-skilled migrants. In contrast with an "utopian" vision of global free movement, she argues more particularly for the *demilitarization* of the US-Mexico border (2019, 149). The worry, as Reed-Sandoval writes, is that low-skilled Latino/a/x migrants may still continue to face oppression under a system of open borders, under the guise of the justified restrictions on migration that are acknowledged by open-borders advocates (2019, 152). For example, in the real-world context, low-skilled migrants might continue to be excluded on the basis that they pose threats to national security, and we can already see this in the "Latino Threat Narrative" that has been reinforced by Donald J. Trump's presidency (Reed-Sandoval 2019, 159). The point is, more open borders are not necessarily coterminous with *less* social inequality; they might even *worsen* it.

For this reason, Reed-Sandoval argues that we ought to prefer the development of "porous, demilitarized borders" (2019, 166). Specifically, this would mean that federal troops should leave the Mexico-US border, and federal military weaponry like weaponized aircraft and armored vehicles should no longer be used (186). Neither should the US military or National Guard be present at the border (186). The demilitarization of the border would effectively cease to subject would-be migrants (most of them low-skilled Latino/a/x persons) to the well-known risks of attempting to cross the border. For example, the current practice of "Prevention Through Deterrence," which militarized the Mexico-US border along urban migration routes, has had the effect of forcing unauthorized migrants into the deadly Sonoran Desert. On top of the risk of getting lost or dying of thirst, hunger, or heat-stroke, they are at tremendous risk of being violently attacked or kidnapped by smugglers (172–173). Reed-Sandoval's stance is heavily consistent with the one I have sketched out throughout the book, which is anchored in the commitment to social equality, rather than open borders per se. We can take valuable steps toward protecting migrants' social equality through policy proposals that do not explicitly call for open borders. Using this approach, how should we address the social subordination of low-skilled migrants? What would states need to do in order to *not* treat low-skilled migrants in a demeaning way?

States might begin by explicitly recognizing and affirming the valuable contributions of low-skilled migrants. As I have discussed in Chapter Three, low-skilled migrants are often framed as a net burden to states whose presence ought to be discouraged and deterred. Yet this characterization and its effects on social perception is often at odds with the necessary or "essential" labor that low-skilled migrants perform for citizens. Many citizens fail to grasp just how dependent their well-being is on low-skilled migrant labor, whether it is their ability to buy tasty fruit and vegetables in the grocery store or their access to caregiving services for themselves, their children, or elderly relatives. At this point, it may be objected that low-skilled labor as a whole tends to be devalued, and it is not fair for states to focus on changing public attitudes about low-skilled migrants without recognizing the value of low-skilled labor as a whole. I am in complete agreement that the devaluation of low-skilled migrants' labor is closely related to negative attitudes toward low-skilled labor and a general disrespect toward persons who are deemed to be "low-skilled." In general, hierarchical attitudes toward labor, which tend to objectionably elevate white-collar professional jobs while denigrating jobs with a focus on manual or physical tasks, urgently need to be unlearned. However, there are still legitimate reasons to differentiate between low-skilled citizens and low-skilled migrants, rather than folding the two together. We need to undertake public education campaigns about the necessary contributions of low-skilled migrants in particular. This is because, unlike low-skilled migrants, low-skilled citizens are *not* at risk of detention and deportation, or other forms of immigration-related coercion, as a result of ignorance about the nature of their work (and by extension, their effect on the economy). Thus, it is especially important that citizens understand the nature of low-skilled migrants' labor contributions, although of course this does not preclude attempts to instill a greater respect for low-skilled labor in general.

That said, states cannot just not stop at recognizing the contributions of low-skilled migrants. There is a worry that an overemphasis on economic contribution may suggest that respect for low-skilled migrants is contingent on their "proving" themselves to be economically useful, and that it can be promptly withdrawn if this begins to be in any doubt (e.g., if low-skilled migrants become sick or elderly and are no longer able to work). As I have claimed in Chapters Three and Four, low-skilled migrants are deserving of equal respect *as persons*, and stereotypical negative beliefs about low-skilled migrants as dangerous or parasitic are wrong because they reinforce xenophobic stigma and gender-oppressive norms, regardless of how economically productive low-skilled migrants are. So, at the very least, states must stop closing off existing legal channels for low-skilled migrants to enter, and create new channels to accommodate a greater supply of low-skilled migrants. To reiterate, I am not arguing for *unrestricted* low-skilled migration, any more than antidiscrimination norms require schools or employers to admit unrestricted numbers of women or ethnic minorities as students or employees. I simply ask for states to stop expressing a blanket preference for highly skilled migrants over low-skilled migrants and creating increasingly high barriers to legal entry for low-skilled migrants who may be just as needed as—if not *more* needed than—highly skilled migrants. While states are permitted to select migrants on the basis of demand for specific skills, all other things being equal, they must be transparent about their need for low-skilled immigration (as the United States typically has not been) and make finer-grained distinctions between high- and low-demand occupations when the distinction between "highly skilled" and "low-skilled" migrants is far too coarse to be useful. For example, under the United Kingdom's post-Brexit immigration rules, anyone earning less than £25.6k per annum is automatically deemed an unskilled worker who does not qualify for entry (BBC News 2020). The new regulations would effectively exclude essential medical workers like nurses, paramedics, midwives, radiographers, care assistants, physiotherapists, and occupational therapists who are now deemed to be "unskilled."

Another serious issue that I have covered in Chapter Five is the ongoing racial exploitation of low-skilled Latino/a/x migrants in the United States. To end these racially exploitative practices, it might be necessary for the United States to allow the free movement of low-skilled migrants from particular countries, like Mexico, El Salvador, and Honduras, which have historically supplied the United States with low-skilled labor and therefore have an economically significant relationship with it, in the sense that an enormous and self-sustaining flow of migrants from those countries is well-entrenched in employer practices and migrants' own expectations. A similar case could be made for Canada opening its borders to citizens of Mexico or Caribbean countries like Jamaica, Trinidad, and Barbados, who have made up the majority of participants in Canada's low-skilled guest worker programs. This is not to say that the freedom of movement would always be limited to those countries in particular. New economic relationships can be forged with time. Suppose that the United States comes to rely on a growing supply of low-skilled migrants from China or Nigeria, who would become increasingly subject to demeaning immigration-related constraints were they not granted the freedom of movement. The freedom of movement would not mean the granting of automatic or immediate citizenship. Rather, low-skilled migrants would be free to enter, work, and reside in the receiving state while also bringing their spouses and dependents with them. Relatedly, neither must we forget about the reparative potential of permissive immigration policies, which I have also discussed in Chapter Five. Inclusion in the polity might be one potent method through which colonizing powers may compensate citizens of ex-colonies for historical injustice. Consequently, certain states may have a duty to prioritize the admission of low-skilled migrants from countries that they previously subjected to colonial rule even if those countries are not presently significant providers of low-skilled labor.

One final clarification is in order. My book has not said very much about highly skilled migrants, other than explaining how they are often used as a foil to low-skilled migrants. As such, I am not committed to any claim about the extent to which highly skilled migrants (myself included) can be included or excluded. I want to make clear, all the same, that I am not denying that highly skilled migrants can also be subject to demeaning, immigration-related constraints. My sense is that at least some highly skilled migrants *may* be demeaned, but not in the ways I have explored. It is also much more likely that they are demeaned because of their race or nationality, rather than their level of skill, which is incidental in such contexts. One example is the obviously racist view that highly skilled South/East Asian software engineers are "taking over" Silicon Valley, and that Americans should be wary of them because they are greedy, materialistic, and have no real commitment to the United States other than using it for a money-making platform. Here, the claims that the software engineers are "greedy" and "materialistic" seem to track racial stereotypes about Asians much more closely than skill-based stereotypes; it is difficult to imagine the same generalizations being made about French or Norwegian engineers, for example.

3. Future research

Before closing, I want to mention two fruitful areas of future research that may spring out of my conclusions.

Firstly, it may be pointed out that social equality cuts both ways. Even though I have focused exclusively on how social equality may *constrain* states' exercise of the right to exclude, social equality may give us states reason to *enforce it more strictly*. Perhaps it could be shown that loosening immigration policies in the ways I have recommended might *worsen* social equality between persons in significant ways. Several versions of this argument have been made, both in the popular discourse and philosophical literature. One is that newly arrived immigrants may harbor deeply racist attitudes toward minority citizens, or sexist attitudes toward women. For example, the purported sexist attitudes of Muslim immigrants toward women in Europe has been a matter of controversy for some time, especially after the multiple cases of sexual assault experienced by women in Cologne, Germany, on New Year's Eve in 2015, by men who were described as "North African" or "Arab" in appearance.

A second, familiar argument that I've addressed earlier in the book is that the presence of immigrants, highly skilled and low-skilled alike, may worsen the social equality of minority citizens—for example, by lowering their wages and pushing them into greater poverty. Of particular concern is the possibility that greater Latino/a/x migration to the United States may exacerbate the social subordination of Black men, who also disproportionately perform low-skilled labor and are therefore hypothesized to be especially vulnerable to economic competition by low-skilled immigrants. As Shihadeh and Barranco write, "Because even a minor drop in the relative supply of low-skill jobs may affect the economic prospects of [Black persons], Latino immigration and [B]lack mobility seem inexorably linked in the United States" (2010, 1394). Here, the worry is not about economic outcomes writ large, but the impact that low-skilled Latino/a/x immigration may have on Black citizens in particular, who may face a competitive disadvantage even if immigration yields generally positive economic results for the receiving state (Shihadeh and Barranco 2010, 1397). Doubts may be raised about whether this undesirable trade-off is a legitimate concern, and not a mere figment of prejudice that serves the interest of the dominant racial group by "dividing and conquering"—that is, through stirring up feelings of competition and hostility between minority-race groups. Such dynamics can effectively detract from broader issues of racial injustice under white supremacy and obfuscate the experience of those with mixed social identities, as in the case of Afro-Latinx persons.

Nevertheless, if it can indeed be shown that increased immigration *does* worsen the social equality of the most vulnerable citizens, especially those who have endured persistent racial stigma, states like the United States may be placed in a very difficult situation: they will have to grapple with the question of *whose* social equality ought to be prioritized. While I do not have a rough-and-ready answer, I will make some tentative suggestions on how to proceed. One seemingly intuitive answer, to the question of who should be prioritized, is that the social equality of *citizens* should take precedence, but this is not obvious. For example, we might choose to prioritize the social equality of the most vulnerable or marginalized groups (whether they are citizens or not). It is also worth bearing in mind that states are not necessarily faced with a zero-sum choice between more or less permissive immigration policies, and we have to be careful about not framing immigration in this misleading fashion. For example, there may be interventions that might help to avoid potential harms to citizens' social equality, and these could be compatible with permissive immigration policies. Additionally, if immigration has the potential to benefit society overall, states might be able to introduce other policy reforms that distribute these benefits in a way that advance social equality for other marginalized groups in society. It's worth noting that, while Shihadeh and Barranco suggest that increased Latino migration is significantly correlated with Black violence, they explicitly describe their research as a "story of Black structural disadvantage and how US immigration policy contributes to the formation of the underclass," rather than an advocation of restricting the flow of Latino migrants (2010, 1409–1410). Regardless of the options at hand, it bears acknowledgment that the realm of social equality is incredibly complex, and greater social equality for some may easily result in greater *in*equality for others if we are not careful. In particular, the tangled and complex relationship between immigration and racial equality warrants further analysis, especially in the context of a multiracial society. My book has underscored the racialized elements of social stigma toward low-skilled Latino/a/x migrants, and above, I've considered the possibility that more relaxed borders might be harmful to the racial equality of Black Americans. Despite contributing to the notion of the "model minority," which I have discussed in Chapter Three, it could also still be argued that skill selection has *on balance* improved the racial equality of Asians and Asian Americans by associating them with high-skill, education, and hard work. All these factors must be taken into consideration when theorizing about how to construct immigration policy that is able to enhance, rather than worsen, racial equality for minority groups.

Thirdly, it is worth thinking about the global applications of my theory. In my book, the United States and United Kingdom have featured prominently as case studies. This is no accident for both personal and political reasons. Admittedly, my focus is motivated and informed by my own immediate experiences as a migrant to both these countries. Yet, more than this, the United States and United Kingdom are both immensely influential global powers. They set global precedents for the permissible limits of immigration policy, and as two of the most popular receiving states, exert tremendous influence over the life-prospects of present and would-be migrants from around the world. What implications, however, does the concept of social equality have for other states? All states, I think, must be reined in by the constraints of social equality. Doubtless, migrants in other countries suffer diverse demeaning immigration-related constraints that I have not addressed in the book. Moving forward, we must identify and understand them to better-protect the social equality of migrants. More controversially, I want to suggest that states must be reined in by migrants' right to social equality, quite apart from whether the states explicitly identify as "liberal" or not. We might think about severe social inequalities suffered by migrant workers employed as domestic helpers and construction workers in "illiberal" countries like Malaysia, Singapore, and Saudi Arabia, whether they may be considered a type of global injustice, and the potential responsibilities that they impose on the global community. This is, however, a conversation for another time.

Above all, I have sought to convince the reader of the central importance of social equality in how we should think about the right to exclude, as well as the value of evaluating the current policies that have been introduced under its banner. It is my hope that social equality, as a core concept, can steady us in a time when low-skilled migrants are so viciously and unconscionably demeaned.

Epilogue

Reflections on COVID-19 and Its Impact on Immigration

The reader is likely to be acutely familiar with the social, political, and economic impact of the COVID-19 pandemic on practically every sphere of human life—consequences that we won't fully understand for a long time. The little things we took for granted, whether it was taking a bus to work, sharing coffee with a friend, or visiting one's family over the weekend, seemed to fall away overnight. Importantly, special attention has already been paid to COVID-19's serious disparate impact on disadvantaged groups. For example, following the implementation of lockdowns that forced people to stay in close proximity with household members, the global rates of domestic violence soared.[1] The coronavirus has also shone a harsh light on racial disparities. Black Americans, in particular, have suffered a disproportionate death rate—as a doctor reported, "In Michigan, over 40% of COVID-19 deaths are African Americans, while only 14% of the population is made up of African Americans" (Malcom and Sawani 2020). Similarly, the Institute of Fiscal Studies found that death rate of British Black Africans and British Pakistanis in English hospitals is more than 2.5 times that of the white population (Siddique 2020). These examples remind us of the intimate ties between social equality and material outcomes. Occupying a position of social inferiority in a particular society, where one is especially vulnerable to persistent discrimination, domination and exploitation, can literally prove to be deadly.

For this reason, I cannot conclude the book without briefly addressing the pandemic's detrimental effect on the social equality of immigrants, as well as how their existing social inequality has compounded the effect of the pandemic.

Immigration and Social Equality. Désirée Lim, Oxford University Press. © Oxford University Press 2023.
DOI: 10.1093/oso/9780197658093.003.0009

1. COVID-19 and travel bans

It goes without saying that COVID-19 has reshaped the immigration landscape. I will begin by noting that, in the interests of protecting public health, travel bans were now de rigueur. New Zealand acted quickly to close its borders to all travelers except citizens, permanent residents, and residents with valid visas from March 19, 2020, and it was not expected to reopen them any time soon.[2] Other countries adopted a more selective approach: for example, foreign nationals originating from China, Iran, the European Schengen area, United Kingdom, and Ireland were prohibited from entering the United States, with exemptions for citizens, permanent residents, immediate family members, and others who qualified for particular exceptions. Unlike the "Muslim ban," which demeaned Muslim citizens and noncitizens alike, I believe that these travel restrictions are compatible with the principle of social equality. This is because, given the highly contagious nature of the virus (unlike HIV, which can be well controlled in the public population without resorting to travel bans on HIV-positive individuals), they are demonstrably necessary for protecting public health. Nor do they inherently single out any single group as the object of stigma. On the whole, New Zealand's travel ban does not discriminate against nationals of any particular country.

While large-scale travel bans are justifiable in principle, they may be troubling for at least two reasons. Firstly, travel bans do not come without significant costs, even if we judge that those costs are reasonable for persons to bear. Suppose that I am now unable to attend my friend's wedding in Japan. On the other hand, suppose that an Italian citizen wishes to be present at the bedside of her dying sister in the United States. While it is regrettable and inconvenient to have to cancel my trip to Japan, the burden is trivial relative to the one borne by the Italian citizen; her final visit to her sister cannot be postponed till later, and the grief of not being able to say goodbye to a close family member is likely to have a serious psychological impact, compared to the disappointment and frustration of missing a friend's wedding ceremony. Indeed, there are costs that can be too much to ask persons to bear—we see this acknowledged in the exemptions that New Zealand and the United States have granted to certain persons, but more exemptions may be required of states (e.g., immediate relatives of persons who are seriously ill). Secondly, the language of public health can easily be co-opted to legitimize existing socially subordinating treatment at the border. For example, citing the public health emergency, the United States used its emergency powers to override immigration laws, expediting removal processes and expelling more than 6,300 undocumented migrants on the US-Mexico border.[3] So, we must exercise due diligence and properly examine the justification for health-related immigration restrictions in the present and future.

2. COVID-19 and social stigma

Apart from ushering in the imposition of severe immigration restrictions, COVID-19 has changed how particular groups of immigrant origin are perceived. It has, no doubt, affected the social standing of persons who are racially coded as "Asian" or "Chinese." A *South China Morning Post* article notes that "[p]eople of Asian descent [based in the United States] have reported being shunned, verbally abused, name-called, coughed and spat on, even physically assaulted as the coronavirus pandemic continues to upend American life."[4] Relatedly, the hashtag #JeNeSuisPasUnVirus was created in light of French-Asian citizens experiencing a new wave of anti-Asian sentiment. Relevantly, many French citizens of Asian descent originate from former French colonies like Cambodia, Vietnam, and Laos and have no relationship to China. There is no doubt that the emergence of COVID-19 (which was, on one theory, linked to a "wet market" in Wuhan, China), has reinforced existing stigmatic beliefs about Chinese people—that they are carriers of disease owing to their lack of hygiene combined with outlandish eating habits (one pernicious Internet rumor falsely suggested that bat soup was to blame for the virus).[5] Furthermore, the spike in anti-Asian racism could only have resulted under circumstances where Asian people are widely viewed as a deindividuated mass, where there is no need to make distinctions between different ethnonational groups and everyone might as well be "Chinese." The failure to distinguish between diverse Asian ethnicities and subethncities is, in my view, a symptom of the tendency to depersonalize and dehumanize Asian people.[6] By contrast, it is difficult to imagine people of European descent being targeted for hateful attacks if a global pandemic originated out of, say, Germany. While my book has focused on demeaning beliefs about low-skilled migrants, particularly those of Latino/a/x descent in the United States, we need to pay attention to the worsening stigma faced by Asian immigrants and people of Asian descent. As my discussion in

Chapter Three has already suggested, the dubious honor of being deemed a "model minority" group has thoroughly failed to insulate Asians and Asian Americans against racial violence and hatred that can be easily reignited in the wake of political events like the coronavirus.

These demeaning beliefs are especially insidious when they seem, at first glance, to align with justifiable travel restrictions like the ones initially imposed on visitors arriving from China. As I have emphasized throughout the book, we have to be careful about the messages that are sent by states' choice of immigration policy, and states must sharply condemn any suggestion that they should ban Chinese immigrants as an ethnic group, rather than *any group or individual* coming from a coronavirus-afflicted area. Furthermore, there is reason to be concerned that travel bans may inadvertently legitimize and promote anti-immigration attitudes that may remain firmly entrenched long after the end of the pandemic.

The United States has certainly not succeeded in this regard; the Trump administration seized the opportunity to demonize immigrants all the more. For example, a "Proclamation Suspending Entry of Immigrants Who Present Risk to the US Labor Market During the Economic Recovery Following the COVID-19 Outbreak" was announced on April 22, 2020. Under this proclamation, every individual "seeking to enter the US as an immigrant" who was outside the United States, lacked a valid immigrant visa on the effective date, and did not have a valid official travel document was banned from entering the United States.[7] Donald Trump's priorities were quite clear: despite the country's half-hearted and poorly organized response to the ongoing crisis, the proclamation boldly gestured toward a future where the country was already "recovering," and said recovery was at risk of disruption by immigrants. To avoid further long-term damage to the social equality of immigrants, states have to make clear that travel bans are exceptional *emergency* measures that are specially warranted by the unique nature of the coronavirus, rather than a convenient tool that can be deployed at will.

3. COVID-19 and low-skilled immigrant groups

Finally, I turn to how the effects of COVID-19 on immigrant populations have been profoundly shaped by the persistent social inequalities I sought to describe in the book. One pertinent example is the case of Singapore. In

2020, owing to its experience with SARS, the small city-state largely succeeded in controlling the outbreak among its citizens. Things were very different however, for its sizable population of temporary migrant workers, who largely come from countries like Bangladesh, India, and China. As the number of COVID-19 cases rapidly rose, the vast majority of infected people are migrant workers who had previously been housed in cramped and often unsanitary dormitories. While the Singaporean authorities tested workers extensively and provided them with free healthcare (the minimally just thing to do), it's worth pointing out that the workers' subpar living arrangements were *already* a foreseeable health liability. I submit that they were only previously justifiable in the eyes of the public because of the *inferior social status* that is assigned to low-skilled migrant workers. A commonplace assumption is that, unlike local workers or highly skilled "expats," it is acceptable and "practical" for migrant workers to be housed in conditions where a room can be shared by up to twenty people, a situation where each workers lacks privacy and communal toilets are often unclean.[8] Meanwhile, the dormitory business appears to be highly profitable for operators. In one case, an operator made a tidy profit of 61 percent.[9]

The United States has seen its own share of COVID-19 outbreaks among low-skilled migrant workers. The comedian and political commentator John Oliver has drawn attention to the dire working conditions at meatpacking factories, many of which failed to adopt safety measures to protect their workers' health. In one instance, management at a Tyson facility took bets on how many workers would contract COVID-19. At the same time, in line with my observations in Chapter Six about the reliance of the US economy on undocumented labor, many undocumented field workers found themselves categorized as "essential workers" who had to continue working despite the stay-at-home directives that are intended to slow the spread of the virus. These workers were told that they are "critical to the food supply chain" and therefore need to continue working for the good of the public, while simultaneously remaining deportable by immigration authorities at any moment. Put differently, they were regarded as necessary *and* disposable in the same breath. It is not at all clear that outbreaks among undocumented workers were successfully handled by the government. The Republican Party sent an exclusionary message to undocumented workers by attempting to disqualify them from receiving the $1,200 stimulus check that was rolled out in April. Their eligibility to receive coronavirus relief funds was bluntly characterized by Senate majority leader, Mitch McConnell, as "[a]nother round of checks for illegal immigrants."[10]

Other undocumented migrants occupy a similarly precarious position with regard to the virus that results directly from their socially subordinated status. Across the United States, there have been outbreaks of the disease in detention centers, and growing evidence that undocumented migrants are not being properly protected and cared for.[11] Again, like the case of migrant workers' dormitories in Singapore, the risk to undocumented migrants' health posed by extremely poor conditions in detention centers would have been apparent even prior to the outbreak. In both cases, we need accountability for the risks and harms to migrants' health. Furthermore, moving forward, respectful treatment of low-skilled migrants requires them to be given minimally decent accommodations that would guarantee each migrant clean facilities and significantly more personal space. It is abhorrent to hide behind the argument that migrants have *agreed* to be housed in such conditions or willingly exposed themselves to the risks of being locked away in detention centers.

To conclude, among other things, the pandemic is a stark reminder of immigrants' vulnerabilities to socially subordinating treatment and its implications for their basic rights. It shows us, more than ever, that social equality must be a cornerstone value of immigration policymaking. Make no mistake: the impact of COVID-19 on immigrants has been devastating. Yet we have strong reason to believe that the world is poised to experience further shocks that could similarly exacerbate migrants' subordination, or create new groups of socially subordinated migrants, as in the case of climate refugees. Our willingness to be attentive to the normative value of social equality, and the requirements or limitations it may place on immigration policy, matters more than ever—we would be gravely mistaken to let it disappear into the background.

Notes

Introduction

1. See: https://www.pri.org/stories/2018-07-26/when-government-wrongly-deports-people-coming-back-us-almost-impossible; https://www.npr.org/2019/07/25/745417268/u-s-citizen-detained-for-weeks-nearly-deported-by-immigration-officials.
2. https://www.timeshighereducation.com/blog/eight-hours-airport-detention-wanting-talk-about-course-welcome-uk.
3. For details on President Biden's policy proposals, see: https://joebiden.com/immigration.
4. See Mills 2006 and Young 1990 (Chapter 2) for examples of philosophical work on the racialized division of labor.
5. I am grateful to Michael Blake for this point.
6. See Amy Reed-Sandoval's *Socially Undocumented: Identity and Immigration Justice* (2019) for an excellent analysis of the social positionality of persons who are legally present in the United States and may even be US citizens, but are nevertheless routinely assumed to be undocumented noncitizens and face oppression on that basis.
7. For more information on racial profiling in immigration enforcement practices, especially the raids on a Pennsylvania poultry transport company and stop-and-search measures by Border Patrol agents, see: https://www.propublica.org/article/racial-profiling-ice-immigration-enforcement-pennsylvania.
8. See: https://www.cnn.com/2019/07/30/asia/singapore-brownface-ad-sparks-controversy-intl-hnk-trnd/index.html.
9. For example, in the interests of global equal opportunity, immigration restrictions could be justified out of a concern for "brain drain"—the large-scale emigration of skilled migrants from developing countries to wealthy Western nations. See Gillian Brock and Michael Blake, *Debating Brain Drain: May Governments Restrict Emigration?* Oxford: Oxford University Press, 2015.
10. I thank Michael Blake for this terminology.

Chapter 1

1. For recent examples of work on the ethics of immigration that incorporate similar concerns, see Mendoza 2016 and Reed-Sandoval 2020. To be sure, migrants are well-known to be socially subordinated in nonliberal states like Singapore and Saudi Arabia, but the scope of this book will be limited to affluent liberal states.
2. This, of course, is a nod to John Rawls's classic articulation of "ideal theory," which assumes all relevant agents' compliance with the demands of justice that apply to them, and the favorability of natural and historical conditions toward the realization of justice (Rawls 1999a, 8).
3. I borrow the term "normatively extraneous" from Sophia Moreau (2010), who refers to the attributes that should not have to feature in our individual deliberations as social costs.
4. Here, I assume that the right to self-determination means that the members of a state have a prima facie right to make their own decisions about the policies they live under (Pevnick 2011, 27). At the same time, while I noted in the Introduction that the right to exclude comprises three conceptually distinct rights (the right to exclude noncitizens from entry, settlement, and political membership), I will focus exclusively on the justifications for states' right to exclude noncitizens from *entry*.
5. It is worth mentioning that Walzer also believes that states can generate duties to certain refugees by dint of doing them past historical injury, such as Vietnamese refugees, whose fate was caused by American interference (49).
6. As Cole has written, "it is not a coincidence that so many of today's affluent societies are among those who colonized and otherwise exploited foreign groups, while many of the most impoverished societies were among those colonized or otherwise exploited; these colonial relationships often contributed directly to the current disparities" (2011, 65).
7. See Naomi Zack, "The Philosophical Roots of Racial Essentialism and Its Legacy," in *Confluence: Journal of World Philosophies* (2014): 85–98.
8. The description of race as a morally arbitrary feature makes sense, I think, in the realm of *ideal theory*. For example, Rawls believes that race should be excluded from the deliberative process of establishing a theory of justice, because it is an "aspect of the social world" that seems arbitrary from a moral point of view (1999a, 14). However, as this is on the idealizing assumption that there has been no previous history of systemic racial disadvantage, and it is not clear how useful this view of race is when applied to nonideal discussions of race and racism. As Charles Mills puts it, "A model predicated on the (past or present) universal inclusion of colorless atomic individuals will therefore get things fundamentally wrong from the start. Races in relations of domination and subordination centrally constitute the social ontology" (2017, 40). I am grateful to Chong-Ming Lim for this point.

Chapter 2

1. See: https://www.latimes.com/nation/la-na-boy-scouts-evolution-2017-story.html.
2. In addition, it bears mentioning that citizens and noncitizens can be severely affected by coercive immigration laws, independently of whether they are themselves subject to coercion. For example, when it still was operational, the "Muslim ban" separated many children from their parents (see: https://www.brennancenter.org/our-work/analysis-opinion/muslim-ban-family-separation-policy). Quite plausibly, in order to be legitimate, exercises of power that profoundly affect the lives of third parties (the children and spouses of excluded migrants in this case) must be justified to them. In other words, states may bear a justificatory burden to affected third parties (and have their exercises of power reined in appropriately) even if their actions fall short of coercion *of* the third party. While I don't elaborate any further on this argument, it's well-worth keeping in mind. I thank Michael Blake for this careful insight.
3. I am indebted to Ben Jones for this suggestion.
4. See Michael Blake's essay, "Distributive Justice, State Coercion, and Autonomy," in *Philosophy and Public Affairs* 30.3 (2005): 257–296, for an excellent explication of this view.
5. This would mirror some arguments that have been made in favor of duties to redistribute wealth *globally*: that the grounds for entitlement to distributive equality may also apply to at least some noncitizens. See, for example, Eric Cavallero's "Coercion, Inequality and the International Property Regime," in *Journal of Political Philosophy* 18.1 (2010): 16–31.
6. It may be that conditions in the sending state are so dire that it is in some sense "unavoidable" or "inescapable" for immigrants to seek opportunities in the receiving state and subject themselves to its power as a result. It may also be that the state's economic presence is so deeply entrenched in the noncitizens' home countries that it is virtually impossible for the noncitizens not to participate in cross-border interactions. However, even with a broader interpretation of inescapability and unavoidability, there remain many groups of noncitizens—relatively privileged professional workers or international students, for instance—who could have chosen *not* to subject themselves to the state's power. Furthermore, I take it that we do not want entitlement to social equality to hinge on adopting a contested definition of "inescapability" and "unavoidability."
7. It is also highly plausible that the second "moral power," our capacity for a sense of justice, could also require the precondition of social equality. I leave this issue aside for now.

8. Of course, we can have senses of self that tend more toward individualistic or collective attitudes. I assume that persons who lean more toward the latter (for example, because they see themselves as merely constituting part of a unified whole) don't lack a "sense of self"; rather, they have a *particular* sense of self that privileges group identities and projects over individual goals.
9. See, also, Ronald Dworkin's conception of autonomy as integrity: https://www.jstor.org/stable/pdf/3349959.pdf?casa_token=T_ss4I8f7BIAAAAA:zKSLGzmeybLqfzN7QbdIEc C50vxkNKP8aYAw51j6aihLQWphBq9ETUeWoU_3_r_mtPtzCtJiWRt_YmukpqHzy597z01RT0GKuyNnlik7Mp5rUXqi1l0.
10. Here, I refer specifically to verbal denigration experienced by socially subordinated groups, which I take to be quite different from insulting and hostile remarks made by socially subordinated groups to more dominant and powerful ones, or intergroup hostilities that may involve negative stereotyping but not necessarily social subordination/the ascription of inferior status (e.g., I am thinking of feelings of animosity between different Chinese subethnic groups like Hong Kongers, Singaporeans, and Taiwanese.)
11. The recent term "microaggressions" has been coined to describe instances of subtle, indirect, and unintentional subordinating behavior; see McTernan 2018.
12. See José Jorge Mendoza, "Enforcement Matters: Reframing the Philosophical Debate over Immigration," in *Journal of Speculative Philosophy* 29.1 (2015): 73–90 for a discussion of humiliating immigration enforcement procedures.
13. This leaves open the possibility that there may be idiosyncratic cases of immigration discrimination that are unlikely to have this impact on those who are excluded: for example, exclusion on the basis of eye color or the first letter of one's surname.
14. I am grateful to Michael Blake for coming up with, and fleshing out this example in detail.
15. To be clear, this is not to say that philosophers cannot be members of socially salient groups by dint of their social identities. It's meaningful to speak of "African American philosophers" or "transgender philosophers" as socially salient groups. In these cases, however, they are not socially salient *qua* their occupation as "philosopher" per se, but their other social identities and how those structure their experience of the occupation.
16. For more information, see: https://www.nationalarchives.gov.uk/cabinetpapers/themes/commonwealth-immigration-control-legislation.htm.

Chapter 3

1. See Sarah Kunz's discussion of the difference between "expatriate" and "migrant": https://archive.discoversociety.org/2019/10/02/expatriate-or-migrant-the-racialised-politics-of-migration-categories-and-the-space-in-between/.

2. I believe this pattern also applies to current public attitudes toward refugees. For example, people do not think that Syrian refugees should be excluded on the basis of race, but of concerns about public safety, as it is claimed that admitting Syrian refugees would doubtless increase the risk of terrorist attacks. However, this seems far more like a poorly grounded belief rooted in demeaning stereotypes about Muslims and their penchant toward terrorist activity, and this connection gives us good reason to reject the exclusion of Syrian refugees on such grounds.
3. In stipulating that membership in a state does not depend on one's capacity to "function"—that is, successfully perform practical tasks—I do not mean to suggest that the exclusion of potential members is morally equivalent to states expelling members who are deemed to be economically unproductive. Expulsion of existing members is, in my view, a greater injustice. My point, rather, is that entitlement to membership in a state (as we currently understand it) does not hinge on our proving our instrumental value for its overall purposes. It is difficult, I suspect, for states to maintain this instrumentalizing view toward outsiders without entrenching stigmatizing views about current members who are perceived to be of low (or no) instrumental value—consider, for example, the widespread perception of racial minorities as "lazy" or parasitic on welfare systems.
4. Caleb Yong, "Justice in Labor Immigration Policy." *Social Theory and Practice* 42.4 (2016): 827.

Chapter 4

1. I leave open the possibility that the gendered pattern of migration I have identified may also serve to worsen sexist norms in *sending* states, and not just receiving ones. For example, if women are also commonly perceived as the passive dependents of men in the sending state, this belief may be further confirmed by the observation that women are only able to leave because of their male partners' overseas job offers.

Chapter 5

1. See: http://ieg-ego.eu/en/threads/europe-on-the-road/economic-migration/pieter-c-emmer-leo-lucassen-migration-from-the-colonies-to-western-europe-since-1800#TheImmigrationFromAfricaIntoSouthernEurope15001800 for more information.
2. I am deeply dubious that such a justification for the right to exclude could exist. It is hard to imagine a theory of exclusion whose core premises could, somehow,

remain untouched by the ethical implications of colonialism. As Phillip Cole writes, "Too often liberal political philosophy is written against the background of a fictional history in which colonial exploitation never occurred. But once we bring this historical element into our considerations, it has a profound impact upon our ethical reasoning concerning migration" (2000, 12).

3. I leave open the means through which the "extent" of injustice could be calculated.
4. See Shachar 2009 for a well-articulated version of this argument.
5. See, also, Peter Higgins's discussion of brain drain in *Immigration Justice* (2013).
6. This is exactly what Gillian Brock argues.
7. Here, I am suggesting that, in some cases, persons can have a "right to do wrong." A similar example might be the right to vote. I might do serious wrong by voting for an evil and corrupt candidate, but our judgment that I act wrongly can be kept conceptually separate from whether I should have the right to vote.
8. While I have focused my discussion on Latino/a/x migrants in the United States, it is worth noting that low-skilled migrants in other countries have also suffered differential and inferior treatment that is detrimental to their well-being. One shocking incident that exposes the vulnerability and disposability of low-skilled migrants would be the Morecambe Bay disaster in 2004, where at least twenty-one undocumented Chinese laborers drowned while picking cockles off the coast in Lancashire, England. Their drowning was at least partly attributable to the workers' lack of knowledge of local geography and language, which led them to pick cockles at high tide and rendered them unable to communicate their distress. That the Chinese laborers were not properly warned about the dangerous tides, combined with the lack of safety protocols to protect their lives, speaks volumes about how those workers were perceived. Consider, also, a recent incident in my home country, Singapore. In 2021, several Indian construction workers were killed/badly injured in two road accidents because they are often transported in the back of lorries without any proper safety measures. This practice is legal, and it continues to be legal because it is only low-skilled migrant workers who are transported in that fashion.
9. Through unions and advocacy groups, low-skilled migrants have actively advocated for their own rights and made significant progress in this regard. For more details, see: https://www.dissentmagazine.org/article/worker-centers-immigrant-organizing, as well as https://www.theguardian.com/us-news/2018/mar/22/unions-undocumented-workers-immigration-deportation-painters. Proper recognition of migrants' political agency, however, is compatible with attentiveness to the rights-violations that they continue to suffer under skill-selective regimes.
10. See: https://www.migrationpolicy.org/programs/us-immigration-policy-program-data-hub/unauthorized-immigrant-population-profiles.

11. See: https://www.citylab.com/equity/2017/04/landlords-are-threatening-immigrant-tenants-with-ice-deportations/521370/.
12. On Reed-Sandoval's view, citizens can also be socially undocumented. However, I focus on noncitizens in this chapter.
13. As I write, there is increasing recognition that detention centers are essentially "concentration camps" that have no place in a liberal, or even minimally decent society.

Chapter 6

1. Here, I use Grant Silva's terminology (2019). Apart from the collective disobedience of migrants themselves, we may also look to the disobedience of sanctuary cities and counties in the United States, which have refused to comply with the federal government's enforcement of immigration law. Such refusal can be appropriately understood, I believe, as another interesting form of migratorial disobedience. Unfortunately, I don't have the space to do the issue justice in this chapter.
2. Hidalgo and Yong also discuss (and disagree on) the right of citizens to refuse to comply with unjust immigration laws. However, for the purposes of this chapter, I will focus on would-be migrants' right to disobey.
3. Note that Candice Delmas excludes certain political goals from the realm of principled disobedience. On her view, in order for their acts to count as principled disobedience, persons must "act with respect for other people's interests, including, but not limited to, their basic interests in life and bodily integrity; their interests in non-domination and in choosing the values that shape their lives; and their interest in protection by a stable, secure system of rights" (2018, 49). From this constraint on the goals of principled disobedience, which requires concern for basic human interests (rather than attempting to set them back), it follows that the disobedient activities of white supremacists or religious extremists who wish to deny others' rights would not count as "principled disobedience."
4. Yong assumes that constitutionally democratic receiving states, in general, have laws with legitimate authority.
5. It is useful to turn back to Joseph Carens's distinction between "general human rights," which states owe to all persons, and "membership-specific right," which states owe only to members of the political community (2015, 93–98). It seems that, for Yong, immigration law can be egregiously unjust if it violates the former but not the latter.
6. Yong's stance on this matter is consistent with John Rawls's claim that "[t]he right to independence, and equally the right to self-determination, hold only within

certain limits" (*The Law of Peoples* 1999b, 38). The limits that Rawls has in mind apply to societies that exercise these rights at the expense of subjugating another population, or when their domestic institutions violate human rights or restrict the rights of minorities on their territory. In such cases, Rawls argues, the right to independence and self-determination is "no shield" from condemnation or even coercive intervention by other peoples (38).

7. For more information, see: https://www.nytimes.com/interactive/2019/07/06/us/migrants-border-patrol-clint.html.
8. Take, for example, a hypothetical state policy mandating that all citizens must cover the costs of healthcare that result from bad "choices," rather than bad brute luck that one has no control over. This seems fair; arguably, it is unjust to expect people to pay for the bad decisions made by their fellow citizens. Yet, under nonideal conditions, this seemingly reasonable healthcare policy would undoubtedly bring about egregious injustice. Consider the possibility that relatively worse-off citizens would be considerably less likely to be equipped with the adequate health education necessary for making "good" choices. Suppose, also, that it is expensive to make "good" or "wise" health choices. Wholesome and nutritious foods are significantly more unaffordable than heavily processed or poorly balanced meals, and gyms with exercise equipment are financially out-of-reach for many worse-off citizens. Given these surrounding structural factors, it is likely that many worse-off citizens would end up with relatively poor health that cannot be attributed to their choices alone, even if it appears to arise from conscious decisions (e.g., a man suffering from heart disease because he has eaten unhealthily over a lifetime and not gotten enough exercise). Furthermore, it is also likely that those citizens would be unable to independently pay the costs of healthcare, leaving them in a scenario where they are bankrupted by medical bills or feel compelled not to seek out healthcare because they know they cannot pay the costs. It is precisely because laws do not operate in a vacuum that health policymakers have a *duty* to be attentive to the unjust social structures that surround them: they must avoid perpetrating further structural injustice.
9. Some examples might include the implementation of a metering policy, or barring refugees from obtaining asylum if they pass through another country before entering. In both cases, the risk of violating refugees' human rights seem both foreseeable and avoidable.
10. Here, I borrow Daniel Markovits's terminology (2005).
11. For a discussion of border coercion, see Arash Abizadeh's "Democratic theory and border coercion: no right to unilaterally control your own borders" in *Political Theory* 36.1 (2008): 37–65.
12. This would certainly be true in the case of, say, classic military intervention. However, in today's political landscape, Beitz's definition of interference might

be lacking. Though widely recognized as a violation of the US citizens' right to independence, Russia's alleged interference fell short of coercive "imposition." For this reason, I suggest a broader account of interference must include actions that do not "force" anything upon individual citizens, but nonetheless *manipulate* them into making political decisions that are friendly to the aims of the intervener (and in some cases, contrary to that of the citizen). I shall take the right to independence, then, to be grounded in citizens' right to autonomously decide on their own political destiny. To violate the right to independence is to undermine citizens' ability to do so, through violence, threats, deceit, or even factual/emotional manipulation (as in the Russian case). However, a proper discussion of manipulation falls outside of the scope of my chapter.

13. An example might be the portrayal of Black Lives Matter activists as inherently violent, dangerous, and unreasonable.
14. For more details, see: https://www.cnbc.com/2018/10/23/over-7000-strong-the-migrant-caravan-headed-for-the-us-pushes-on.html.
15. See, also, Delmas on "deliberative inertia" (78).
16. Relevantly, Markovits observes that "[i]n the context of American democracy, for example, prison practices that abandon rehabilitation in favor of segregation and retributive criminal punishment have more or less excluded considerations concerning prisoners' rights and prison reform from democratic politics" (2005, 1897). A similar parallel can be found in the criminalization of unauthorized migration and how it has shaped policy discourse.

Conclusion

1. For more information, see: https://www.aclu.org/news/immigrants-rights/reproductive-abuse-is-rampant-in-the-immigration-detention-system/.
2. See: https://www.propublica.org/article/ice-guards-systematically-sexually-assault-detainees-in-an-el-paso-detention-center-lawyers-say.

Epilogue: Reflections on COVID-19 and Its Impact on Immigration

1. See, for example: https://www.nytimes.com/2020/04/06/world/coronavirus-domestic-violence.html.
2. https://www.scmp.com/news/asia/australasia/article/3082903/coronavirus-new-zealand-wont-open-borders-tourists-long-time.

3. https://www.bbc.com/news/world-us-canada-52244039.
4. See: https://www.scmp.com/news/world/united-states-canada/article/3085589/shunned-abused-spat-hate-crimes-against-asian.
5. See: https://foreignpolicy.com/2020/01/27/coronavirus-covid19-dont-blame-bat-soup-for-the-virus/.
6. We see similar tendencies in the commonplace misconception that "Africa is a country," or the assumption that a person of Latin American descent has to be "Mexican."
7. The proclamation does not apply to permanent residents and immediate relatives of US citizens, among other exempted groups.
8. See: https://www.nytimes.com/interactive/2020/04/28/world/asia/coronavirus-singapore-migrants.html.
9. http://theindependent.sg/psps-hazel-poa-says-dorm-operator-reaps-the-profit-taxpayers-pay-for-covid/.
10. https://www.vox.com/2020/5/16/21260906/house-stimulus-check-immigrants-heroes-act.
11. https://www.bbc.com/news/world-us-canada-52476131.

Bibliography

Abizadeh, Arash. "Democratic Theory and Border Coercion: No Right to Unilaterally Control Your Own Borders." *Political Theory* 36 (2008): 37–65.

Alexander, Michelle. *The New Jim Crow*. New York: The New Press, 2012.

American Immigration Council. "Immigrant Women in the United States: A Portrait of Demographic Diversity." (2014). Accessed at: https://www.americanimmigrationcouncil.org/research/immigrant-women-united-states on 15 March 2017.

Amighetti, Sara, and Nuti, Alasia. "A Nation's Right to Exclude and the Colonies." *Political Theory* 44.4 (2016): 541–566.

Anderson, Bridget. *Us and Them*. Oxford: Oxford University Press, 2013.

Anderson, Elijah. *The Cosmopolitan Canopy*. New York: W.W. Norton, 2012.

Anderson, Elizabeth. "What Is the Point of Equality?" *Ethics* 109.2 (1999a): 287–337.

Anderson, Elizabeth. "Reply to Richard Arneson, Thomas Christiano, and David Sobel." 22 December 1999b. Accessed at: http://www.brown.edu/Departments/Philosophy/bears/9912ande.html on 17 May 2016.

Anderson, Elizabeth, and Pildes, Richard. "Expressive Theories of Law: A General Restatement." *University of Pennsylvania Law Review* 148.5 (2000): 1503–1575.

Apgar, Lauren. "Authorized Status, Limited Returns: The Labor Market Outcomes of Temporary Mexican Workers." *Economic Policy Institute*, 2015. Accessed at: https://www.epi.org/publication/authorized-status-limited-returns-labor-market-outcomes-temporary-mexican-workers/ on 19 November 2020.

Appiah, Kwame Anthony. "Racisms" in *Anatomy of Racism*. Ed. D. T. Goldberg, 3–19. Minneapolis: University of Minnesota Press, 1990.

Aristotle, Jowett, Benjamin, and Davis, H.W.C. *Aristotle's Politics*. New York: Cosimo Classics, 2008.

Balch, Alex, and Balabanova, Ekaterina. "Ethics, Politics and Migration: Public Debates on the Free Movement of Romanians and Bulgarians in the UK, 2006–2013." *Politics* 36.1 (2016): 19–35.

Batalova, Jeanne and Lowell, Lindsay B. "The Best and the Brightest: Immigrant Professionals in the U.S." in *The Human Face of Global Mobility: International Highly Skilled Migration*. Eds. Michael Peter Smith and Adrian Favell, 81–102. New Brunswick, NJ: Transaction Publishers, 2006.

BBC News. "Immigration: No Visas for Low-Skilled Workers, Government Says." 2020. Accessed at: https://www.bbc.com/news/uk-politics-51550421 on 20 February 2020.

Beitz, Charles. *Political Theory and International Relations*. Princeton: Princeton University Press, 1999.

Birchall, J. Gender, Age and Migration: An Extended Briefing. *BRIDGE* 2016. Accessed at: http://www.rosavzw.be/digidocs/dd-001417_2016_Gender_Age_Migration_IDS.pdf on 15 March 2017.

Blake, Michael. "Distributive Justice, State Coercion, and Autonomy." *Philosophy and Public Affairs* 30.3 (2001): 257–296.

Blake, Michael. "Immigration and Political Equality." *San Diego Law Review* 45.4 (2008): 963–980.

Blake, Michael. "Immigration, Association, and Antidiscrimination." *Ethics* 122.4 (2012): 748–762.

Blake, Michael. "Immigration, Jurisdiction, and Exclusion." *Philosophy and Public Affairs* 41.2 (2013): 103–130.

Blake, Michael. *Justice, Migration, and Mercy*. New York: Oxford University Press, 2020.

Blauner, Robert. "Internal Colonialism and Ghetto Revolt." *Social Problems* 16.4 (1969): 393–408.

Blinder, Scott. "BRIEFING: Deportations, Removals and Voluntary Departures from the UK." 19 August 2016. Accessed at: http://www.migrationobservatory.ox.ac.uk/sites/files/migobs/Briefing- Deportations.pdf on 2 March 2016.

Bodenhausen, Galen. "Model Minority" in *The Routledge Companion to Race & Ethnicity*. Eds. Stephen Caliendo and Charlton McIlwain, 173–175. London: Routledge, 2011.

Borjas, George J., and Katz, Lawrence F. "The Evolution of the Mexican-Born Workforce in the United States" in *Mexican Immigration to the United States*. Ed. George Borjas, 13–55. Chicago, IL: University of Chicago Press, 2007.

Boyd, Monica, and Pikkov, Deanna. "Gendering Migration, Livelihood and Entitlements: Migrant Women in Canada and the United States." United Nations Research Institute for Social Development, Occasional Paper 6 (2005): 1–40.

British Social Attitudes. "Attitudes to Immigration." 2013. Accessed at: http://www.bsa.natcen.ac.uk/media/38108/immigration-bsa31.pdf on 17 May 2017.

Brock, Gillian, and Blake, Michael. *Debating Brain Drain: May Governments Restrict Emigration?* New York: Oxford University Press, 2015.

Brownlee, Kimberly. *Conscience and Conviction: The Case for Civil Disobedience*. Oxford: Oxford University Press, 2012.

Bryden, Daniele, and Storey, Ian. "Duty of Care and Medical Negligence." *Continuing Education Anaesthesia Critical Care Pain* 11.4 (2011): 124–127.

Bureau of Labor Statistics. "Foreign-Born Workers in the U.S. Labor Force." 2013. Accessed at: https://www.bls.gov/spotlight/2013/foreign-born/home.htm on 17 February 2020.

Bureau of Labor Statistics. "Foreign-Born Workers: Labor Force Characteristics—2017." 2017. Accessed at: https://www.bls.gov/news.release/pdf/forbrn.pdf on 17 February 2020.

Business Standard. "Gender Pay Gap in India at 27%: Monster Salary Index." *Business Standard*, 18 May 2016. Accessed at: http://www.business-standard.com/article/management/gender-pay-gap-in-india-at-27-monster-salary-index-116051700807_1.html on 15 March 2017.

Butt, Daniel. "Colonialism and Postcolonialism" in *The International Encyclopedia of Ethics*. Ed. Hugh LaFollette, 892–898. Chichester, UK: Blackwell, 2013.

Camarota, Steven. "Welfare Use by Immigrant and Native Households." September 2015, 1–53. Accessed at: http://cis.org/Welfare-Use-Immigrant-Native-Households on 17 May 2016.

Card, David. "Is the New Immigration Really So Bad?" April 2004. Accessed at: http://discovery.ucl.ac.uk/14323/1/14323.pdf on 17 May 2016.

Carens, Joseph. "Aliens and Citizens: The Case for Open Borders." *Review of Politics* 49.2 (1987): 251–273.

Carens, Joseph. "Realistic and Idealistic Approaches to the Ethics of Migration." *International Migration Review* 30.1 (1996): 156–170.

Carens, Joseph. "Nationalism and the Exclusion of Immigrants: Lessons from Australian Immigration Policy" in *Open Borders? Closed Societies: The Ethical and Political Issues*. Ed. Matthew Gibney, 41–60. Westport, CT: Greenwood Press, 1988.

Carens, Joseph. *The Ethics of Immigration*. New York: Oxford University Press, 2015.

Chishti, Muzaffar, and Bolter, Jessica. "'Merit-Based' Immigration: Trump Proposal Would Dramatically Revamp Immigration Selection Criteria, But with Modest Effects on Numbers." Migration Policy Institute 2019. Accessed at: https://www.migrationpolicy.org/article/merit-based-immigration-trump-proposal-immigrant-selection on 26 November 2021.

Christman, John. "Relational Autonomy, Liberal Individualism, and the Social Constitution of Selves." *Philosophical Studies* 117.1/2 (2004): 143–164.

Cole, Phillip. *Philosophies of Exclusion: Liberal Political Theory and Immigration*. Edinburgh: Edinburgh University Press, 2000.

Cole, Phillip. "Open Borders: An Ethical Defense" in *Debating the Ethics of Immigration: Is There a Right to Exclude?* Eds. C. H. Wellman and P. Cole, 159–313. New York: Oxford University Press, 2011.

Cole, Phillip. "Taking Moral Equality Seriously: Egalitarianism and Immigration Controls." *Journal of International Political Theory* 8.1–2 (2012): 121–134.

Cole, Phillip. "Beyond Reason: The Philosophy and Politics of Immigration." *Critical Review of International Social and Political Philosophy* 17.5 (2014): 509–520.

Costa, Daniel. "The H-2B Temporary Foreign Worker Program." Economic Policy Institute, 2016. Accessed at: https://www.epi.org/publication/h2b-temporary-foreign-worker-program-for-labor-shortages-or-cheap-temporary-labor/#epi-toc-1 on 19 November 2020.

Costa, Daniel. "Modern-Day Braceros: The United States Has 450,000 Guestworkers in Low-Wage Jobs and Doesn't Need More." *Workplace Fairness*, 2017. Accessed at: https://www.workplacefairness.org/blog/2017/03/31/modern-day-braceros-the-united-states-has-450000-guestworkers-in-low-wage-jobs-and-doesnt-need-more/ on 19 November 2020.

Costa, Daniel. "Employers increase their profits and put downward pressure on wages and labor standards by exploiting migrant workers." *Workday Magazine* 2019. Accessed at https://workdaymagazine.org/employers-increase-their-profits-and-put-downward-pressure-on-wages-and-labor-standards-by-exploiting-migrant-workers/ on 10 April 2023.

Costa, Daniel. "Trump Administration Looking to Cut the Already Low Wages of H-2A Migrant Farmworkers While Giving Their Bosses a Multibillion-Dollar Bailout." Economic Policy Institute, 2020. Accessed at: https://www.epi.org/blog/trump-administration-reportedly-looking-to-cut-the-already-low-wages-of-h-2a-migrant-farmworkers-while-giving-their-bosses-a-multibillion-dollar-bailout/ on 19 November 2020.

Darwall, Stephen. "Two Kinds of Respect." *Ethics* 88.1 (1977): 36–49.

Delmas, Candice. *A Duty to Resist: When Disobedience Should Be Uncivil.* New York: Oxford University Press, 2018.

Douglas, Karen M., and Saenz, Rogelio. "The Criminalization of Immigrants and the Immigrant-Industrial Complex." *Daedalus* 142.3 (2013): 200–227.

Du Bois, W. E. B. *The Souls of Black Folk.* Oxford: Oxford University Press, 2007.

Enchautegui, Maria. "Immigrant and Native Workers Compete for Different Low-Skilled Jobs." *Urban Institute,* 2015. Available at: https://www.urban.org/urban-wire/immigrant-and-native-workers-compete-different-low-skilled-jobs.

Fanon, Frantz. *Wretched of the Earth.* New York: Grove Press, 1963.

Fine, Sarah. "The Ethics of Immigration: Self-Determination and the Right to Exclude." *Philosophy Compass* 8.3 (2013): 254–268.

Fine, Sarah. "Immigration and Discrimination" in *Migration and Political Theory: The Ethics of Movement and Membership.* Eds. Sarah Fine and Lea Ypi, 125–150. Oxford: Oxford University Press, 2016.

Fine, Sarah, and Sangiovanni, Andrea. "Immigration" in *The Routledge Handbook of Global Ethics.* Eds. D. Moellendorf and H. Widdows, 193–209. Durham: Routledge, 2014.

Fiss, Owen M. "Groups and the Equal Protection Clause." *Philosophy and Public Affairs* 5.2 (1976): 107–177.

Fourie, Carina. "What Is Social Equality? An Analysis of Status Equality as a Strongly Egalitarian Ideal." *Res Publica* 18 (2012): 107–126.

Fourie, Carina, Schuppert, Fabian, and Wallimann-Helmer, Ivo. "The Nature and Distinctiveness of Social Equality: An Introduction" in *Social Equality: On What It Means to Be Equals.* Eds. Carina Fourie, Fabian Schuppert, and Ivo Wallimann-Helmer. New York: Oxford University Press, 2015.

G v. St. Gregory's Catholic Science College. British and Irish Legal Information Institute, 2011. Accessed at: http://www.bailii.org/ew/cases/EWHC/Admin/2011/1452.html on15 March 2017.

Gheaus, Anca. "Care Drain as an Issue of Global Gender Justice." *Ethical Perspectives* 20.1 (2013): 61–80.

Griggs v. Duke Power Co., 1971. Accessed at: https://supreme.justia.com/cases/federal/us/401/424/case.html on 15 March 2017.

Goffman, Erving. *Stigma.* London: Penguin Books, 1963.

Golash-Boza, Tanya. "The Immigration Industrial Complex Why We Enforce Immigration Policies Destined to Fail." *Sociology Compass* 3.2 (2009): 295–309.

Gov.uk. "Tier 2 Shortage Occupation List." 2015. Accessed at: https://www.gov.uk/government/uploads/system/uploads/attachment_data/file/486107/Shortage_Occupation_List_-_November_2015.pdf on 15 March 2017.

Gov.uk. "The UK's Points-Based Immigration System: Policy Statement." 2020. Accessed at: https://www.gov.uk/government/publications/the-uks-points-based-immigration-system-policy-statement/the-uks-points-based-immigration-system-policy-statement on 20 March 2020.

Government of Canada. "Facts & Figures 2015: Immigration Overview—Permanent Residents." 2015. Accessed at: http://open.canada.ca/data/en/dataset/2fbb56bd-eae7–4582-af7d-a197d185fc93?_ga=1.235939911.772865243.1488928689 on 15 March 2017.

Griggs v. Duke Power Co. (1971). Accessed at: https://supreme.justia.com/cases/federal/us/401/424/case.html on 5 July 2015.

Guerra, Crystal Vance. "Why Hondurans See Migration as an Act of Civil Disobedience." *Yes Magazine*, 2018. Accessed at: https://www.yesmagazine.org/peace-justice/why-hondurans-see-migration-as-an-act-of-civil-disobedience-protest-20181213 on 17 February 2020.

Hanson, Gordon, Liu, Chen and McIntoch, Craig. "The Rise and Fall of U.S. Low-Skilled Immigration." *National Bureau of Economic Research* Working Paper 23753. Accessed at: https://www.nber.org/system/files/working_papers/w23753/w23753.pdf on 10 April 2023.

Hartmann, Heidi, Hayes, Jeffrey, Huber, Rebecca, Rolfes-Haase, Kelly and Suh, Jooyeoun. "The Shifting Supply and Demand of Care Work: The Growing Role of People of Color and Immigrants." 2018. Accessed at: https://iwpr.org/publications/supply-demand-care-work-immigrants-people-of-color/ on 17 February 2020.

Hainmueller, Jens, and Hopkins, Daniel J. "Public Attitudes towards Immigration." *Annual Review of Political Science* 17 (2014): 225–249.

Haslanger, Sally. "What Are We Talking About? The Semantics and Politics of Social Kinds." *Hypatia* 20.4 (2005): 10–26.

Heath, Malcolm. "Aristotle on Natural Slavery." *Phronesis* 53.3 (2008): 243–270.

Hegeswisch, Ariane, Liepmann, Hannah, Hayes, Jeffrey, and Hartmann, Heidi. "Separate and Not Equal? Gender Segregation in the Labor Market and the Gender Wage Gap." Institute for Women's Policy Research, Briefing Paper (2010): 1–16.

Hellman, Deborah. *When Is Discrimination Wrong?* Cambridge, MA: Harvard University Press, 2011.

Hidalgo, Javier. "Resistance to Unjust Immigration Restrictions." *Journal of Political Philosophy* 23.4 (2015): 450–470.

Higgins, Peter. "Immigration Justice: A Principle for Selecting Just Admissions Policies." *Social Philosophy Today* 25 (2009): 149–162.

Higgins, Peter. *Immigration Justice*. Edinburgh: Edinburgh University Press, 2013.

Hunter, Rosemary C. "Disparate Impact Discrimination: American Oddity or Internationally Accepted Concept." *Berkeley Journal of Employment & Labor Law* 19.1 (2014): 108–152.

Ikuenobe, Polycarp. "Conceptualizing Racism and Its Subtle Forms." *Journal for the Theory of Social Behaviour* 41.2 (2010): 161–181.

Iredale, Robyn Rae. "Gender, Immigration Policies and Accreditation: Valuing the Skills of Professional Women Migrants." *Geoforum* 36.2 (2005). Accessed at: https://www.sciencedirect.com/science/article/abs/pii/S0016718504000673 on 10 April 2023.

Kim, Claire Jean. "The Racial Triangulation of Asian Americans." *Politics & Society* 27 (1999): 105–138.

Kofman, Eleonore, Phizacklea, Annie, Raghuram, Parvati, and Sales, Rosemary. *Gender and International Migration in Europe*. London: Routledge, 2000. Cited in Kofman, Eleonore and Raghuram, Parvati. "Gender and Global Labour Migrations: Incorporating Skilled Workers." *Antipode* 38.2 (2006): 282–303.

Kofman, Eleonore, and Raghuram, Parvati. "Gender and Global Labour Migrations: Incorporating Skilled Workers." *Antipode* 38.2 (2006): 282–303.

Kraut, Richard. *Aristotle: Political Philosophy*. Oxford: Oxford University Press, 2002.

Ku, Leighton, and Bruen, Brian. "Poor Immigrants Use Public Benefits at a Lower Rate Than Poor Native-Born Citizens." *The Cato Institute's Economic Development Bulletin*. 4 March 2013. Accessed at: http://object.cato.org/sites/cato.org/files/pubs/pdf/edb17.pdf on 17 May 2016.

Kukathas, Chandran. *Immigration and Freedom*. Princeton: Princeton University Press, 2021.

Kymlicka, Will. *Contemporary Political Philosophy*. New York: Oxford University Press, 2001.

Law Library of Congress. "Points-Based Immigration Systems: Canada." March 2013. Accessed at: https://tile.loc.gov/storage-services/service/ll/llglrd/2013404868/2013404868.pdfon 10 April 2023.

Lee, Emily S. "The Ambiguous Practices of the Inauthentic Asian American Woman." *Hypatia* 29.1 (2014): 146–163.

Lee, Emily S. "Model Minority" in *50 Concepts for a Critical Phenomenology*. Eds. Gail Weiss, Ann V. Murphy, and Gayle Salamon, 231–236. Evanston, IL: Northwestern University Press, 2020.

Lenard, Patti, and Straehle, Christine. "Temporary Labour Migration: Exploitation, Tool of Development, or Both?" *Policy and Society* 29.4 (2010): 283–294.

Lenard, Patti, and Straehle, Christine. "Temporary Labour Migration, Global Redistribution, and Democratic Justice." *Politics, Philosophy & Economics* 11.2 (2011): 206–230.

Library of Congress. "Immigration and Relocation in U.S. History: Irish-Catholic Immigration to America." Accessed at: https://www.loc.gov/classroom-materials/immigration/irish/irish-catholic-immigration-to-america on 27 December 2021.

Lind, Dara. "The US Has Made Migrants at the Border Wait Months to Apply for Asylum. Now the Dam Is Breaking." *Vox*, 2018. Accessed at: https://www.vox.com/2018/11/28/18089048/border-asylum-trump-metering-legally-ports on 27 December 2021.

Lippert-Rasmussen, Kasper. "The Badness of Discrimination." *Ethical Theory and Moral Practice* 9 (2006): 167–185.

Lister, Matthew. "Dreamers and Others: Immigration Protests, Enforcement, and Civil Disobedience." *APA Newsletter on Hispanic/Latino Issues in Philosophy* 17.2 (2018): 15–17.

Loury, Glenn. *The Anatomy of Racial Inequality*. Cambridge, MA: Harvard University Press, 2003.

Macedo, Stephen. "When and Why Should Liberal Democracies Restrict Immigration" in *Citizenship, Borders, and Human Needs*. Ed. Rogers M. Smith, 301–323. Philadelphia: University of Pennsylvania Press, 2011.

MacKay, Douglas. "Are Skill-Selective Immigration Policies Just?" *Social Theory and Practice* 42.1 (2016): 123–153.

Malcom, Kelly and Sawani, Jina. *Racial Disparities in the Time of COVID-19*. Michigan Medicine: University of Michigan, 2020. Accessed at: https://www.michiganmedicine.org/health-lab/racial-disparities-time-covid-19 on 10 April 2023.

Markovits, Daniel. "Democratic Disobedience." *Yale Law Journal* 114.1897 (2005): 1896–1952.

Matalon, Lorne. "Extending 'Zero Tolerance' To People Who Help Migrants Along The Border." NPR, 2019. Accessed at: https://www.npr.org/2019/05/28/725716169/extending-zero-tolerance-to-people-who-help-migrants-along-the-border on 10 April 2023.

McTernan, Emily. "Microaggressions, Equality, and Social Practices." *Journal of Political Philosophy* 26.3 (2018): 261–281.

Mehta, Suketu. "Why Should Immigrants 'Respect Our Borders'? The West Never Respected Theirs." *New York Times*, 7 June 2019. Available at: https://www.nytimes.com/2019/06/07/opinion/immigration-reparations.html.

Mendoza, José Jorge. "Enforcement Matters: Reframing the Philosophical Debate over Immigration." *Journal of Speculative Philosophy* 29.1 (2015): 73–90.

Mendoza, José Jorge. "Illegal: White Supremacy and Immigration Status" in *The Ethics and Politics of Immigration: Core Issues and Emerging Trends*. Ed. A. Sager. London: Rowman and Littlefield, 2016.

Migration Advisory Committee. "Migrants in Low-Skilled Work." July 2014. Accessed at: https://www.gov.uk/government/uploads/system/uploads/attachment_data/file/333083/MAC-Migrants_in_low-skilled_work__Full_report_2014.pdf on 17 May 2016.

Migration Observatory. "Thinking behind the Numbers: Understanding Public Opinion on Immigration in Britain." Accessed at: http://migrationobservatory.ox.ac.uk/understanding-uk-public-opinion/executive-summary on 17 May 2016.

Miller, David. *On Nationality*. Oxford: Oxford University Press, 1995.

Miller, David. "Equality and justice." *Ratio* 10.3 (1997): 222–237.

Miller, David. "Immigration: The Case for Limits" in *Contemporary Debates in Applied Ethics*. Eds. A. I. Cohen and C. H. Wellman, 193–206. Oxford: Blackwell, 2005.

Miller, David. *Strangers in Our Midst*. Cambridge, MA: Harvard University Press, 2016.

Miller, David. "Is There a Human Right to Immigrate?" in *Migration and Political Theory: The Ethics of Movement and Membership*. Eds. S. Fine and L. Ypi, 11–31. Oxford: Oxford University Press, 2017.

Mills, Charles. "Ideal Theory as Ideology." *Hypatia* 20.3 (2005): 165–184.

Mills, Charles. "Racial Exploitation and the Wages of Whiteness" in *The Changing Terrain of Race and Ethnicity*. Eds. Maria Krysan and Amanda E. Lewis, 235–262. New York: Russell Sage Foundation, 2006.

Mills, Charles. *Black Rights/White Wrongs: The Critique of Racial Liberalism*. New York: Oxford University Press, 2017.

Moreau, Sophia. "Discrimination as Negligence." *Canadian Journal of Philosophy* 40: 2013 (2013): 123–149.

Morrison, Angela D. "Executive Estoppel, Equitable Enforcement, and Exploited Immigration Workers." *Harvard Law & Policy Review* 11 (2017): 295–336.

Murray, Alasdair. "Britain's Points Based Migration System." *CentreForum* (2011): 1–62.

Nath, Rekha. "On the Scope and Grounds of Social Equality" in *Social Equality: Essays on What It Means to Be Equals*. Eds. Carina Fourie, Fabian Schuppert, and Ivo Wallimann-Helmer, 186–208. Oxford: Oxford University Press, 2015.

Nozick, Robert. *Anarchy, State and Utopia*. New York: Basic Books, 1974.

Oberman, Kieran. "Immigration as a Human Right" in *Migration in Political Theory: The Ethics of Movement and Membership*. Eds. S. Fine and L. Ypi, 32–56. Oxford: Oxford University Press, 2016.

Okin, Susan. *Justice, Gender and the Family*. New York: Basic Books, 1991.

Ortega, Mariana. "Multiplicity, Inbetweenness, and the Question of Assimilation." *Southern Journal of Philosophy* 46 (2008): 65–80.

Pettit, Philip. *Republicanism*. Oxford: Oxford University Press, 1997.

Pevnick, Ryan. "Social Trust and the Ethics of Immigration Policy." *The Journal of Political Philosophy* 17.2 (2009): 146–167.

Pevnick, Ryan. *Immigration and the Constraints of Justice*. Cambridge: Cambridge University Press, 2011.

Phillips, Anne, and Taylor, Barbara. "Sex and Skill: Notes towards a Feminist Economics." *Feminist Review* 6 (1980): 79–88.

Piper, Nicola. "Gender and Migration." *Policy Analysis and Research Programme of the Global Commission on International Migration* (2005): 1–54.

Quijano, Aníbal. "Coloniality of Power and Eurocentrism in Latin America." *International Sociology* 15.2 (2000): 215–232.

Rawls, John. *Political Liberalism*. New York: Columbia University Press, 1993.

Rawls, John. *A Theory of Justice*. Cambridge, MA: Harvard University Press, 1999a.

Rawls, John. *The Law of Peoples*. Cambridge, MA: Harvard University Press, 1999b.

Reed-Sandoval, Amy. *Socially Undocumented: Identity and Immigration Justice*. New York: Oxford University Press, 2020.

Reuters. "UK post-Brexit rules to 'turn off tap' of low-skilled foreign labour." February 15, 2020. Accessed at: https://www.reuters.com/article/uk-britain-eu-immigration-idUKKBN20A007 on 11 May 2023.

Sangiovanni, Andrea. *Humanity without Dignity: Moral Equality, Respect, and Human Rights*. Cambridge, MA: Harvard University Press, 2017.

Scheffler, Samuel. "Choice, Circumstance, and the Value of Equality" in *Equality and Tradition: Questions of Value in Moral and Political Theory*, 208–235. Oxford: Oxford University Press, 2012.

Scheffler, Samuel. "The Practice of Equality" in *Social Equality: On What It Means to Be Equals*. Eds. Carina Fourie, Fabian Schuppert, and Ivo Wallimann-Helmer, 250–268. New York: Oxford University Press, 2015.

Seglow, Jonathan. "The Ethics of Immigration." *Political Studies Review* 3.3 (2005): 317–334.

Selmi, Michael. "Indirect Discrimination and the Anti-Discrimination Mandate" in *Philosophical Foundations of Discrimination Law*. Eds. Deborah Hellman and Sophia Moreau. Oxford: Oxford University Press, 2013.

SG v St Gregory's Catholic Science College. (2011). Accessed at: http://www.1cor.com/1315/?form_1155.replyids=1414 on 10 April 2016.

Shachar, Ayelet. *The Birthright Lottery*. Cambridge, MA: Harvard University Press, 2009.

Shachar, Ayelet. "Picking Winners: Olympic Citizenship and the Global Race for Talent." *Yale Law Journal* 120.8 (2011): 2088–2139.

Shachar, Ayelet, and Hirschl, Ran. "Recruiting 'Super Talent': The New World of Selective Migration Regimes." *Indiana Journal of Global Legal Studies* 20.1 (2013): 71–107.

Shachar, Ayelet, and Hirschl, Ran. "On Citizenship, States, and Markets." *Journal of Political Philosophy* 22.2 (2014): 231–257.

Shelby, Tommie. "Race and social justice: Rawlsian considerations." *Fordham Law Review* 72 (2003): 1697–1714.

Shelby, Tommie. "Race" in *The Oxford Handbook of Political Philosophy*. Ed. David Estlund, 337–353. New York: Oxford University Press, 2012.

Shihadeh, Edward S., and Barranco, Raymond E. "Latino Employment and Black Violence: The Unintended Consequence of Immigration Policy." *Social Forces* 88.3 (2010): 1393–1420.

Shin, Patrick. "The Substantive Principle of Equal Treatment." *Suffolk University Law School Legal Research Paper Series* 09–31 (2009): 1–34.

Siddique, Haroon. "British BAME Covid-19 death rate 'more than twice that of whites.'" *The Guardian*, 2020. Accessed at: https://www.theguardian.com/world/2020/may/01/british-bame-covid-19-death-rate-more-than-twice-that-of-whites on 10 April 2023.

Silva, Grant. "Embodying a 'New' Color Line: Racism, Anti-Immigrant Sentiment and Racial Identities in the 'Postracial' Era." *Knowledge Cultures* 3.1 (2015): 65–90.

Silva, Grant. "Migratorial Disobedience: The Fetishization of Immigration Law." *RPA Mag*, 2019. Accessed at: https://www.rpamag.org/2019/01/migratorial-disobedience on 17 February 2020.

Silverman, Stephanie, and Nethery, Amy. "Introduction: Understanding Immigration Detention" in *Immigration Detention: The Migration of a Policy and Its Human Impact*. London: Routledge, 2015. Accessed at: https://www.academia.edu/9957462/Understanding_Immigration_Detention_Editorial_Introduction_to_Immigration_Detention_The_Migration_of_a_Policy_and_Its_Human_Impact_Routledge_2015 on 12 January 2020.

Steinberg, Ronnie J. "Social Construction of Skill: Gender, Power, and Comparable Worth." *Work and Occupations* 17.4 (1990): 449–482.

Stemplowska, Zofia. "Luck Egalitarianism" in *the Routledge Companion to Social and Political Philosophy*. Eds. Gerald F. Gaus and Fred D'Agostino. New York: Routledge, 2013.

Stemplowska, Zofia, and Swift, Adam. "Ideal and Non-Ideal Theory" in *The Oxford Handbook of Political Philosophy*. Ed. David Estlund, 373–390. New York: Oxford University Press, 2016.

Strawson, Galen. "Against Narrativity." *Ratio* 17 (2004): 428–452.

Sumption, Madeline, and Papademetriou, Demetrios G. "Legal Immigration Policies for Low-Skilled Foreign Workers." Migration Policy Institute Issue Brief, 2013: 1–12.

Sundstrom, Ronald, and Kim, David. "Xenophobia and Racism." *Critical Philosophy of Race* 2.1 (2014): 20–45.

Tan, Kok-Chor. "Colonialism, Reparations, and Global Justice" in *Reparations: Interdisciplinary Inquiries*. Eds. Jon Miller and Rahul Kumar. Oxford: Oxford University Press (2007): 280–306.

Taylor, Charles. *Multiculturalism and the Politics of Recognition*. Princeton, NJ: Princeton University Press, 1994.

Taylor, Diane. "Man to Be Removed from UK So Ill Home Office Will Send Four Medics on Flight." *The Guardian*, 2018. Accessed at: https://www.theguardian.com/uk-news/2018/oct/13/home-office-sending-medics-to-accompany-man-on-removal-flight-australia-three-stokes on 17 February 2020.

Taylor, Matthew. "School's Ban on Boy's Cornrows is 'Indirect Racial Discrimination.'" *The Guardian*, 2011. Accessed at: http://www.theguardian.com/uk/2011/jun/17/school-ban-cornrows-indirect-discrimination on 10 April 2016.

Underwood, Emily. "Unhealthy Work: Why Migrants Are Especially Vulnerable to Injury and Death on the Job." *Knowable Magazine*, 2018. Accessed at: https://knowablemagazine.org/article/society/2018/unhealthy-work-why-migrants-are-especially-vulnerable-injury-and-death-job on 19 November 2020.

United Nations. "Declaration on the Granting of Independence to Colonial Countries." 1960. Accessed at: https://www.ohchr.org/en/instruments-mechanisms/instruments/declaration-granting-independence-colonial-countries-and-peoples on 10 April 2023.

Universal Declaration of Human Rights. United Nations. Accessed at: http://www.un.org/en/universal-declaration-human-rights on 17 May 2016.

Usbourne, Simon. "Katie Hopkins Has Just Written a Piece so Hateful That It Might Give Hitler Pause—Why Was It Published?" *The Independent*, 18 April 2015. Accessed at: http://www.independent.co.uk/voices/katie-hopkins-when-is-enough-enough-10186490.html on 17 May 2016.

Valentini, Laura. "Ideal vs. Non-Ideal Theory: A Conceptual Map." *Philosophy Compass* 7.9 (2012): 654–664.

Volpp, Leti. "Divesting Citizenship: On Asian American History and the Loss of Citizenship through Marriage." *UCLA Law Review* 52 (2005): 405–484.

Waldron, Daniel, and Ali, Sanwar. "UK Tier 2 Visa Immigrants must earn £35,000 to settle from April 2016." 7 July 2015. Accessed at: http://www.workpermit.com/news/2015-07-07/uk-tier-2-visa-immigrants-must-earn-35000-to-settle-from-april-2016 on 17 May 2016.

Wakefield, Juliet R. H., Hopkins, Nick, and Greenwood, Ronni M. "Thanks, but No Thanks: Women's Avoidance of Help-Seeking in the Context of a Dependency-Related Stereotype." *Psychology of Women Quarterly* 0361684312457659 (2012): 1–9.

Walzer, Michael. *Spheres of Justice: A Defense of Pluralism and Equality.* Oxford: Martin Robertson, 1984.

Wellman, Christopher Heath. "Immigration and Freedom of Association." *Ethics* 119.1 (2008): 109–141.

Wright, C. F., Clibborn, S., Piper, N., and Cini, N., 2016. "Economic Migration and Australia in the 21st Century." Lowy Institute [online]. Accessed at: https://www.lowyinstitute.org/sites/default/files/wright_et_al_economic_migration_and_australia_in_the_21st_century_0_0.pdf on 15 March 2017.

Ypi, Lea. "What's Wrong with Colonialism." *Philosophy and Public Affairs* 41.2 (2013): 158–191.

Yong, Caleb. "Justice in Labor Immigration Policy." *Social Theory and Practice* 42.4 (2016): 817–844.

Yong, Caleb. "Justifying Resistance to Immigration Law: The Case of Mere Noncompliance." *Canadian Journal of Law & Jurisprudence* 31.2 (2018): 459–481.

Young, Iris Marion. *Justice and the Politics of Difference.* Princeton, NJ: Princeton University Press, 1990.

Young, Iris Marion. "Responsibility and Global Justice: A Social Connection Model." *Social Philosophy & Policy* 23.1 (2006): 102–130.

Young, Iris Marion. *Responsibility for Justice.* Oxford: Oxford University Press, 2011.

Zack, Naomi. "The Philosophical Roots of Racial Essentialism and Its Legacy." *Confluence: Journal of World Philosophies* 1 (2014): 85–98.

Index

For the benefit of digital users, indexed terms that span two pages (e.g., 52–53) may, on occasion, appear on only one of those pages.